JIM TELFER

**To Mum and Dad,
Frances, Mark and Louise**

JIM TELFER

Looking Back . . .
                    For Once

JIM TELFER *with*
DAVID FERGUSON
Foreword by
HRH The Princess Royal

MAINSTREAM
PUBLISHING
EDINBURGH AND LONDON

First published in Great Britain in 2005 by
MAINSTREAM PUBLISHING COMPANY
(EDINBURGH) LTD
7 Albany Street
Edinburgh EH1 3UG

ISBN 1 84596 062 9

A catalogue record for this book is available
from the British Library

Typeset in Sabon and Univers

Printed in Great Britain by
Clays Ltd, St Ives plc

Contents

Foreword

by Her Royal Highness the Princess Royal,
patron to the Scottish Rugby Union

Jim Telfer is well known throughout the world of rugby both for his exploits on the field and as a coach with Scotland and the British and Irish Lions, and through my role as patron of the Scottish Rugby Union, I have had the pleasure of meeting him at games and various functions on many occasions. I am delighted he has chosen to write about his very full and colourful life in rugby, as he has given so much to the game and sought nothing in return other than the joy of seeing his teams and players achieve.

Our contact has not been limited to the rugby arena, however, and what is less well known, at least outside Scotland, is the great success Jim achieved as an educator. I was delighted to be asked to open the refurbished Hawick High School in 1993, at the time when Jim was headmaster at the Borders school. As a teacher, Jim knew that rugby has its place in education in developing an understanding of rules and working with others. Rugby demands a range of skills and risk-taking, and inculcates in its players a sense of responsibility by one's self for one's teammates.

He is often seen and portrayed as a rugged Scotsman who rarely enjoys himself, one who rarely smiles, and there is no doubt that he takes the fortunes of Scottish rugby very seriously. However, you cannot be a popular and successful headmaster and not have a sense of humour. Even his players know he has a highly developed sense of humour, some might say slightly too highly developed. In October 2003, I had lunch with the Scottish squad in Sydney and wished Jim, Ian McGeechan and all the players good luck in the World Cup, which turned out to be Jim's farewell tournament.

I have known this unique Borderer for over 20 years and his commitment to rugby at all levels, be it in striving to develop rugby as a team sport in schools, or steering Scotland or the British and Irish Lions to success, has been inspirational. Jim deserves his place in rugby history as a leading innovator and coach, but his achievements as an educator should not be overlooked. I know you will enjoy reading Jim's autobiography and I wish him well, as we all do, in his retirement.

Introduction

by Martin Johnson CBE
British and Irish Lions (1993, 1997 and 2001)

Martin Johnson remains the only player to have captained the
British and Irish Lions on two tours. He was part of the 2–1 series
defeat in New Zealand in 1993, and in 2001 he led his side in the
2–1 defeat to Australia, so it is no surprise that he considers the
2–1 win in South Africa in 1997 to be among his greatest lifetime
achievements.

A rugby player will look back on titles, trophies and successes on
the field with some pleasure but what most players desire from the
game is respect – respect from peers, from teammates and
opponents, and from coaches – and not everyone achieves that.

If you won the respect of someone like Jim Telfer, it meant
something, and in the British and Irish Lions success of 1997,
every single forward, and most other players, I suspect, quickly
made gaining his respect a priority. To be honest, I don't know if
I ever achieved that, because he would never tell you – forwards
don't go in for that soft stuff – but I would like to think that I did.
He certainly won my respect.

I only knew of Jim Telfer, the veteran Scottish coach, by
reputation before 1997 and although I'd come up against his
Scotland teams, I had never worked with him before then. The
Lions players knew he was quite a tough character, that he
demanded high standards and worked players very hard. I have to

9

admit, he was generally painted by players and the media as some kind of ogre who you really didn't want to get to know. He was nothing like that.

For a start, he was not as hard away from the training field as we expected. He was straightforward and honest, but he listened and was a coach who showed respect to players. Rather than being an ogre, he was quite simply committed. He does not suffer fools gladly, nor does he like mucking around when there is serious rugby to be played and I have found that forwards coaches who have that strong, disciplined approach are the better ones.

But once on tour, travelling across the sometimes hostile rugby environment of South Africa, Jim Telfer came into his own. We started the tour very well and it was going along nicely when, two weeks away from the first Test match, we hit a week which was the major turning point of that whole experience. We were to play Northern Transvaal, Gauteng Lions and then Natal in just over a week, and we knew these games would be very tough. Having won every match up to that point, there was a momentum building with us but also in South Africa as the proud rugby nation urged each team to become the first to topple us.

We probably had become a bit too confident by the time we met Northern Transvaal – the Super 12 team also known as the Blue Bulls – and we lost the game 35–30; that knocked us out of our stride. Jim called us all together after that game and told the players in no uncertain terms that we were not good enough, that we were not playing at a standard to worry anyone and that we had a choice: adapt or go under.

He then took us down to Loftus for a forwards training session and gave the guys a really tough time. It was a no-holds-barred session which would make grown men wince. International players now would probably say they wouldn't do that a few days before a match but we all knew what it was about: this was a challenge and our character was being put to the test. So everyone got on and did it – no moans.

We went out and beat the Gauteng Lions at Ellis Park with a great try from John Bentley and then really stuffed Natal, in a week when Paul Wallace and Jeremy Davidson came through to push their Test claims. We didn't lose another game on the tour until the final Test match and I believe that was because of what happened that week. Jim had forced everyone to stand up at a point where there was a risk the tour would fall flat, a time when players were questioning and perhaps doubting themselves.

There were a lot of first-time Lions on that tour and the squad needed someone to show the way and have belief in them. Jim pulled it together and pushed many of us to the level required to win a Test series and I don't think, as a team, we would have achieved that without him. He and Ian McGeechan were a great partnership – the quiet, thoughtful McGeechan and Jim with the big stick. It worked perfectly and both styles were needed on that tour.

There were funny times as well. The footage in the *Living with Lions* film of Jim and Ian sitting in the stand, with local supporters all around them hurling abuse, getting frustrated as they watched us in the Second Test is absolutely priceless. They were like an old married couple!

It is a great privilege to have played on and captained a winning Lions tour, particularly having suffered defeat in 1993 and 2001, and I feel it is fitting that Jim's career included such a high point, as he, also, had endured some hard times on Lions tours as a player and as a coach before then.

I think Jim is a guy who inspires loyalty, respect and hard work. People misread Jim when they say players live in fear of him: it is not fear but an acknowledgement of the passion in him which motivates players. Players in his charge quickly get to a point where they simply don't want to let him down.

Our paths have crossed many times since 1997 and we still look at each other with a glint in the eye, a smile – that is all it takes to recall the memory of what we achieved together. Jim Telfer is a wonderful person and a coach who deserves a significant place in the history of world rugby for what he has contributed to the game.

Preface

by David Ferguson

You may feel at times reading this book that Jim Telfer is a man quite full of himself, a strong character with a confidence in his own abilities which he is not reluctant to share. It is a confidence delivered with a seriousness which has jarred with some people over the years and made him enemies, and one has often wondered where this desire to convince people that he is successful stemmed from; it was, in fact, one reason for encouraging Jim to write his life story.

Jim Telfer is not a conceited man and all who know him will attest to that. But with them, he does not feel the same need to point out his successes. Having reached the end of his story, I do feel we have uncovered some explanations for this innate eagerness to convince. As you will soon discover, much of Jim's approach to his rugby career, his never-ending pursuit of improvement, has come from his upbringing in the remote Borderland.

Jim is the son of a Borders shepherd. The environment in which he grew up is one where people live straightforward lives: they work hard, take a wage and ask few questions, and praise is deemed superfluous. His upbringing also developed in him socialist leanings. He abhorred the class divides in rural Scotland and sought to break or shun them throughout his life, always from the perspective of the working-class underdog. He therefore grew keen to challenge authority and champion the successes of the working class, his own included.

Another, more latent contributor to his fiery exterior is the criticism he received towards the end of his career, some fair but much more wholly undeserved. That resulted to a large extent from the fact that his straight-talking, serious demeanour made him an easy character to attack, and there are always plenty of dips in Scottish rugby for those keen to begin the season of hunting for scapegoats.

Jim has taken much of this on the chin but, with an in-built defence mechanism that manifests itself in angry and often controversial outbursts, he would at times confront criticism without thinking of the consequences. He has, therefore, upset people and explains in this book some of his regrets.

But, one hopes, what comes through clearly is that Telfer is a man who has quite simply devoted himself to Scottish and British and Irish Lions rugby, seeking nothing for himself in the process. His background shaped a man who no longer needs to convince, someone who has given more to Scottish rugby than any other single individual, and whose commitment and determination may never be matched.

He made mistakes and he achieved incredible successes but he was always prepared to push the boundaries, push those working with him and push himself as hard as he could. The main reason I pressed Jim to write this autobiography was simply because I could not believe that there was not already a book among the countless publications on shelves around the world chronicling his near 50 years at the heart of rugby.

Now there is and it has been a privilege to walk the path to this point with a character as wonderful, honest and likeable as Jim Telfer.

It would not have been possible without the terrific support of Jim and his family – particularly Frances, his wife, and his daughter Louise – and my understanding wife Fiona and daughters Kate and Olivia. We are indebted to HRH the Princess Royal and Martin Johnson for their input. This book will, hopefully, take you on a journey much more vivid and interesting than many autobiographies can and much of that is down to the number of people who have contributed to the chapters: Peggy, Frances and Kenneth Telfer, Derek Brown, Derrick Grant, Colin Meads, Gareth Edwards, Terry Christie, Richie Dixon, Andy Irvine, Willie John McBride, John Rutherford, Ian Landles, Finlay Calder, Roy Laidlaw, Ian McGeechan, Gregor Townsend, Gary Armstrong and Bryan Redpath. The tremendous statistical help from Michael Scouler, a Scotland and Lions devotee, and Jack Dun of Melrose has helped ensure as much factual accuracy as possible, while the work of many of Scottish sport's best photographers has ensured some great images. We thank them all for the great help.

We also acknowledge the indispensable assistance provided by the passionately written books on the Lions by Terry McLean, J.B.G. Thomas, John Reason, David Frost, Bill Beaumont, Ian Robertson, Andy Dalton, and Clem and Greg Thomas, and on Scottish rugby by Nick Oswald and John Griffiths, and John Davidson. Many others have helped ensure that a full and rounded story emerged, and the tremendous support and expertise of Mainstream Publishing, and, in particular, Bill Campbell, Graeme Blaikie and Claire Rose, turned the idea into reality. I must also thank my employers, *The Scotsman*, for their encouragement to pursue this project.

1

A Difficult Birth

Kenneth James Telfer
Age: 13
Caps: many (most worn backwards)

It is good that he's retired now. It was nice having a papa that was well known, though I can't believe that he was famous for being a rugby player and coach, and I don't even like rugby. I prefer cricket and swimming, and outdoor sports like sailing and canoeing.

It can be annoying as well, now he's retired. Papa likes to give me homework to do – he always tries to get me to do lots of spelling and who likes that? And he checks up on me when it's not done. I particularly do not like him waking me up in the morning when I stay at the weekends!

He still watches rugby constantly but he has time to take me on a lot more trips now. He's great fun when we go away visiting places. We've been to bird sanctuaries, museums, safari parks and Disney World in Florida – he wasn't very brave because he wouldn't go on the rollercoaster. I always try to get him to go to Blackpool but he won't ever since he discovered there was a rollercoaster there!

But I am proud of what he has achieved and I am glad Jim Telfer is my papa.

In his year of presidency of the English Rugby Football Union (RFU), just after the game had gone professional, Peter Brook

17

made a most profound statement when speaking of the need to commit to the exciting new sport that was appearing before us. He said: 'A woman cannot be half-pregnant.'

It was a strange metaphor but it set me thinking. It actually created a vivid picture of how I perceived the birth of professional rugby and the differences between the leading nations. If we were to think of rugby as a married couple, then pre-1995, they could be said to have had no children. Post 1995, a child in the shape of professionalism came along. There had been attempts before then to have children, with talk of professional circuses and 'shamateurism', whereby the child was born but hidden away and looked after by a sugar daddy.

In 1995, some families (unions) began planning for a birth while others ignored the signs. France and the southern-hemisphere countries had actually seen it coming for some time and planned for years to have a family, but the home nations had shunned the very idea.

When it came, I believed there would be no hiding any more and was surprised that rugby families acted differently from one another. The Irish family quickly accepted the new child. In England, the new baby was adopted by businessmen. The parents (the RFU) were allowed to see it from time to time and they gave it gifts (currently around £1.8 million a year). Only in Wales and Scotland were they at a loss as to what to do with it. In Scotland the couple – the SRU and the clubs – simply couldn't cope as they didn't have a solid relationship in any case. Some people in the country wanted to abort it, others wanted to push it back into the womb after it was born; we finally let it live but it was hidden away, starved and neglected.

In England, it was born into a rich family, with resources and love. In Scotland, it was born into a poor family with meagre resources and little love. When a child is born, a family changes forever, and the new opportunities and experiences it encounters as the child grows up are numerous and enriching. The Scottish family closed its mind to these opportunities.

In Wales, they eventually came to their senses. The parents accepted the child and it now has a chance of going from strength to strength. But in Scotland, we now have a ten-year-old child which is still only five in mental age and physical development.

To some, this metaphor may not seem appropriate, but as you read this book, hopefully it will become clearer how important children, family, education and ambition have been to me, both in rugby and away from it. I am not growing so senile with age as to believe professional rugby was my 'baby', but I do wish we had cared for it much better.

In other countries, it was a great adventure to have professional rugby but in Scotland, it was a chore. A couple of years ago I was on a radio programme with John Beattie, the former internationalist, now a leading broadcaster, and he asked me, 'How long will it take for us to accept professionalism?' I replied that it would take 15–20 years at the present rate of progress, and he was surprised it could be as long as that. I explained that we had wasted ten years and that even when everybody in Scotland finally comes together like a family to offer each other and the game support, it will take another five years to get to the level we want to achieve. I have often said that we need twenty-first-century solutions for twenty-first-century issues.

Until the culture changes, we will always struggle. Some people are only beginning to accept that professional rugby is here to stay, that it is both an entertaining spectator sport and a profession for elite players, and that amateur rugby can acquire great benefits from it.

Some old internationalists say, 'I'm glad I played when I did because we got the best of it,' but I feel sorry for them. They are not talking about the rugby they played, but about the socialising in the game. Saying that is an insult to young players of today, who are just as sociable, who respect and talk to their opponents and build up lifelong friendships. The 2005 British and Irish Lions, for example, when they left for New Zealand, carried the same hopes, excitement, enthusiasm and squad spirit as Lions squads before them.

In 1996, Scottish rugby could have taken great steps forward when we had the chance to separate the game into professional district rugby and amateur rugby, but that opportunity was not taken because some clubs would simply not accept it. In 2000, the Lord Mackay Report presented another opportunity and a greater one, with the Union split into an executive, installed mainly to run pro rugby, and a committee, in charge of club rugby. Yet the general committee and some clubs would not accept even that.

In 2005, we were given a third chance. Finally, Scottish rugby seemed to understand the split and the executive were handed complete control of professional and international rugby while a new council was elected to be responsible for running the amateur game. So, after ten years, if this opportunity is taken and all politics and personal gain are put aside, we will finally be able to move forward. Unfortunately, the main architects of the latest changes – David Mackay, the chairman of the executive board; Phil Anderton, the chief executive; and Ian McGeechan, the director of rugby – are all gone, the first two as a result of the vote of no confidence in Mackay in January 2005, which forced him to stand down and precipitated the resignations of three non-executive directors and Anderton. To me, this was something Scottish rugby could have done without. I do not fall into the camp of those who denigrate all the work of the general committee, but I believe they made a mistake there which harmed the game at that juncture. The one positive aspect to emerge, however, is a new structure of governance which, one hopes, will be a step towards a brighter future.

People in Scottish rugby must realise that the international side is the most important team in Scotland. It is at the top of the food chain; it must be nourished and that can only happen if all the parts of the body have a strong, unified involvement and strive to make each part as strong as possible, working not in isolation but in harmony with each other.

Gavin Hastings made a very accurate statement just after one of the countless special general meetings of the SRU this year. He said, 'To be perfectly honest, nobody gives a shit about Scottish rugby outwith Scotland . . . people outwith the country, and within it as well, will judge Scottish rugby on the success of the international team.'

It thus struck me as ironic this year when both Gavin and Finlay Calder, two of the players who led the clubs' campaign against the districts in 1996 and 1997, failed to win the support of the clubs in seeking election to the new council. It often doesn't pay in Scottish rugby to have reached the top! Journeymen are preferred, I sometimes feel.

The plain fact is that very few people outside Scotland and not many who pay good money to watch the Scotland team at Murrayfield care about who wins our domestic championships or cup. We may not like that but it remains a fact.

Before 1995, there were lengthy British and Irish Lions tours but there were not the numbers of supporters or the global attention the 1997, 2001 and 2005 tours attracted, because the top level of the sport has now joined the professional elite. It is more attractive, has become more accessible, and the commercial side has taken rugby far further than it has ever been before. This is not the same game or sport which club committeemen were part of a decade ago. The 2005 Lions tour to New Zealand was described by Sean Fitzpatrick, the former All Black captain, as 'the greatest rugby show on earth'.

We hear people say the players were much better in the past, yet players now are fitter, stronger and more skilful at the top level than they were. Jonah Lomu arrived in the big time in 1995 as a powerful indication of the changing nature of the game, and Jason Robinson, George Gregan, Richie McCaw, Martin Johnson, Joost van der Westhuizen, Olivier Magne, Tom Smith, Gareth Thomas and Brian O'Driscoll have proved there are many outstanding sportsmen playing professional rugby.

In fact, I am now coaching 15-year-olds and the skills of players this age have gone up enormously since I last worked with that age group 10 years ago. They know about defence systems and communicate far better, they have different styles of passes and kicks, they lift heavier weights and train much more.

Right at the start of professionalism, in 1996, a report by Roy Laidlaw and Douglas Arneil, as members of the Rugby Division which oversaw the development of the game, recommended to the SRU that they split the game into amateur and professional, largely because of what they had discovered studying rugby league at Bradford Bulls. If we didn't, they warned, our teams would be left behind and we would struggle to produce players capable of competing with the top nations in the world. Then, we had recently contested three Grand Slam deciders and won one, finished fourth in the 1991 World Cup and lost only to New Zealand in the last eight in 1995. We are ranked ninth in the world at the time of writing.

In Scottish rugby, we accept mediocrity far too readily. The vast majority of people involved in the game, be they players, coaches or officials, though very valuable, will be hard-working journeymen. However, there has been and will continue to be real star quality coming through in Scotland. Yet too often obstacles are placed in the paths of the truly talented, almost as a form of keeping ambition in check, because that is the Scottish way. Nonetheless, everyone wants a piece of that young star and wants credit for him, while at the same time wanting to decide when and how he progresses, and ultimately holding him back.

Coverage of rugby has completely changed in the last decade. I got on well with the press and enjoyed the banter and the way some would write something nasty about you then cuddle up to you the next day wanting more quotes. I used to look forward to going to the press conferences because it was like a discussion about what we were trying to do; we were giving an honest appraisal of where we were. The criticism did not bother me, though I did not enjoy the effect uninformed reporting had on my family, particularly my mother and father. But it was different after 1995: more interest, more widespread reporting and more uninformed, salacious styles.

I remember being at a function at Jordanhill College in Glasgow, just after the game had turned professional, and I spoke about how much more intrusive the media had become. Ernie Walker, the former SFA chief executive and now a member of UEFA, said to me, 'Welcome to the club, Jim. We've had this for 100 years and now it's your turn to get some of it.'

It was quite a change from the men I remember growing up with, writers like Hugh Young, Jack Dunn, Reg Prophit, Peter Donald, Norman Mair, Harry Pincott, Bill McLaren and Bill McMurtrie, to name a few. They would simply write about the game quite positively and did not seem to be under any pressure to find exclusive angles or write about negative aspects. The editors and owners of the quality papers and many of their readers came from middle-class backgrounds and wanted to read about rugby. It was all quite straightforward.

But as soon as a sport becomes professional, the media and the public at large believe you are there to be shot at. We have also witnessed a lot of jealousy from people who were involved in amateur rugby and think it's wrong to have people being paid now for doing what they did in their spare time.

Some of the things written in opinion columns, or worse, in letters to the papers and on internet chatrooms, especially about coaches, committeemen and officials, are appalling. The media has now travelled beyond traditional boundaries but with that travel it has also become very spiteful, narrow-minded and incredibly uninformed. Chatrooms can be like Chinese whispers to the nth degree: they lose all links with reality. The media had a chance to be different in terms of how they reflected a new professional sport, rather than follow the tired old route of football reporting.

I used to go into Murrayfield and ask my secretary, Carolyn, 'Who are the press crucifying today?' She would tell me to remember that it was just one man's opinion and it was worth no more than that of anyone else. Now, when I read the papers, it is easier to take each opinion with a pinch of salt.

Having rarely been able to give my own opinion as Scottish rugby progressed through a turbulent period, I now have my opportunity. In 2003, working with Scotland players again but for the final time, I was a different coach. I sanitised a lot of what I did and said because some players then had the ear of the press and were more intent on exploiting it, almost hurrying to leave training to complain that this or that was wrong. So I stepped back and, to be honest, it did not feel right working in an environment where I could not be myself. That was when I knew I had to walk away for good.

2

Home in the Borders Hills

Peggy Telfer, Jim's mother

Jim was a happy laddie. His grandfather was Jim and that is who we named him after, and Willie wanted William as his middle name. Jim quite enjoyed the farming but it was a hard life and I wanted him to enjoy his life more, so I encouraged him to look further afield.

He got on very well with his sisters and I don't remember many rows. Jim was always very keen on the rugby and we encouraged him in that as well, though I never imagined he would play for Scotland and be Scotland coach one day.

I felt very proud watching him playing for his country; he comes from working folk and he has done well – though I wouldn't tell him that. We were absolutely delighted to see him win his first cap and we went to watch him play for Scotland at Murrayfield.

Jim has a reputation now for always speaking his mind but he has surprised me with his comments at times. He was quite shy at home and his dad is so quiet, you see. We were both very proud of him when he became a coach of the Lions but I didn't like watching that Lions video where he was swearing all the time. I was a bit upset by that but that must be what he's like and how he gets the players moving on.

I am delighted that he is retired because he had a lot of hard times and people knocking him; it is difficult to see your son being attacked in the papers the way Jim was at times. Away from the rugby, he is very different, a very kind man who would do anything for anybody. He has done a lot with his life and it has been an honour for us to watch him rise up in his rugby and in teaching, where he worked very hard to realise his ambition of becoming a headmaster. Until he came along, us Telfers preferred to stay in the background!

My birthplace of Pathhead might have you believe that I am a Midlothian boy, starting out in life near Dalkeith on the outskirts of our capital city, Edinburgh. But anyone who has spent more than a minute or two in my company will realise that I'm a proud Borderer to the bone.

I was born on 17 March 1940 – the same year as Pelé and Jack Nicklaus – and at that time, in these parts anyway, children were often born at home. Our family lived in a very remote place in the Borders, up the Bowmont Valley, which disappears south of Kelso into the Cheviot Hills. My father was a shepherd on a farm called Calroust Hopehead, near the village of Yetholm, where the burn runs right up to the border with England.

My mother tells me she was taken to have me at the farm of her aunt and uncle at Dodridge, near Pathhead. She had been brought up by them and they feared that we might be snowed in at our farm and unable to get to a midwife if one was needed. My father's parents lived only a mile down the valley from us, which was in the middle of nowhere as well, so Dodridge it was.

Though my passport says 'Birthplace: Pathhead', I have never lived there. I have had a few homes around the Borders, however, and in Glasgow and Edinburgh during my teaching days, and they have all played major parts in shaping my life and views on society. But, really, it's a case of 'once a Borderer, always a Borderer'.

If you pay heed to the people who reckon I've been an explosive character all my life, then it is perhaps no surprise to learn that on the night I was born, a warplane crashed and exploded on the farm where my father worked. It was a very thick misty night and a Wellington bomber apparently lost its bearings, hitting the hill on the Scottish side, just above Calroust Hopehead.

My father was the first to find the wreckage and had to report it. He told me that one of the plane's bombs exploded when it hit the hill, killing the four airmen in the plane. Hearing this story as a lad years later was fascinating and, even after we moved to Kedzlie and Wester Housebyres, my sisters and I would get the bus back down to Yetholm to stay with my grandparents, and I would go looking in the hills for bits of the plane to collect as souvenirs.

My childhood was always linked with farms because of my father's shepherding work and it was as a result of this that I began to develop my left-wing politics, I think. We moved when I was four or five to Nether Tofts, near Denholm, and went to Kirkton School – which is not there now – and also Denholm School for a little while when the Kirkton teacher was off. We then moved to Kedzlie, near Earlston, and I was two or three years there. I still remember going with my father to the agricultural shows after he'd spent Fridays doctoring the show sheep up by putting white stuff (zinc oxide, I understand) on their faces.

But what sticks in the memory is seeing the farmer's sons during the holidays and not being able to understand why they were not there all the time. It was a while before I discovered that they went to boarding school and so could only come back in the holidays, when they'd spend time sledging and so on with my sisters and me. The wee socialist was growing, though, because I remember thinking, 'Hold on, my father works seven days a week, does not get a holiday at all, just a day off here and there to take the sheep to the sales, and yet his hard work is helping to pay for the farmer's sons' education.' I thought there was a real unfairness there.

It's a fact of life in the Borders, though. We used to spend holidays back with my grandparents at Calroust, and latterly down at Mowhaugh Schoolhouse. The landowner was the Duke of Roxburghe and they always referred to him as 'The Duke'. I always thought that was so unfair, that one man could own so much land. The shepherd and his family were clearly servants.

It has always been a part of me, ever since then, the feeling that life can be unfair, that some people have to work extremely hard to make ends meet whilst others are given so much to start with. It might sound a naive sentiment in today's world but it stems from those early days which certainly shaped my strong socialist

26

leanings and perhaps subconsciously filtered into my approach to playing and coaching rugby. As a coach, I would always try to ensure that everyone was treated the same and that only what you did on the training pitch or on the field of play – not your background – determined your standing as a rugby player.

Don't get me wrong, I was not a wee politician in the making or anything; I did not sit on hay bales philosophising or planning a route to No. 10. I was more interested in making catapults to kill birds or chasing rabbits at the harvest. I don't think I necessarily had the same opinions as my parents either, as my dad just tended to get on with life and never moaned much about things. At the same time, my mother and father have always been major influences on me and I think you appreciate that more the older you become.

My mother had gone into service at the age of 14 in the 'big house' – the local farmer's house. She had been quite good at primary school but, because there was no secondary school close to her house, she had remained at the advanced primary until leaving. She then went straight into work, which was quite normal at that time. My father became a young herd, which was a popular choice for young men, first near the border with England at Carter Bar and then on a farm near Langholm. I had four uncles on my father's side and three of them were all herds up the Bowmont Water. The fourth worked for a while on a farm and then moved to Edinburgh to work and still lives there. I had two aunties, also on that side of the family, and one of them still lives in Yetholm, with another uncle, not far from where I grew up.

My mother was an only child brought up by her uncle and auntie. Craig Chalmers' grandfather was her cousin and they were brought up together as brother and sister, so there is a family link between us pair. The reason Craig is a Melrose lad is that his grandfather came to work as the gardener for the owner of Darnlee House, the large house opposite the Waverley Hotel on the way into Melrose.

I'm also related to Scott Aitken, who has just, in 2005, completed 300 games for Melrose. His mother is a sister of Craig's mother – their maiden name is Minto, which is Craig's middle name. Carl Hogg, the former Scotland back row, is one of my sister's sons. I can't go on or people will begin to believe that the whole of the Borders is actually related – though that's not something I could disprove.

I enjoyed living and growing up on a farm but my mother always said that if she had anything to do with it, I would never follow my dad. She wanted me to get a 'collar-and-tie job', as she put it. There was no future on the farm unless you were the farmer's son, she would tell me. I am indebted to my mother, particularly, for pushing me towards an academic career. I've got nothing against farmers – my sister married one – but my mother was right: it was not for me. She thought the best job for me would be in a bank, however, and that never happened either!

My mother was a strong character and she was always first around us. I remember two instances that summed her up. She used to come and meet us when we got off the bus at the road end, about a mile from our house, in the pitch black and she'd walk with us all the way home despite the fact that she was absolutely petrified of the dark. The other vivid memory I have is of my elder sister Elma dropping a ring into the embers of a coal fire. Immediately, my mother stuck her hand into the fire and pulled it out. She was burned quite badly but she saved the ring. I remember thinking, 'What a crazy thing to do!'

My father is a different character: quiet and straightforward, no great emotion. He was brought up just to get on with life and I was too. I spent a lot of time with him, especially during the school holidays.

There were parts you liked and others you did not. I used to enjoy the lambing, the shearing and going to the sales. During the summer holidays, my sisters, Elma and Sheila, and I often went to our grandparents house at Calroust and we were supposed to help with the chores. But we'd spend most of the time chasing each other through the haylofts or going for walks up the surrounding hills. I remember what used to really turn me off farm work, though, was when my father and I used to go up and put the sheep on the turnip breaks, the strips of fields set aside for feeding them in the winter. We would put the hay in wire baskets and my hands would be absolutely frozen. That was murder!

The shepherd on the farm also had the job of killing the pigs and most of the workers had one. I remember watching my father hitting the pig over the head with a big hammer to stun it and before it came to, he would slit its throat with a razor-sharp knife and the blood would gush out everywhere. I don't suppose tackling big ugly New Zealanders would seem a problem after that!

I can't recall my dad giving me many rows, although I'm sure he did. There was one time when we lived at Nether Tofts. I had caught an ailing sheep and was riding on its back. My father saw me, his belt came off and whoosh – I got it. After that, whenever the belt came off, I knew I was in trouble. Getting the belt seemed to have a salutary effect on me but I suppose my father would now be taken before the European Court of Human Rights for such an act.

When I was a boy, unlike in these days of factory farming, there was always plenty of other children on the farms, so they were great communities to grow up in. The fathers used to join in with the sons, playing football and cricket during the summer nights. The football was usually a blown-up pig's bladder; we were not stuck for them on a farm. But sport was just sport then – something to fill in the time.

That began to change for me when we moved again. This time a particular change of farm would shape the rest of my life. It was when my parents took us to Wester Housebyres when I was about nine. We enjoyed living in the other places, don't get me wrong, but that move brought us close to both Melrose and Galashiels, and so opened up great new opportunities, in both sport and education.

I joined Melrose Grammar School, the local primary, and when I started, I was placed twenty-fourth in a class of twenty-eight. Within six months, I had moved up to fourth and I remained near the top for most of my secondary education. I just seemed to thrive among larger numbers of children, with more competition and being pushed harder. I'd been at Blainslie Primary School before that, a one-teacher school – Miss McQueen in my time – and there is no doubt that it was of great benefit to me to go from a small school to a large school; I relished it.

In sporting terms, I started going along to a nearby village called Darnick where they played rugby and I got into the Under-12s sevens team. Our coach was Bob Mitchell, whose son Brian played in the team. We won the local Boyd Cup on our first outing and then another parent, Ian Millar, took over from him. These competitions were played on the famous Greenyards pitch. The Darnick team graduated to the Jubilee Cup and then the Crichton Cup, like hundreds of Melrose youngsters before and since.

Around the time I moved to Melrose Grammar School, I also acquired the nickname 'Creamy'. There have been various explanations over the last 50 years as to where the name originated and people will still come up to me and say 'Hi, Creamy.' The most feasible one, I believe, is that I admired a horse called Cream Of The Border which ran in the Grand National in the late '40s. I must have talked about it a lot, because I was given the nickname by my school friends and it stuck. It caused me embarrassment when I taught at Galashiels Academy later and pupils used to shout the name behind my back. The well-known rugby journalist Norman Mair, himself a former Melrose and Scotland forward, always refers to me as 'Creamy', as well.

I was actually a small boy for my age but I was lucky that at Wester Housebyres there were two tough older boys. The Morris Boys liked to scrap with the 'toonies' of Melrose and I used to back them up, usually when most of the fighting had been done. I liked being in their 'gang'. When I started playing rugby, I was a hooker and very lightweight, but then I moved to prop when I started to grow a bit. There was a burn close to our house with large stones at the side and my first endeavours in weightlifting were trying to hoist those stones above my head. I had a focus by that stage and knew even then that if I was going to succeed in rugby, I would have to be strong.

Despite living on the farm most of the time, I used to spend many of my weekends with the Hastie family who stayed at Newstead and then Darnick, both villages just outside Melrose. They had also come from the Bowmont and knew my parents well, and they were a real sporting family, with three boys – Alex (Eck), Bill and Rob. Eck, known as 'Moose', played for Melrose and Scotland at the same time as me.

At that time, the school-leaving age was 15 but as my parents wanted me to go on, I went to Galashiels Academy for a few years and I was glad, because they were good years at a good school. Because my house was in Roxburghshire, I had the option of going to Hawick High School, but Hawick was more than 30 miles away by train so I went to Gala. One lad from the same farm, Jake Wheelans, did choose Hawick and he later became a stalwart of Selkirk Youth Club – always one to be different was Jake!

I really developed at the Academy, rugby-wise and academically. I played cricket and was reasonably good at athletics. I wasn't a star but I captained my house, Eildon, in my fifth and sixth years, and then the school cricket and rugby teams in my final year, which I enjoyed. My housemaster was the international rugby referee Sandy Dickie, who was principal teacher of Classics in the school. In order to stir up some inter-town rivalry in the Latin class, Sandy used to ask the question 'What happened in 1066?' Before anybody could respond, he would say, 'That's the last time Melrose won the Border League.' It was different then, there was a lot more extra-curricular sport. Sandy and other staff would take the house for athletics twice a week in the summer evenings and organise us into events and relay teams for the school sports.

It is interesting, looking back, to see that I was captain then even though I wasn't the greatest sportsman. My shyness had gone and I must have already developed an enthusiasm for giving orders and organising people. It seemed natural, to be honest. But I can still remember making one mistake which suggests I was not hugely confident. The first representative game I ever played was for the South of Scotland Schools Under-16s against Wales and I was asked if I wanted to be captain. I thought there would be a lot of speeches to make, so I turned it down. Another Gala boy was chosen and he never needed to make any speeches at all! I vowed that I would not be so hesitant again.

That game was at Cardiff Arms Park and my lasting memory is of the cacophony of noise as we walked onto the pitch. I could not hear the piper playing and he was only ten metres away!

On the academic side, too, Galashiels Academy was good for me. I was never the brightest, never a school dux, and after moving from Melrose to Galashiels Academy, I found myself amongst a lot of bright children. But I won the senior school prizes in geography and science, and I was also good at French and Latin. I never really got on with my French teacher at the Academy – he preferred to teach his favourites – and failed the external exam twice. That's my story anyway and I'm sticking to it!

Strangely, I did not take PE as a subject in my final years at the Academy. I took Latin instead. I was going to study applied chemistry at Heriot-Watt College – later to become a university – and because so many old chemistry papers were allegedly written in German, I also took a crash course in it. I can't remember ever using the German on the course!

I had considered studying geography but, interestingly, I felt that the only career to follow would have been teaching and I didn't want to be a teacher at that stage. And science seemed to attract me, experiments in particular. I actually got a job as a lab technician in the science department while still a pupil. The principal teacher of chemistry was Charlie Rogers, a Melrose man, so maybe that was why I got it. My job was to lay out equipment and chemicals for the next day's classes and I remember making a real faux pas once.

I was diluting concentrated sulphuric acid; a golden rule was always to put the water in first and then add small amounts of acid. Well, I put the acid in this huge glass container first, then poured the water in. When I lifted the glass container up, it was cut clean right round the bottom and the acid/water mixture poured everywhere.

My school days were enjoyable, though, and I was quite popular with my fellow pupils and teachers. It wasn't something that worried me much, I just tried to lead by example, work hard and get on with things. My fellow pupils would probably say I was dedicated, someone who when he set his mind to something, he did it. It is a philosophy that has never changed throughout my life.

I have my critics, but I don't think anyone, be they teachers, players, coaches, colleagues or even the media, could say that I was ever not dedicated or committed to working as hard as I could. The start and support I received from staff and fellow pupils at Borders primary schools and then Galashiels Academy inspired that in me.

3

My Sporting Choice

Derek Brown
Melrose RFC (1956–64)

Jim came out of school as a big, strong laddie who was pretty confident and from the first time he pulled on a Melrose jersey, we could see that he was bound for the very top.

He had the ability and he had this desire to reach the top. Jim was a student at Heriot-Watt College in Edinburgh in 1957 when he started with Melrose but he would travel down for training and never missed it. In fact, he would train even more on his own and was fitter than any of us.

We had some great players at the time – internationalists Eck Hastie, David and Robin Chisholm, Wattie Hart and Frank Laidlaw – but Jim was never frightened to contribute. He brought new ideas to the training, which maybe didn't go down too well initially with some people, but he quickly turned their heads because his ideas were good ones and in a reasonably successful side, everyone wanted the club to be better.

He played in the second row to begin with and didn't like it much; he wanted to play number 8 but the problem for him was that I was number 8 and a bit more senior to him at that time. To show how things changed, at the end of my playing career, in 1964, I was pushed into the second row and he was number 8!

He prided himself on his appearance and was always very smartly turned out, setting high standards on and off the field. Jim was actually quite a severe and deep-thinking youngster who thought a lot about the game of rugby and read a lot of politics. He never imposed his views on anyone but he was keen on righting injustices.

He went on to become a great Melrose, Scotland and Lions player and, as Melrose coach, he turned many ordinary players into winners to put the club at the top of Scottish rugby for a consistent period. From boys like my son Robbie and his generation of the 1990s to people like myself, Eck, Frank and that of the 1960s, there is a great respect for Jim. Players still think the world of him. I still think of him as a big soft-hearted laddie.

Rugby was not my first love and those who used to watch me as a committed youngster trying to improve my cricketing skills may have been surprised to see me spend a lifetime with a rugby ball.

I was very keen and played a lot of cricket as a youngster, and still believe that there is more skill in cricket than in rugby. But in the Borders, the opportunities for becoming a successful rugby player were greater than those for becoming a top-class cricketer. Actually, I wasn't that good, so I would not have made it as a top cricketer anyway.

But sport did take a grip of me. From a very young age, I was always excited about competing and of course the location of our house, equidistant between Melrose and Galashiels, gave me unlimited opportunities. My sister Sheila was a better sportsperson than me; she was good at athletics and hockey. The strange thing is that whilst I was fortunate to spend my developing years amongst top-quality rugby players, which undoubtedly pushed me to the levels I reached, the opportunities for Sheila were limited. She reached the South District level as a hockey player, and became a long-serving coach and umpire, but she would have had to move to the city to progress to international honours, which was tough. My other sister, Elma, was not so sporty – she preferred a more sedentary life, I think.

That's no great surprise, because I did not come from a sporting family. My relatives were shepherds in outlying farms and so had little opportunity to become interested in sport. However, like many rural workers at that time, they entertained themselves by playing music and I am told that my grandfather was an accomplished fiddler and played at local dances, while all my uncles played a variety of musical instruments. The best I can manage is the paper comb! Yet, much later, as a headmaster at Hawick, it gave me tremendous pleasure and pride to watch my pupils performing in choirs and musical groups to a very high standard. It also highlighted to me how by pursuing one career as slavishly as I did, you can neglect so many others.

But sport was my passion and the teenage Jim Telfer used to play three games most weekends – two of rugby and one of football. I played for the school in the morning, then Gala Wanderers, a semi-junior club, in the afternoon and then football on the Sunday morning. I was either centre-half or goalkeeper.

Funnily enough, having grown up in Scotland, and in the wide open spaces of the Borders, one sport I did not play as a boy was golf, but then my family didn't live near a golf course and we didn't own a car. Anyone who has seen me on the course recently will conclude that I still can't play. The Melrose cricket pitch was a lot closer and from my house it was almost completely downhill for two miles, so it only took about fifteen minutes to get there on my bike. Unfortunately, it took three times longer to get home.

Leaving school was a crossroads for me in sport – I had to decide where I was going to play seriously. Almost all my teammates at the Academy and the Wanderers were moving up to the Gala club or to the city to play. Most of my rugby development had been due to Jim Shearer, the head of PE at Galashiels Academy and a very good rugby coach. Lots of Melrose boys had gone through his hands and I suppose he gave them the same advice he gave me, which was, 'You are a Melrose boy and you should go back there.'

He was a Gala supporter, so he must not have thought I was all that good! All his favourites, I remember, were called by their first names while I remained 'Telfer' even when I was captain. He did relent and start calling me by my first name when I returned to the school as a member of staff a few years later!

The final decision on where I should go was really taken by my father. Gala Seconds had asked me to play for them and when I went home to tell him, his curt reply was, 'You're no playing for them.' I 'decided' to join Melrose Rugby Club.

At that stage in my career, I don't think my father rated me very highly either. I made my debut for the 1st XV a few months later, in October 1957, and he made a rather rash promise. He said, 'Every time you play in the 1st XV, I'll clean your boots.' He gave that up long before I played 300 games.

Going to the Greenyards was a wise choice for me. As I have said many times, I am indebted to the club for almost everything I have achieved in playing and coaching. Just how privileged a route I was taking came home to me very early in my career. In those days, the South Schools were regularly well beaten by the Edinburgh Schools and, by chance, one of the Edinburgh players became a classmate at lectures in my first year at Heriot-Watt College.

I had joined Melrose by then and he had joined Watsonians Juniors straight from George Watson's College. Within a year I was playing regularly for Melrose and within three for the South, yet he never moved up to his senior club XV and after a few years gave up altogether. There could be many reasons, of course, but the different paths always intrigued me.

There is no doubt that the opportunities available to me at Melrose and in the Borders generally were instrumental in shaping my future as a player, coach and administrator. Interestingly, when I was working at the SRU, some of my Rugby Division colleagues set up what we called a National Pathway for young players throughout Scotland, to enable them to progress from schools to senior level more simply and effectively. It proved so successful that other home unions have copied it and it is viewed as a great model for twenty-first-century rugby. And yet there was a seamless competitive-performance pathway for young players in the Borders 50 years ago when I played through school, semi-junior, club and district all the way to international level.

Melrose has always been a small town in the Borders, with a population of only around 2,500, and today it has no secondary school but when I joined the club straight from school, it was one of the most successful in Scotland. Leslie Allan, Robin Chisholm and Norman Mair were internationalists, and Wattie Hart, David Chisholm, Eck Hastie and Frank Laidlaw were soon to follow. We also had quite a number of South district stalwarts as well.

The season was very regular then, in the late '50s. It started on the first Saturday in September with Earlston Sports, followed on successive Saturdays by Kelso Sports and then Selkirk Sports (all sevens tournaments). The season finished on the last day of April, with Langholm Sports on the final Saturday. Our opening 1st XV game was always against Trinity Accies on the Edinburgh Monday holiday in the third week of September and the next weekend, the Glasgow holiday weekend, we had two games – against Kelvinside Accies on the Saturday and Hutchesons' Grammar School on the Monday. Regular as clockwork and easy for players and supporters to follow – there's something to be said for that.

My debut for the Melrose 1st XV was in October 1957, against Heriot's FP at Goldenacre. I got my chance because Derek Brown had the flu. I played second row, we won, but Derek came back and I was dropped the following week. However, by the end of the year, I was established in the team and it was memorable to be part of winning the Border League. I was still underage to drink and I remember Wattie Hart took it upon himself to look after me, which meant ensuring I did not touch the demon drink until after my 18th birthday! The two of us often went to the cinema after a game instead of going to the pub.

I wouldn't like you to get the idea that Melrose players and officials at that time did not drink or that we were not sociable, of course! All of the senior players had done National Service (I missed that by only six months), so drinking large amounts after the game was an art many had acquired and which they willingly passed on.

Melrose has always been a very open club and because most of the city clubs were exclusively for former pupils of particular schools, quite a number of players were attracted down to the Borders to play. Our playing strength was always augmented by incomers, which was a bonus for a place as small as Melrose. Mike Bewsher, Mike Chipolato, the former Scotland A team manager Rob Flockhart, Raymond Pia, Paddy Hart, Bill Ingram and Gordon Blyth are names that come to mind.

There was also a real feeling of ambition at the club and that you would take up the challenge of pushing yourself towards higher honours was taken as read. On my 19th birthday, I played my first game for the Scottish Border Club, a pseudonym for the South, at Mansfield Park, Hawick, on 17 March 1959. I remember the game because all the Scottish selectors were there casting an eye before deciding a few days later on the team to play England. I was not yet on their radar but Derek Brown was in line for a cap. He had an outstanding game, scoring two or three tries, but, incredibly, he still did not get the nod.

Jock Davidson from Edinburgh Wanderers did, and Derek never got a cap. He was very unfortunate, because he had been a stalwart for the South for a number of years and played against the Springboks in 1951. I found that disappointing but it did not dent my belief that playing for Melrose and the South was more of a help than a hindrance in trying to become an internationalist.

When I stepped into the full South side the following season, it was similar to when I'd joined Melrose, with so many quality players, some of them household names. Players like Hugh McLeod, Adam Robson, Oliver Grant, Ken Smith and Christy Elliot, along with Melrose's David Chisholm, Eck Hastie and Derek Brown, were the backbone of the team. At that time, four teams – South, Glasgow, Edinburgh, and North and Midlands – competed in the Inter-district Championship.

The South were dominant then – they shared seven championships and won seven outright between 1954–55 and 1970–71, my last season as a district player. As you can imagine, I was quite lucky to get in, but once you were involved, you could not help but learn from such a good team.

McLeod, the Hawick prop, was at his peak then. He had been playing for Scotland since 1954 and went on to play 40 consecutive matches, until he retired in 1962. In one South game at Selkirk, I was in the second row and early in the game, as the scrum broke up, this player sprinted past me like a tornado and tackled the opposition inside-centre, killing the movement stone-dead. It was all a blur and I thought, 'What was that?' It was just Hughie making his presence felt early in the game.

That small cameo of play remained with me for some time, as it had provided a glimpse of the level of urgency and intensity of men playing at a higher level. A British Lion in 1955 and 1959, Hughie impressed me in many ways, not just on the field. To me, he was the first true professional rugby player in Scotland: a dedicated fitness enthusiast as well as an excellent technician. When he retired, he did not rest on his laurels, instead making sure that what he had learned from his experiences in New

Zealand, South Africa and the international stadia around Britain was ploughed back into helping his club. Along with his protégé, Derrick Grant, he kept Hawick at the top of club rugby throughout the late 1950s, the '60s and the '70s. His example had a significant effect on me and when I came back from Scottish and Lions tours, I tried to use what I'd learned to Melrose's advantage.

But then, in the 1961–62 season, I was still experiencing the highs and lows of trying to make myself better. I was dropped from the South team for the entire season and the Springboks were on tour. The selectors wanted bulk and picked a prop in my position, supposedly to match the Springbok strength. The game was played at Hawick before a very large crowd and the score was 19–3 to South Africa. I'll never forget one fact: we were completely outplayed in the lineout, one of my strengths! The following season, I was back into the team. I established myself and played against the All Blacks in 1963, again at Hawick. But we lost that one 8–0.

My rugby was becoming more intense but my academic work at Heriot-Watt was also becoming more demanding. I could see that my chances of finding a job linked to my studies were remote. Initially, I saw myself working in a big industrial complex like ICI or BP, but there were also small chemical companies in the Borders. I gained some experience at Kemp Blair dyeworks in Galashiels before college and later spent a few months at Turnbull dyeworks in Hawick. But these companies tended to train their own dyers through apprenticeships.

I even spoke with Wilson Shaw, Scotland's famous captain in the Triple Crown year of 1938. He was then president of the SRU and as a chemist, he had worked for ICI for a long time. But my own tutor, Professor Bell, provided the answer. Near the end of the course, he advised the final-year students that the labour market for chemists was not too good but that there were ample opportunities in teaching. Now that could be done in the Borders, near Melrose, I thought, and I duly enrolled at Moray House Teacher Training College when I graduated.

Moving into teaching is something I never regretted and I thoroughly enjoyed working with children and adults in an educational environment. After teaching practice at Boroughmuir High School in Edinburgh (where my tutor was Ernie Anderson, the legendary sevens scrum-half of Daniel Stewarts FP), Tynecastle High School and Hawick High School, it was a matter of finding a job.

Whilst at Moray House, I had been capped for Scotland and I briefly toyed with the idea of joining the Army as a Scotland teammate, Pringle Fisher, had done. He was a dentist and had joined as an officer, initially for three years with the option to come out with a fairly large gratuity. Mike Campbell-Lamerton, another fellow internationalist, was a captain in the Duke of Wellington Regiment at that time and also recommended a career in the Army as a teacher. It was thought that if I joined, it might have been possible to get a posting near London and play for London Scottish.

It is interesting looking back now at what paths I might have taken, because I also received enquiries from rugby league scouts who were keen for me to turn professional, although that wasn't an option I took seriously. To some rugby officials in the Borders at that time, turning professional was tantamount to committing murder! Those who did were often spurned by former teammates or even debarred from their own clubhouse. The culture has changed over the years but to this day, there is still resentment in some clubs towards players and officials making money out of rugby union.

The first teaching post I was offered, I turned down. It was at the Royal High School in Edinburgh – the top rugby school in the city at that time. I didn't take it because I felt they only really wanted me because I had played for Scotland.

Then two jobs came up in the Borders. I returned from a Canada tour with Scotland in 1964 to be welcomed at Edinburgh Airport by my sister Sheila, who gave me a clean shirt and tie and told me to get to the County Buildings in Galashiels for interviews for Selkirk High School and Galashiels Academy. There was a fellow student, Ian McKellar, being interviewed for the same two jobs just before me and he told me some time later that during his interview he was asked if he knew whether Jim Telfer was home yet – he knew then he'd have to wait until I decided where I was going before he'd know which job he'd get! I chose Galashiels Academy and he went to Selkirk but that blatant favouritism always left guilt with me. He was an excellent teacher and should have been judged on merit.

In both rugby and teaching, in truth, I never set myself targets like wanting to play for Scotland or be a head teacher. My aim in both was simply to be as good as I could be. A touch naively, I thought that after three or four years teaching I would have a full set of science lessons and wouldn't need to prepare any more for the rest of my teaching life. I soon realised that my subject kept changing and that, just as in rugby, in teaching you are always developing and improving.

In rugby, that attitude probably began with personal fitness. People remind me still of how I used to climb through the window into the changing-rooms at the Greenyards when no one else was around, train on my own, get changed again and leave through the front door. Strangely, there was actually no point to it. I could have done all the training at home, in the field in front of my house, to acquire the same effect. The only difference was that the Greenyards was marked out in lines whereas the field at home was not. And there was no cow dung on the rugby pitch!

On one night visit to the changing-rooms, there was about a foot of snow lying and I could not run on the pitch. But someone had cut a path through the snow from the street to the clubhouse and I did my fitness work along the path. It might seem a bit strange, or masochistic almost, but I would train thinking to myself, 'No one else will be training in this tonight, so I'm one up.' From an early age, I realised that I was not going to be the best player in Scotland, but I believed I could be the fittest.

As a player, I acquired a reputation in the Borders for being negative but I don't think that was fair. There was a lot more diving on the ball in those days and I quickly realised the importance of winning and keeping possession. In the modern idiom, I was prepared to put my body on the line, and I still carry many scars to show for it. I maintain that often I won the ball quite legitimately but my teammates were not there quickly enough to support me and so left me exposed to the opposition. It never stopped me, though, and I can provide an example of where it worked to my team's advantage.

It was in 1964 when Scotland played the All Blacks at Murrayfield. With the score at 0–0, New Zealand were pressing on the Scottish line and it looked inevitable that their pressure would lead to a try. The ball appeared at the side of a ruck and I dived on it. I hung on to it like grim death and as the All Blacks drove over me, I took quite a few boots to my back and head.

There was a shrill blast of the whistle and I got up expecting to be penalised for holding on to the ball. But instead, Colin Meads, the All Black forward, was taken aside, given a stern warning by the referee for dangerous play and the penalty was awarded to Scotland. The pressure was relieved and we finished the game level at 0–0. To this day, we have never beaten New Zealand, and only then and in 1983 have we drawn.

Like most Borders rugby players, my introduction to rugby was through sevens. I played a lot at senior level for Melrose, and won four winner's and nineteen runner's-up medals – most of the latter coming second to a very good Hawick seven, if memory serves me well.

There was one particular sevens tie against Hawick when I was very young and up against experienced international forwards Adam Robson, Hughie McLeod and Jack Hegarty. I was hooker and every time our scrum-half put the ball into the scrum, Jack would bore in and twist my head so I couldn't see the ball coming. I suggested to my loose-head prop that he help me out but he did nothing.

So at the next scrum, I took the law into my own hands and as Jack bored in on me, I bit his ear and the scrum broke up in disarray. There was some blood from the wound but the referee could not work out what had happened. Well, the boring stopped after that but I suppose I'd probably get about six months' suspension for that nowadays.

In truth, young players probably would not believe how dirty the game used to be. The laws of rucking were far more lax and players were literally rucked out the back if they lay near or around the ball. Fights were a frequent occurrence, even at international level, and I'm glad that the advent of TV and citings has made the game a lot cleaner. Then, young players had to grow up quickly and be prepared to defend themselves or go under. As I grew older and possibly wiser, I acquired a reputation for being able to 'help' the referee administer the game to such an extent that I was sometimes accused of actually refereeing it.

It did not always work. In 1966, I went on the Lions tour to New Zealand and, as I write elsewhere in the book, it was very tough. After three months of battling to survive, my rucking skills were honed to perfection and I was prepared to stand on legs, arms and backs to legitimately win the ball. In one of my first games back at Melrose after the tour, I went in to ruck the ball and there was a loud blast on the whistle. The referee, Barry Laidlaw, an experienced internationalist, penalised me and said, 'Penalty for dirty play.'

I said, 'Look, I have been doing that for three months in New Zealand,' to which he replied, 'You're not in New Zealand now!'

I had to accept the decision but it was the first of many times when I have had reason to believe that domestic rugby in Scotland is soft compared to other countries we compete with. Don't get me wrong, I have never encouraged dirty play. But rugby is a hard physical game and our domestic rugby should prepare our international players from youth level upwards to compete successfully on the world stage and I often questioned whether that was the case.

It is difficult to pick one reason as to why Melrose was such a good grounding for an aspiring internationalist because it was probably a combination of things. In my early days, there were no floodlights and training was pretty basic, mostly running round the pitch and doing sprints. During the light nights, there was some ball work. Most of the young players were very keen but it was the older ones like Wattie, Eck and Les Allan who would drive the rest of us. Just as it is today, touch rugby was a great favourite at Melrose and, like most teams, we had some players who could have played touch rugby for Scotland but were not much cop when it came to the real thing.

Training began to change quite dramatically in the late '60s, largely due to the lessons learned by myself and others on tours. Clubs were very self-sufficient in those days and facilities like new training lights were starting to be put up by the players and officials themselves, without any prompting from the SRU. Players I have coached at various stages have complained about me working them too hard but it is a fact that the hardest sessions I have ever taken (apart from the Lions scrummaging sessions in 1997) have been at Melrose Rugby Club and nobody ever complained – not to my face, anyway! I know it came from my own approach, where I felt I could overcome a lack of ability in some areas by being fitter than opponents. When working with poorer resources, compared with larger rugby nations, in a country like Scotland, I felt you had to look for an edge like that.

As a player in the 1960s, I trained five times a week – twice with the club and three times on my own. But it was not all work and no play. It was great fun playing games away from home, going to Glasgow by train to play Glasgow High School FP on New Year's Day or taking the ferry across the Firth of Forth to play Dunfermline, followed by drinks and team songs on the bus home.

In those days, the pack leader was probably the most important man in the team, organising the lineouts and scrums, and generally driving the forwards, and I enjoyed that role. I tried to make a point of getting to the lineout first and speaking to each forward as they arrived. At that time, of course, the wingers threw the ball into the lineout, but eventually common sense prevailed, mainly because it was sensible to have the same player, usually the hooker, doing it all the time. It also allowed the wingers to practise with the backs when the forwards were on their own.

The hooker was often a completely different shape to the rest of the forwards, normally very small and very good at hooking for the ball, both for and against the head. But it was far more of an art than it is today, with possession contested at almost every scrum and so many going against the head. Props and hookers could be dropped from international sides if they lost too many scrums and teams used to have specific moves planned in case their tight-head was under pressure. Nowadays, most number 8s have no idea what to do if a tight-head is taken. It is not only in the Super 12 that scrummaging arts have been lost.

I spoke earlier of the influence my mother had on my academic career, but my father had quite an influence on how I approached my playing and coaching of rugby. For one, he was never totally satisfied with how I played. If I asked him about my performance, he would screw up his face and say, 'Well, you weren't too bad but you could have done better.' It rankled me a bit but I accepted that I should try to do better next time.

The fact that he had not played rugby at all didn't seem to deter him from giving expert advice! Mind you, he was not alone – most 'experts' in the press have never played rugby either. I think there

44

is little doubt that his attitude rubbed off on me, because I have never been one to accept low standards in the classroom or on the playing field and tended to tell players even when they'd won that they could have done better.

Some readers might remember Bruce Woodcock, a heavyweight boxer in the early 1950s. His father was his trainer but he was very hard to please. I read an article which said Bruce had knocked his opponent out and the usual hangers-on were celebrating around him. But before he joined in the celebrations, he turned to his father and asked for his verdict. 'You did all right, son' was the response and only then did Bruce feel happy.

I never have suffered fools gladly but, contrary to some reports, I very seldom criticised players in a beaten team immediately after a game. I would always wait until things had calmed down and the team met at the next training session. However – and this was what surprised some people – I might have a go at my team if they won. I did give some praise but I would point out that they could have done better. Clearly, as I have noticed from their comments in the press, some players and coaches have had problems with that but I don't think they understand the psychology behind it.

To take the Melrose team of the late 1980s and early 1990s as an example, players like Craig Chalmers, Bryan Redpath, Carl Hogg and Robbie Brown, just to name a few, never rested on their laurels and were always striving to improve. Even after games they had won easily, they were prepared to take criticism on the chin – in fact they would look for it from myself and the other coaches, Rob Moffat and Alan 'Gel' Tait, and from each other. We used to talk about the perfect performance both at training and in the games. That was what we were striving for – but we never reached it, of course.

At international level, the Grand Slam teams of 1984 and 1990 were the same. The players accepted constructive criticism from me and from each other. They were squads full of characters who made sure that the mentally weaker members lifted their performances. They demanded the best of each other and my approach fitted in well with those kinds of people.

It did not please everyone, however, even coaches. David Johnston, the Scotland assistant coach between 1995 and '98, criticised me in a newspaper article for the way I spoke to the team in 1996 after the French match which they had won 19–14. It was an open, exciting match made even more so by the fact that Scotland almost contrived to lose even although they were at least 15 points better than France. I did have a real go at them, because they nearly let France win and, knowing full well how long some of these players could go without beating a team like France, I felt it was important they realised that that performance had almost cost them a precious victory. They had to seek improvement rather than get carried away with having won.

A fortnight later in Cardiff, Rob Wainwright, the captain, gave the team a similar dressing-down for almost losing the game against Wales. The score was 16–14 and again Scotland were far better than the opposition and should have won by some distance, and while Rob may not have quite the same style as me, he let the players know how he felt.

To my mind, some players are naive; they feel I am just letting off steam, when really the things I say and how I say them have been, in the main, deliberately thought out. There has always been a lot of 'black' psychology in my approach, both to teaching and coaching, in truth; sometimes you have to be negative to provoke a positive response. The use of intonation of the voice and an animated style have formed a strong part of my method. It has been developed over many years and from different experiences in an effort to find what will get the best out of people. Some ideas have been tried and left behind because they did not work, but the fact that I was able to get a lot out of the 1984 squad, the 1990 forwards, the Melrose League winners, the 1997 winning Lions pack and the 1999 Five Nations champions gives me some measure of satisfaction.

A huge part of winning is to do with pride – a pride in being the best you can be and exhorting others to be the best they can be. Melrose and the South of Scotland began that education but my Scotland career and my travels around the world brought home to me how we simply had to push very hard in Scotland if we wanted to compete in world rugby.

4

Wearing the Thistle

Derrick Grant
Scotland (14 caps), British and Irish Lions (1966)

The 1960s was an enjoyable time to be playing rugby. Certainly it was at Hawick, with the South and with Scotland. Coming from Hawick, there were always great rivalries with the other Border teams and I used to like meeting Jim Telfer when Melrose visited Mansfield Park – preferably at the bottom of a ruck!

We were a bit similar and liked doing the hard work in the game but Jim was a very brave sort, to the point of being careless with his body. The New Zealanders used to say, 'Put your body down there and there'll be 16 feet coming and kicking you out the back in no time.' And did that stop Jim? Did it hell.

A very fit and clever player, he captained us in South Africa with the Scottish Border Club in 1967 and worked us very hard. People reckoned he may have gone too far at times but I agreed with everything he did. The coach sets the standard. If you aim for the top, you might get something slightly below that, but better that than aiming for halfway. He demanded a lot of himself and never asked anyone to do anything he was not capable of.

We had some superb backs then and very hard-working forwards, and Scotland played some great rugby at times. Jim and I were rivals in Borders rugby but the key was that we always felt we were Scottish and on the same side against the rest of the world.

I was unfortunate to have a serious groin problem on the 1966 Lions tour to New Zealand, which kept me out of a lot of games,

47

and I was looking forward to touring with them again, in 1968, to South Africa. The coach, Ronnie Dawson, had seen me during the season and told me I was definitely going to be picked. But I was getting bad headaches and double vision during games, and being sick, so I had to go and see a specialist. He told me I had suffered concussion too many times and couldn't continue playing rugby, so that was me, suddenly finished with Hawick, Scotland and the Lions.

There are individuals who can do marvellous things but they can be a bit selfish; Jim Telfer was a player's player. He would do the jobs that no one saw needed doing or that no one wanted to do – covering up for people, putting in vital tackles and stopping big men, placing his body in the middle of lots of rucking feet – the kind of player you never miss until they're not there.

We struck up a good friendship as coaches and I worked with Scotland teams off and on right up until the end of the 2003 World Cup, latterly as a manager, then selector, retiring when I was 65. Jim's ability to move with the times and change his coaching to suit modern rugby was tremendous. We didn't always agree and had different viewpoints on how to approach certain problems but there was a genuine respect for Jim.

To play for your country is the greatest honour a rugby player can have and the memory of my first cap at Murrayfield still remains very fresh in my mind.

A lot has happened since that day, 4 January 1964, and the game of rugby has taken me on an incredible roller-coaster journey, both mentally and physically. Although I wasn't aware of it at the time, the path you have to tread in Scotland to gain a cap is easier than in some other countries but the one which takes you to victory is more arduous than most realise.

In that first season, I thought I was flying – Scotland was a team which hardly lost! Having played seven seasons in senior rugby as a second row, it was a surprise when I was chosen to play flanker in my first game for Scotland. Those who have played both positions will appreciate that the duties can be quite different. I felt very exposed as a flanker in the scrum and I remember getting some advice from Les Allan on running angles from scrum and lineout. Considering he was a centre who occasionally played stand-off, he had limited practical experience himself but I was indebted to him for his advice!

I also had the added responsibility of leading the pack, which was somewhat strange because the captain, Brian Neill, was in the pack as well. Brian was actually a good captain, who spoke well and spoke French, but I was leading the pack for the South at the time and had that experience. There were four new caps in my first game – Peter 'P.C.' Brown, who was still at West of Scotland then; the Hawick second row Willie Hunter; Stewart Wilson, the full-back from Oxford University who went on to become a good captain and Lion as well; and myself – so there must have been change in the air.

No Scotland player has it easy but when I first came into the team, we had France first up and then the All Blacks two weeks later. We beat France 10–0 at Murrayfield, two converted tries to nil. A good win, but I lost my dinner! I remember afterwards sitting at the team dinner beside Michel Crauste, my opposite number. He was older than me and had started playing for France in 1957, going on to win 63 caps, which was a formidable achievement in those days.

When the cold meat starter was put in front of us, he leaned across and, with his fork, took all of mine. I just sat and looked at him and never said a word; he couldn't speak English and I couldn't speak French. Failing my French at school was proving a good thing. But I had my fork primed ready for the steak main course! I played against him again the next year but, thankfully, he was captain then so he sat at the top table and I didn't go hungry. I never found out if he pinched Brian Neill's meat or not.

We then drew 0–0 with New Zealand, lost to Wales 11–3, beat Ireland 6–3 – not a classic – and then we defeated England 15–6. That was a great game to finish with, for me personally and for Scotland. I scored my first international try and gave the scoring passes for Norman Bruce and Ronnie Glasgow's tries. I've been told it was the first time that a crowd ever ran onto the pitch at Murrayfield after a try was scored. And you could see why, because it was such a great season – the first time we'd beaten England since 1950 and Scotland's most successful season since 1938. I certainly enjoyed that Calcutta Cup game and it was called by some newspapers 'Telfer's match', which is a great memory.

At the end of that season, to be honest, I thought I was king. We toured Canada in the summer and, though no caps were awarded, we won all five games, so that was a good way to finish the season.

And then in 1965 it all came crashing back to earth. I played in the first three games of that year, in which we lost 16–8 to France, 14–12 to Wales and 16–6 to the Irish, and I was dropped. At this time, there were four Melrose players in the Scotland team – myself, Frank Laidlaw, Eck Hastie and Davie Chisholm – which was a tremendous achievement for such a small club, and I was not happy at becoming the odd one out.

The team then drew 3–3 with England in a match which became known as 'Hancock's game' after the winger Andy Hancock from Northampton. I can still see that Hancock try yet – as travelling reserve, I was sitting high up in the stand at Twickenham and had a bird's-eye view of it.

Scotland were attacking down the right-hand side of the field through David Whyte, our winger, who came inside and got caught. The ball was turned over and Mike Weston, the English stand-off, noticed the space out left. He immediately passed the ball to his left-winger Hancock, who ran for about seventy metres and at least four Scottish tacklers missed him one after the other. Thankfully, he scored at the corner, England missed the conversion and the game ended in a draw. The players reckoned that Davie Chisholm scored a try in that match and did not get it, which just added to the game's notoriety.

I had realised by then that playing for Scotland, and being dropped, was no bed of roses. Scotland beat South Africa 8–5 a month later and I still was not in the team – P.C. Brown was in my place then. I resolved just to put my head down and work harder, and I got a chance to play against the Springboks for the Scottish Districts at Hawick. The Springbok captain in that game was Dawie de Villiers. He was a wee blond-haired scrum-half who, interestingly, was born just three months after me in 1940 and, like me, finished on 25 caps in 1970. However, he was also a minister of the Dutch Free Church who later became a government minister, so we were not that close!

Mike Campbell-Lamerton had been our captain during that difficult period and when I lost my place, he also lost the captaincy, the full-back Stewart Wilson taking over. Mike was a real genuine bloke, a career soldier who put his heart and soul into everything he did. He had appeared out of the mist, literally, when he had played at Murrayfield for Combined Services a few years earlier. He was later captain of the 1966 Lions, when he suffered terribly at the hands of the media. Thinking back, it was probably the first time I witnessed at close quarters a real character assassination of a fellow sportsperson.

But 1966 was a big year because it was a Lions year, and everybody knew that. Remember the tour started then on 21 April and finished on 20 September, so it was a big, big thing. There were to be 35 matches, 8 in Australia, 25 in New Zealand and 2 in Canada and everybody involved at international level wanted to be on that tour. Forty years on, the honour of being a Lion is still just as great.

Like many players, I imagine, the target I set myself at the start of that season was to regain my Scotland place and try to win a shot with the British and Irish Lions, so it was a tremendous achievement when I was informed I'd been selected for the Lions. I don't know if the club thought as much of it, though. Supporters in Melrose expected Eck and Davie to become Lions, but they did not go and instead Frank and I were picked.

We seemed to be 'the wrong two' in the eyes of many and even at a presentation before we left for the tour the president of the club used most of his speech to complain about how the Lions selection had been poor because Eck and Davie were not there, hardly mentioning Frank and me. I didn't really notice the slight but, naturally, some of my family did. Anyway, we couldn't have been that bad, because both of us went on Lions tours again – me with the 1968 tour to South Africa and Frank with the successful 1971 tour to New Zealand.

At that time, the coach didn't have a say in selection. There were selectors from Scotland, England, Ireland and Wales, and they and the manager picked the squad. I'm certain there would have been some horse-trading, because it was still in vogue when I was a selector in 1983. The Lions tours were wonderful experiences and there is many a story to tell about New Zealand in 1966 and South Africa in 1968, which we will come to later, but playing for Scotland is the pinnacle of most players' careers and remains the environment in which you must first prove yourself. That is where you become an international and only when you can perform regularly at that level does the dream of a Lions jersey come into view.

So wearing the blue jersey remained my priority. Season 1966–67 was a quiet one for me; I missed the autumn Test and the first match of the Five Nations due to injury. The Australians toured here in the autumn and I was resigned to watching. My place at number 8 was taken by Alasdair Boyle, whose brother Cammy had already played a few times at prop in the early 1960s. Scotland played well, beating the Wallabies 11–5 – the South had already beaten them under Norman Suddon's captaincy, so it was disappointing to be sitting out two good performances – and were well set for the Five Nations to follow. Scotland also won against France in Paris in the first Five Nations match, which was a great feat in itself, and I was back for the rest of the season – we beat Wales and I scored a try in the 11–5 win but we then lost to Ireland and England.

That summer, I enjoyed my first tour to South Africa and, while it wasn't with the Lions, it was very special, as it was with the Scottish Border Club. It was a short tour but a good tour. The squad became known as 'The Ambassadors' due to an informative book about the tour with that title written by the venerable Borders journalist John Dawson – a great character. We played four games in Aliwal North, Johannesburg, Bloemfontein and Durban.

The quality of the team had a lot to do with the success of that tour. Colin Telfer was a young boy then, and we had Eck, Frank, George Stevenson, Christy Elliot, Dougie Jackson, Harry Whitaker – who went to rugby league – Derrick Grant, Charlie Stewart, Willie Hunter, Norman Suddon, Jock Turner, Peter Robertson: all great players. Davie Chisholm was not there because he had had his knee injured, late-tackled in a meaningless match with Allan Glens FP at the end of the season.

We won our first game and then drew with Transvaal at Ellis Park, at altitude, which was a great achievement. We were narrowly beaten by Orange Free State – 'nae oranges, naebody's free and it's in a hell of a state' we used to say back then – and then we went to Durban and our players were almost panicking because of the heat. It was late May and it was the first time many of us had experienced sitting in the dressing-room preparing to go out soaking with sweat; many of us were worried how we were going to get through the game. We played quite well but were beaten for stamina in the last 20 minutes and lost the game.

As captain, the way the Borders squad conducted itself and became real ambassadors for South and Scottish rugby gave me great pleasure. We were taken to Johannesburg Airport at the end of the tour and given a farewell by Dr Danie Craven, who was chairman of the South African Rugby Board, and before we got onto the plane we had to make speeches. Cardiff had been there at the same time. The Scottish Border Club were all dressed in blazers and well behaved, and I made a speech on our behalf, as did Andrew Bowie, the co-manager.

The Cardiff captain could hardly speak, he was so drunk – he had to be held up beside me and Danie. We were there in blazers, the Cardiff boys were just out of bed, pretty scruffy, and I remember comparing the two squads and being proud I was with the Borders players. The tour had showed Scottish rugby in a great light and projected Scotland as a well-disciplined, professional group. Almost every time I met Dr Craven after that, he commented on that tour and I struck up a great friendship with him. After he died, I went to visit his statue at Stellenbosch whilst on holiday in 1999.

It was pleasing to be able to return to South Africa in 1968 with the Lions, including a lot of Welshmen, and have my respect for Welsh rugby restored. But there were times in the 1967–68 season when a second Lions tour seemed a world away.

To be fair, I didn't suffer many injuries in my career but in October 1967, against Kelso, I remember jumping, running through a lineout with the ball, which you could do then, and someone coming in from the side and whacking me on the knee. I was carried off the field and needed a cartilage operation which ruled me out until February of that season.

I missed the autumn tour to the UK by New Zealand and having to watch the All Blacks playing on my home territory was very disappointing. Before facing Scotland, they played a Scottish Districts match at Melrose and won easily – Colin Meads offered his commiserations to me afterwards. But I remember that match because of a technique they used in a maul. I can still see Waka Nathan standing up in a tackle in midfield and turning with the ball towards the scrum-half. Players came in to join him and formed a 'V', all facing the scrum-half. He took the pass from Nathan and, with the forwards then set up to follow the ball wherever it went, he moved it through his backs.

I watched the international at home on television. Scotland played reasonably well but were beaten 14–3. It was the first time, but not the last, when I thought that while Scotland had a chance in theory – both teams had 15 players, after all – in practice they had none.

The game is famous for the sending-off of Meads, arguably the greatest All Blacks forward of all time, by Kevin Kelleher. Colin was more reckless than malicious, swinging a boot at the ball but just missing Davie Chisholm, who had stooped to get it. Meads had been warned about dangerous play in a ruck and so was sent off but he was really a victim of his own robust style. Davie appealed to the referee not to send him off, I remember, but to no avail. It was not the first time an All Black had been sent off either – Cyril Brownlie had that dubious honour in 1925.

The All Blacks were coached by Fred Allen on that tour, one of the best coaches New Zealand have ever had – they went home unbeaten. Their game with Ireland was called off due to a foot-and-mouth epidemic. Unfortunately, the English centre Danny Hearn broke his neck in the Midlands and Home Counties game when he tackled Ian MacRae and was left paralysed from the neck down, which was greeted with widespread shock and sadness.

There was a lesson to be learned from that game at Leicester about underestimating the difference between representative and Test rugby. New Zealand had struggled to beat the Midlands even with Hearn off. So what did the England selectors do? They picked the whole Midlands pack and three of their backs for the Test match a week later, not realising the huge difference in intensity. New Zealand won easily at Twickenham, 23–11.

Interestingly, I had a visit around 20 years later from the All Black winger of that tour, Tony Steel, who had become a head teacher in New Zealand and decided to look me up when I was rector at Hawick High School.

I returned in the final Championship game against England and it was enough for me to prove my fitness and win selection for the 1968 Lions squad. The tour is clearly a whole story in itself so we will come to that later, but my Scotland career continued throughout the 1960s, and there were highs and lows still to come. The start of season 1968–69 was marked again by the visit of the Aussies in November and, as well as being fit this time, I was also Scotland captain.

We played well in the Test match, beating them 9–3, and then went to France for the first Five Nations match of 1969, a game that proved to be one of the most memorable I have ever been involved in. At that time, France played their home matches at Colombes, the famous stadium where Eric Liddell, the Scottish sprinter, won his Olympic gold medal in 1924. The stadium was really a running track with a pitch in the middle. To get to the pitch, players had to walk underneath the track and then come up through steps onto the end of the pitch.

Even before the game started, there was drama. Salut, the French flanker nicknamed 'The White Corsican', twisted his ankle and was replaced by a prop. The French reshuffled their pack, with Benoit Dauga moving into the back row and the prop Jean Iracabal taking his place in the second row.

During the game, our scrum-half, Gordon Connell, was injured and had to be replaced by Ian MacRae – a notable moment as Ian became the first replacement in world rugby. He made his presence felt almost immediately by dispossessing his opposite number at a scrum in the French 25. He then passed the ball to me, and I ran over the top of Pierre Villepreux and scored. I was quite pleased Ian had come on!

The French showed plenty of flair in that game, however, and outplayed us for most of the time. I can remember Joe Maso, now the French manager, doing scissors moves behind his own line. They were over the line at least twice but could not score and we held on for a most unlikely victory.

Predictably, the French crowd were incensed, and the referee had to be escorted from the field by the police. Norman Mair, the doyen of Scottish rugby writers, wrote in *The Scotsman* on the Monday that the Scottish team would not need to fly home, as they could just walk across the English Channel! As most Scottish rugby supporters know, that victory became part of our folklore as we had to wait until 1995 for Scotland to win in Paris again. Mercifully, the black-and-white images shown every two years by the BBC were finally confined to the dusty film can.

Two matches later, against Ireland, I became involved in a bizarre replacement situation. At a short lineout, I was standing in the Scottish back division beside the referee. Ireland won the ball and moved it to their backs. Both the referee, Merion Joseph, and I started to run but as his elbow came back, he caught me in the eye – Joseph should have been sent off for that! I was concussed, taken off and had to spend a night in hospital. Peter Stagg went on to replace me but I remember that, before he did, the 6 ft 10 in. lock accidentally sat on me – he was obviously eager to play!

By this time, we were looking forward to finishing the season with a tour. While it did little for summer holiday fun with friends and family, it was great for developing players. Argentina was next on the schedule for Scotland and that was planned for September. Argentina had a reputation for being a very difficult country to win matches in and so it turned out to be.

Some countries from the northern hemisphere had toured there previously and not taken the Pumas seriously; we were determined not to make that mistake. Caps were not awarded at that time for such matches but that did not alter our resolve. I was chosen as captain for the tour and two SRU committeemen, George Crerar and Lex Govan, were appointed co-managers. They organised the tour off the field and I was responsible for all the training and coaching.

We went with a squad of just 21 but it was very well prepared, with plenty of fitness work and skills training. As the tour was scheduled for September, the pre-tour training was done in excellent weather. We spent the last few days at Middleton Hall, near Gorebridge, under the direction of Lyn Tatham, who worked for the Scottish Sports Council and later became the chief executive of the Sports Council for Wales. Unfortunately, Kenny Oliver of Gala pulled a calf muscle in the lead-up to departure and there was serious doubt as to whether he would make it. The medical opinion was that his calf muscle would recover sufficiently to allow him to play early in the tour, but, as a precaution, we took Tom Elliot of Langholm down to London. As it turned out, Kenny responded well, the management decided to take him and Tom returned home, only for Kenny then to trip in a hole in the pitch at our first training session in Buenos Aires and also have to go home!

With 21 players, a replacement should have been simple enough, but not when you're dealing with the SRU. We asked for Tom Elliot to be sent out, knowing that he was fit, but the message came back that we could not have him. At the time, I thought it must have been an IRB (International Rugby Board) ruling but years later I learned that the decision was made by the SRU! We were now down to 20 players even before the first of six games was played. In fact, Rodger Arneil and I had to play in all six matches, with Sandy Carmichael, a prop, twice drafted into the back row.

Argentina felt a very unstable place, with the legacies of revolution and civil unrest apparent. The tour was based predominantly in Buenos Aires and as we walked out from our hotel, we would see lots of bullet and shrapnel marks on the walls of the main buildings. We travelled by bus from Buenos Aires to Rosario and one of our supporters, Dr McMyn, a former SRU president, told us on the way that, during a previous visit he'd made in the 1920s, there had been strikes in the city. Right on cue, the strikes returned and the team was confined to the hotel almost all the time we were there, as it was not safe to venture out.

We even had to walk to the ground for the game in small groups, as all the buses had been commandeered by the strikers. If you add in that every crowd we played in front of was hostile and the referees were all home-based, you begin to appreciate the enormity of our task and perhaps why the tour left such a mark on me. Many players 'grew up' on that tour. We won the four provincial matches and, although we lost the first international 20–3, we regrouped for the second and came through a gruelling battle to win 6–3.

For most of the first international, we had to play with 14 men because centre Ian Murchie broke his collar bone early in the first half and, as it was not a Test match, no replacements were allowed. He was straight-armed by Alejandro Travaglini, a 6 ft 4 in. centre, and carried off. We were beaten twenty points to three, Travaglini going on to exploit the absence of his opposing centre to score two tries. In the Scotland dressing-room after the game, I saw for the first time grown men crying, not from cowardice, but from an overwhelming sense of frustration and hopelessness.

But cometh the hour, cometh the man. The players responded magnificently the following week when we met Argentina again. We had steeled ourselves for a real battle and took the Pumas on at their own game, with very basic, physical rugby, and fully deserved our victory of 6–3. I broke off a maul and the ball went through lots of hands before Sandy Carmichael scored at the corner and just before half-time, Colin Blaikie scored a penalty from the halfway line. The effort that went into holding that 6–3 lead throughout the second half was immense.

At his height, Peter Stagg was easily identifiable and the Argentinians would always kick towards him at the restarts. A huge roar would go around the ground as the home players charged at him, shouting something in Spanish which identified him, and us Scots ran out of the way in case we got thumped! Colin Blaikie, our full-back, tried to kick goals while coins from the crowd were hitting him on the head.

It was on that tour that the ploy known as '99' used by the Lions in 1974 originated, I believe. Because of some of the intimidation and off-the-ball incidents, the forwards decided that if one player was picked on by the opposition all the rest would go to his aid. We calculated that the referee couldn't send off all eight forwards. The ploy worked and in that second international, we won the forward battles and the match.

The display that day was the most gutsy performance I ever witnessed as a player for Scotland and it was just a shame that it took place thousands of miles away from home, so that only the players and a few others witnessed a famous win.

As I intimated, several players grew up mentally on that tour but the one I believe put hardness into Scottish rugby at that time was Ian McLauchlan. He was one of the hardest blokes I ever played with and I give him great credit for taking Scotland to another level. He was one who learned from that tour to Argentina. It taught a lot of those players, especially the forwards, how to look after themselves and it was no surprise to me that so many of them went on Lions tours. Players like Ian, Alastair McHarg, Gordon Brown, Sandy Carmichael and

Rodger Arneil became the backbone of the Scottish pack through the 1970s.

In my captain's speech at the farewell dinner, I took the opportunity to say what I felt about Argentinian rugby – you will read later of how I upset New Zealanders with a similar typically honest assessment in another captain's speech. But I simply stated that if Argentina continued with their cynical approach to the game, they would alienate themselves from the rest of world rugby. I was a bit concerned about how it would be received in the room as the translator got to his feet and did his job. The speech seemed to go down quite well and I got a standing ovation. Only on the way out of the dinner did I realise that he had translated it along the lines of 'I think Argentina is a great place and I have been very happy to be here'!

We arrived home in late September and immediately started to prepare for a controversial visit by the Springboks in the autumn of 1969. It was at the height of the anti-apartheid demonstrations. I had no personal reservations about playing against the Springboks – I had already played them the year before with the Lions – but the atmosphere in the country and at their games was very tense. I remember coming off the pitch after the game for the South at Netherdale in Galashiels and being spat on in the tunnel.

The atmosphere at Murrayfield for the Test match was extremely antagonistic: tense and bordering on evil. There were people at that game who didn't know what a rugby ball looked like and large parts of the crowd were sectioned off. It was the only time at a rugby match I've seen hordes of people – police and stewards – facing the crowd and not watching the game at all.

My own feeling on the apartheid issue was quite straightforward: I felt that rather than avoiding apartheid, rugby and sport generally could be used as a vehicle for getting rid of it. Sport, I have always believed, can transcend politics because it is a part of so many lives across the world. I knew apartheid was wrong and the savage massacre of African patriots at Sharpeville in 1960 left an indelible mark on me. When touring South Africa in 1999, we took the Scotland squad to a township near Vanderbijlpark, which, with Langa, Nyanga and Sharpeville, was one of the scenes of the massacres of peaceful African demonstrators. We wanted to help the squad understand what had gone on. I could not see the benefit to Africans, however, of sportsmen avoiding the country and ignoring the problem of apartheid. To me, apartheid was two-fold – between black people and white people, and also between white English-speaking people and the Afrikaans-speaking whites. Sport, and rugby in particular, I still hope helped play some small part in bringing an end to apartheid and, having witnessed at first-hand the success of the 1995 Rugby World Cup, I would hope it might help the country in the future.

In '69, the South African players had been put under enormous pressure off the field and it showed in their play on it. They had some very famous Springboks at that time, including de Villiers, Hannes Marais, Frik du Preez and a world-renowned back row of Jan Ellis, Tommy Bedford and Piet Greyling. However, Scotland played very well on the day and won 6–3, after an excellent try by Ian Smith, who made an intrusion from full-back and cut the defence to score out wide.

My international career started to tail off in 1970. I was still captain when we lost three games on the trot – France (9–11), Wales (9–18) and Ireland (11–16) – so I was dropped for the Calcutta Cup match at Murrayfield. I remember Lex Govan, the chairman of selectors, being good enough to telephone me before the news went to the press. I was disappointed but accepted that the team hadn't been playing very well.

P.C. Brown took over my position at number 8 and Frank Laidlaw, my Melrose colleague, was made captain. Scotland played very well in that match and won it quite convincingly 14–5. I didn't accept that that was the end for me as a Scotland international but, although I tried very hard to get back in the team, I never made it and so my 25th cap did indeed turn out to be my last.

When I reflect now on the highs and lows of that Scotland career, there is a great feeling of pride in what I achieved. I never set out to play for Scotland, and for a long time never believed I would, but I would not swap those honours and experiences for anything in the world.

5

Pride and Passion – Off the Field

Frances Telfer, Jim's wife

I didn't know him at all but I was friendly with his sister Sheila through playing hockey with her at the school. There were four of us girls who had gone along to a dance at the Waverley Hotel in Melrose, where they had live bands in the '60s. I had actually just gone out for a walk and some friends persuaded me to go for a drink because two of them had just got engaged – I wasn't even dressed for dancing and had no money with me!

He was standing there at the side of the dance floor reading *The Pink* – the Edinburgh sports paper which came out on Saturdays. The girls often dared each other to ask someone up to dance who you hadn't danced with before, and they pointed to Jim and told me to go and ask him. I thought, 'Oh God, he's reading the paper!'

But he danced and I remember asking things about him, and he said he had a picture of me in a hockey team with his sister. I was quite puzzled and then I realised he was talking about Sheila. I remember saying to Jim I didn't know she had a brother. He was mortified because he was a well-known international.

I don't know what it was about him – he had nice teeth, I remember – but we just clicked. We blethered for hours that night as if we'd known each other for years. We were complete opposites – he was quiet and I . . . well, I wasn't. I was always 'bubbly', you'd say.

I found out quite quickly that he was very committed to his

61

rugby and the only night he didn't train was Friday, when we'd often go the cinema – never late, though, with a game the next day. But I played hockey and tennis, so it didn't bother me. I loved my sport, too, and so we were probably made for each other.

I had girlfriends at school and college but I remember meeting Frances and thinking she seemed nice. I actually had had my eye on her when she came and asked me to dance – maybe through the paper!

It was not a lot of fun, however, as we spent the first few minutes trying to work out who I was through my relations! It sounds conceited, probably, but I'd been playing for Scotland for a whole season and just thought everybody in Melrose knew who the hell I would be. But Frances obviously didn't. We were complete opposites – she stopped her hockey because it was too cold for her! – but she came from a 'big hoose' in Melrose and I probably thought she was rich! I knew what side my bread was buttered on.

Frances was born in Galashiels on 18 February 1943, but her father, Harry Denton, a marine, was killed at Normandy just 18 months later, in August 1944 after the D-Day landings. Her mother, Nancy, was pregnant with Harry, her brother, at the time.

Nancy, who has always followed my career with pride and been hugely supportive, married Ken Harrington, an electrical engineer, and he was a tremendous character who I had a lot of time for. He died from cancer of the throat on 31 March 1990, a fortnight after Scotland's Grand Slam, so while Scottish supporters only really saw the joy I felt being involved with another Grand Slam, we were going through a difficult time personally then as well.

Ken and I had great, enjoyable debates. He was a rabid socialist, a communist actually, and loved Russia and took our son Mark there once. He was one of the most able men I've ever met, especially on the DIY front. I learned a lot from him. We even became pretty competitive with each other at gardening and regularly used to get quite animated about the size of vegetables! He was from London but when he came to the Borders he fell in love with the area, the rural countryside and friendliness, and though he had many opportunities to earn promotion, he always refused if it would mean leaving the Borders.

Frances and I were married in St Cuthbert's Church in Melrose on 10 August 1967. It was a Thursday, I remember, and that was planned because I did not want to affect the cricket team, who had a match on the Saturday and some of them were coming to the wedding. We had got engaged before I went to New Zealand with the Lions in 1966, so Frances already knew what she was in for, because I was away for five months. We chose the summer of 1967 to be married because there was no major tour that year.

We had the reception at the Waverley, where we had first met, and I had to work on a pretty decent game plan to avoid the traditional send-off that newlywed men received at the end of their wedding night in those days. We were expected to head south on the train from Melrose Station but instead slid out secretly from the hotel at the end of the reception. I discovered some time later that my fellow Scotland back row Derrick Grant and his wife Elsie had suffered as a result and were 'helped' onto the train back to Hawick by some of our guests, but in carriages at opposite ends of the train – and that was before you could move between carriages!

In fact, we were off in the car to Edinburgh for the night before heading down to Southsea in the south of England for our week away. We had chosen Southsea because Frances had a lot of family there who couldn't make the wedding. Frances also paid for our 'great escape'; when she was back at a wedding the following year, while I was on tour with the Lions, our friends enjoyed placing confetti in areas confetti should never be!

It was strange for me to be away for a whole week not thinking about rugby, but I still caused a bit of a stir in our hotel. Frances had been out getting postcards one morning when she came back to find a crowd in the lobby staring at this chandelier swinging above them. Frances overheard them saying it was that young Scottish couple who had just got married obviously carrying on a bit. She was mortified and came running upstairs to find me doing press-ups on the bedroom floor. I couldn't not train, could I?

There was another occasion down there when I embarrassed myself. Frances thought it would be romantic if we went out on the lake in a boat but I'm no sailor, never have been. Anyway, when it came to being called in – those were the days when they did shout 'Come in number nine, your time's up . . . oh, sorry, are you in trouble, number six?' – well, we were called in and could I get the bloody boat turned round and into the side? Could I hell. I succeeded only in soaking Frances behind me and it ended up with people pulling us in while I sat there with a red face. Never again.

Rugby had been a great passion since my teenage days but there is no doubt that Frances has been a wonderful and strong partner through a 40-year period full of more ups, downs and roundabouts than we could have imagined when we started out. In those early years, everything lay ahead of us and it was great to have someone who shared my ambitions, both professionally and in rugby; Frances always encouraged me to go for promotion in my job. After six schools and seven homes (including owning a hotel for four years), we decided to retire in Galashiels, the town where our first house was.

There seems always to have been plenty of people willing to criticise my personality, suggesting I was not a warm or friendly person, or that I lacked interpersonal skills or was not easy to get to know. There are two sides to every story. At times, I have become quite frustrated and angry at comments made about a Jim Telfer I don't recognise or seem to know very little about, and I have a go back. I have often regretted outbursts and yet, to be honest, there were times I feel I should have said something rather than bitten my lip and kept my own counsel.

But while you grow used to the criticism, you find that it hurts those closest to you, and Frances has experienced more than her fair share of that, living with and supporting me. I have never been one for self-analysis to the nth degree but in the process of writing this book, I have had to delve a bit deeper. My co-author has forced me to think, asking 'Why?' an awful lot. 'Why did you not praise players?' or 'Why were you hard to get along with?' and while I don't have the answers to everything, I know that my character has not suited everyone.

Looking back, I suppose most of my friends shared my sense of humour and understood me better than those with whom I had to work closely but who never took to me. Isn't that the case with everyone? In our early married years, Frances and I had a good group of friends. I remember us spending a lot of time with Frank Laidlaw, the Melrose and Scotland hooker, and his wife Wilma; my sister Sheila and her husband Dave Hogg; and Gordon Blyth and his wife Isobel.

We socialised a lot together but the men would hate coming to our house on a Saturday night because we didn't have a television to watch *Sportscene* or whatever the sports programme was called at that time. It was quite embarrassing not to able to entertain them but Frances and I didn't see the need for a TV at that time.

Then, one night, they all turned up and Gordon came out with this very small TV. We only got BBC1 on it until we got a wee box a bit later that could receive ITV and BBC2. It was probably more for their pleasure than ours that they gave it to us, though!

We lived in Galashiels when we were first married, just across the river from Gala Rugby Club, one of Melrose's great rivals, and it used to give me some sadistic pleasure to go down and train on the back pitches all on my own when I could see that there was no one from Gala training.

However, in October 1967, I was badly injured playing at Kelso. I suffered a cartilage injury and was carried off.

I was in hospital for two weeks after the operation and it took three more months to recover, so life was a bit frustrating then. There was at least one benefit to being injured and off work for a few weeks: we redecorated the hall and stairs in our new house thanks to the insurance money, which we couldn't afford to do when we first moved in.

The great rival for my position in the Scottish team at that time was Rodger Arneil. He was quite literally the great white hope (he was very blond), and a very good player. Ironically, he also came from Gala, though he played for Edinburgh Accies. Anyway, one particular night just after I was able to start running again, I went down and, though my knee felt like broken glass, I kept pushing myself on round the big expanse of grass pitches by repeating over and over to myself, 'Rodger Arneil, Rodger Arneil, Rodger Arneil – you won't get my place.'

As it turned out, we often played in the same team and went on the 1968 Lions tour together. I never did thank him for that motivational help. As part of that recovery, I also used to sit in the kitchen with the milk rack full of tins of beans, lifting it up and down on my ankle to strengthen my knee. There were no fancy fitness rooms then but at least the technology had moved on from lifting stones from the burn.

Frances never batted an eyelid. She knew I took my sport seriously and she would always be there to help. I once came home with a cut knee which turned septic. Frances, the dutiful wife, was keen to help, so she prepared a poultice with kaolin, a heat-absorbent substance which would draw the poison out. She'd been told this was what to use, so she put some on a bit of lint and then onto my knee. I nearly hit the roof – it was agony. When the doctor came the next day, she told him what she'd done and he couldn't believe it. 'It's all right to use kaolin, Mrs Telfer, but don't put it straight onto skin!' he said. Apparently, it should be covered by lint on both sides – but it cured it!

Frances also liked nothing better than to do my kit washing when Melrose had beaten Gala and hang as many of my Melrose jerseys as she could find out along the washing line!

We were like any other couple enjoying forging a path together and they were good times. But there was one thing that didn't follow the plan we had and provided a massive shock. It's something I think most couples probably plan without thinking twice – that next step of having a family of your own.

Frances had suffered two miscarriages and was in and out of hospital throughout the pregnancies. I was coaching rugby at the school on one occasion when the hospital phoned, and I left to go straight there. We had been trying since we got married in 1967 – between Scotland and Lions tours of course – but despite Frances falling pregnant quickly, it became apparent that we were not going to be able to conceive naturally. That was incredibly difficult, I think particularly because both of us were so fond of children. Frances had babysat for friends and relatives since she was a young girl, I had always loved working with children and we had plenty of nieces and nephews. In late 1969, we began to turn our thoughts to adoption.

We applied to the adoption society run by the Church of Scotland and though we heard nothing, we pressed on and worked through local organisations. We did not actually have to wait long – about eight months – before we got a call to say there was a baby boy, just ten weeks old.

It was a local half-day, a Wednesday, I remember, and we had been a bit taken by surprise and so had nothing ready except a cardigan Frances had knitted which did not yet have buttons on but we went to see Mark. He grabbed Frances's finger and that was that! We rushed out to a popular baby shop, Little Ones in Galashiels, to try and get some baby stuff, though my sisters had children by then and they were a great help as well.

No sooner had we got Mark home than I had to go off coaching and it was always a bit like that then – me dashing between home, school and coaching. But thankfully, he was a very good, contented boy from the start. Some people might be surprised but I was very much a hands-on dad, and did my bit with the nappies and taking the children for walks in the pram.

I think people have this image of me as being the traditional, brusque ogre because of what they've seen of me in dressing-rooms, in classrooms or on the training field. But what I do on the rugby field and how I am away from the game are quite different. It's just that not many people see the other side and, to be honest, that's the way I've liked it. I like to keep myself and my family quite private, I always have. Actually, I've not courted the media in my professional life either. My home telephone number is ex-directory for that reason, although a few journalists have acquired it over the years. But I tried to keep a low profile because I was away quite a lot, so when I was at home I wanted to spend as much time as I could with the children without interruptions.

We had wanted to have a second child from the day we got Mark. The following year, we were contacted again and Louise, who was born in the Borders like Mark, weighing just six pounds, was with us in late 1971. It was an exciting time for us, as for any new parents, and we could not actually agree on a name for Louise. I quite liked Suzanne, for some reason, and Frances preferred Colette but we ended up with Angela Louise. Nothing was ever simple with us and the reason we then decided to call her Louise was that neither of us fancied the idea of people calling her 'Angie'! So she was Louise. Mark was much simpler, Mark James.

Mark and Louise spent most of their early lives in Edinburgh and went to Parsons Green Primary School, then to Philiphaugh Primary and eventually Selkirk High School when we bought the Glen Hotel in the Borders town.

When he left school, Mark joined the Scots Guards and spent ten years with them, including two tours of duty in Northern Ireland. He now lives and works in Camden in London, with his partner Colette and their two children Joel and Skye. He also has another daughter, Jenna, from his first marriage and she lives with her mother in Longniddry outside Edinburgh. Jenna won a scholarship to George Heriot's School; she is a great reader and shows a keen interest in all kinds of dancing, from tap to jazz. Louise works for a large housing association in Melrose and lives in Galashiels with her son Kenneth, who I see every day and who is a water sports enthusiast. Frances and I thoroughly enjoy being grandparents and are very proud of them all.

They say children bring you down to earth and Kenneth has a knack of doing that for me. I phoned home after the British and Irish Lions had won the Second Test and hence the series in 1997 and Kenneth answered the call. I was ecstatic with the result, desperate to pass on the news. He was five years old and excited too. I told him what had happened and he replied, 'Yes, but, Papa, Papa, I've got something to tell you – I can ride my bike without the stabilisers!'

There was also the occasion when I picked him up at his primary school, St Peter's in Galashiels, about ten days after I'd retired. We were walking back towards my house and three older boys overtook us. They stopped about ten metres ahead and one came back and asked, 'Are you Jim Telfer?'

I said, 'Yes.'

He stood for a moment and then asked, 'Are you famous?'

And before I could reply, Kenneth said, 'He used to be.'

It says it all.

6

Entering the Lions' Den

Colin Meads
New Zealand (55 caps, 1957–71)

Jim Telfer should have been an All Blacks forward. It is
something myself and teammates Brian Lochore and Kel
Tremain used to say – he, more than any of the others, was our
kind of player, we felt.

The British and Irish Lions came to New Zealand in 1966 and
it appeared to us that they were a team beset by problems,
mostly in selection. The choice of another Scot, Mike Campbell-
Lamerton, as the Lions captain was not a good one because, as
much as we liked Mike, who was a great man, he was not a
good enough player in that Lions squad to be guaranteed his
place and so lead them through the Test series. We felt Jim
Telfer and Willie John McBride were the leaders and with Jim
being the more senior, he probably should have captained the
Lions on that tour.

He was a hard bugger: a very staunch, hard-working and
honest Scots forward. It was on that tour that you recognised
Jim's qualities as a forward who could have slipped into an All
Blacks side. His high work rate, courage and rucking skills were
good qualities but, more than that, he was the kind of valuable
loose forward who could be a third lock; he could take part in all
parts of the game. There was a player like that in all New
Zealand sides, which is why I always said of Jim that he would
have made a great All Black forward.

He did make a name for himself on that tour, of course, when

JIM TELFER

he dominated the headlines with a speech in Canterbury. He received a lot of criticism in the press but, to be fair, we admired him for it. It was a dirty game and Jim Telfer is the sort who will only ever say things the way he saw them. That's the way it should be said.

Canterbury were a great side and always have been but they were renowned in New Zealand for that type of thing. They were a 'take no prisoners' kind of side, an attitude which was more a part of rugby in those days. The Lions were trying to get on a roll and play a more exciting game at that stage but Canterbury were out to stop them, simple as that. The game has changed a lot since then and Canterbury have adapted better than most. As a result, they are the current Super 12 champions, which is a great credit to their rugby.

But we had some great times in the 1960s. In those days, of course, you only came together on the Thursday before the Saturday Test match; but we did have a consistency in selection which the Lions didn't, with players like my old mate the late Kel Tremain, and then when we lost a great captain in Wilson Whineray, in came Brian Lochore, who was an outstanding choice to lead the All Blacks. Ken Gray was another great player, a colossus who never got the credit he was due.

We had happy times when we played rugby, enjoying dinners after games and getting to know other players as great friends. I loved touring Scotland as well, first in 1963, when we spent time up in Aberdeen – I was given time off up there and had a marvellous time with wonderfully hospitable people – and then in 1967, when we came back with Fred Allen as coach. We spent a lot of time in the Borders, and the people and the rugby there were tremendous. Then, of course, I had one moment of regret at Murrayfield.

I'll always blame Jim's wee friend, the Melrose hooker Frank Laidlaw, for my sending-off! I had actually helped the ball out for them from a ruck and was then trying to get to the ball to kick it away from David Chisholm (another Melrose man – how many of them were there?). But he got it first and my boot swiped past him. It was not intentional, of course, but the referee, Kevin Kelleher, an Irishman, had given me a formal caution earlier for over-vigorous rucking (the 'formal caution' had just come in and

70

was, I suppose, the equivalent of the modern-day yellow card) and though I maintain to this day that he never saw it, he heard little Laidlaw screaming, 'Did you see what that dirty bastard did, ref?' and I was off.

I have since had good times with Kevin and there's no ill feeling, even with all those Melrose guys! But I loved it in Scotland and it was nice to see where Telfer came from. It was no surprise to me that he developed into a world-class coach and it is only a pity that Scottish rugby has lost ground in recent years. Perhaps they need another Telfer to take it forward.

Des O'Brien
British and Irish Lions manager, 1966
Speaking at the dinner after the Lions v. Canterbury match, 23 July 1966

'We were delighted to win today. Rugby is a game we love and a game we enjoy playing but we are heartily sick of the obstruction, short-arm tackling and other illegal tactics employed by teams we have met in New Zealand.

'We went out today to counter those tactics and this is the spirit we intend to preserve in the remaining games. We have had enough. The tour has been most enjoyable apart from the 90 minutes of each game. I say 90 minutes advisedly: 80 minutes for playing and 10 minutes for the inevitable injuries.'

Jim Telfer
British and Irish Lions captain v. Canterbury, 1966
Speaking at the after-match dinner

'I don't apologise for the type of game we played today. We have been told we should play open rugby and run with the ball but it takes two teams to play open rugby. I play match-winning rugby, the only way I know. I am not going to say today's game was dirty, because every match I have played in on this tour of New Zealand has been dirty.

'When the All Blacks were touring the British Isles in 1963–64,

71

they were often 20 points up and yet kept the game tight and continued with their stereotyped rugby. And thank you for the way you booed Stewart Wilson when he took that vital conversion today.

'I have to propose the toast to the referee and I might say it is the manner in which referees in New Zealand allow play to run that starts all the fighting. The interpretations of the laws are vastly different here. I can only wish the referee a safe journey home.'

The 1966 British and Irish Lions tour to New Zealand left the deepest, most indelibly etched scars on me, physically and mentally, of my rugby career.

I attracted a lot of media attention halfway through the tour when I spoke out against what I believed was seriously dirty play and lost the captaincy. However, it was an incredible introduction to Lions rugby for me and a five-month period that would shape me as a player and coach more than anything else in my life.

It all started so simply, controversy-free. There wasn't the same speculation as there is today in the press about who would be picked. You were asked if you were available – I had to get permission from my school and Selkirkshire County Council to go, because it meant five months off work – so I knew I was on the long leet. Then we were told we were in and the squad was announced to the public the next day.

I was a teacher at Galashiels Academy. There were only three players on that tour not being paid by their employers, as I recall, Brian Price, Alun Pask and myself, all teachers. I remember Gary Prothero, the Bridgend forward, coming into the room in the London hotel with his pockets stuffed full of pound notes and fivers. He had received them walking along the street in his home town on his farewell.

After the tour, I went to the council buildings in Galashiels to ask about holiday pay and I was told that a teacher is never officially on holiday and can be brought back from wherever they are if necessary. To be fair, I did get some payment.

I went to Jed-Forest Sevens on the Saturday, 21 April, and then later that day got the sleeper train to London from Newtown St

Boswells. Frank Laidlaw had got on at Melrose and then Derrick Grant got on at Hawick. We trained at Bournemouth for a week and then flew out to Perth in Western Australia, our first port of call.

It was interesting for me meeting up with all these great players from the other home nations but I wasn't the shy wee Borders boy by then. I was 26 years old and had been leading the Scottish pack for two years; I'd gone through being dropped after that great first season and had had to fight my way back.

So I went down there fairly confident. I knew I was behind Alun Pask for the number 8 position – he had captained Wales to the Triple Crown. Mike Campbell-Lamerton, the Scotland second row, was chosen as captain, really as a compromise to try and bring all the nations together. He had had a very successful 1962 Lions tour and had captained Scotland a few times. With an Irishman, Des O'Brien, as manager and John Robins, a Welshman, as coach, there was some logic in making an Anglo-Scot the captain.

The Lions are unique in that you are together for such a short time; the real challenge is to bring players from four nations together as a squad, into one team, playing and supporting each other. Without real cohesion, you stand no chance. Squad unity is the key to success.

There were worries then, and have been since on Lions tours, that when Welshmen were away from home they tended to be cliquey and homesick, whereas Irishmen and Scots seem to go the other way and blossom more on tour. They would go away as underdogs and come through into Test teams. As I wrote earlier, I have long admired Welsh rugby and many players from there became good friends, but there was some evidence of a cliquey approach at times.

I remember a Welsh clique would regularly sit at the back of the bus and sing 'We are the Triple Crown boys', and quite openly shun Delme Thomas, the Llanelli forward who hadn't been capped. That I found disappointing, because Delme became a great stalwart of Welsh rugby and went on three Lions tours. He became one of my best friends on that tour, along with Derrick Grant.

With the bulk of the squad Irish and Welsh, it was viewed as a pretty good one. There seemed a healthy mixture of older and younger players. There were 12 Welshmen in the 30-man squad, plus Terry Price, the full-back, who came out later. We'll come back to that because that's a whole story in itself. Including replacements, there were only five players from England, nine Irishmen and six Scots.

On the South African tour in 1968, there was a great crop of Welshmen who were starting to come through but that was interesting, because they were different characters. People like Gareth Edwards, Barry John, Gerald Davies and John Taylor, who would go on to become world figures, came across as fairly extrovert and got on with everybody.

We had some characters, though, in 1966. You tend to think of Welshmen as all being from the Valleys, like Denzil Williams, Alun Pask and Alun Lewis, but Ken Jones was an Oxford University student and I remember going to the films with him one night. That great Welsh actor Richard Burton was in it and Ken sat there telling everyone, 'It makes such a difference when one actually knows the actor, doesn't it?' Big show-off! He actually buggered off from training later in the tour and refused to play at one point – what about, I can't remember.

We actually had the first full-time coach on a Lions tour in John Robins, who was very good. He had been a prop on the 1950 tour to New Zealand and Australia, and was a PE lecturer in Sheffield. John did a lot at training, some sessions lasting two hours, with running and stamina work, but we saw a fair amount of the ball as well. He was a very accomplished and thoughtful coach. The manager, captain and coach picked the team in those days. There were four players, one from each country, who advised on selection for Test matches and I was the Scottish one.

We had kicked off the tour with eight games, including two Tests, in Australia and had played well, winning seven and drawing one. I'd scored my first two Lions tries, including the winner, a push-over, against a Combined Country XV in New South Wales. We won the First Test 11–8 in front of a record crowd – 42,303 – for a rugby match in the Sydney Cricket Ground. That wasn't a bad Australian side, either, with the famous Ken Catchpole and Phil Hawthorne at half-back, and forwards like Jules Guerassimoff, Greg Davis, Tony Miller, Rob Heming and John Thornett, the captain.

We then went on to Brisbane and set a record for a Lions victory, winning 31–0, only after we'd got IRB permission to play at Lang Park to ensure we didn't become 'professionals' just by playing at what was a rugby league ground!

That remains the biggest Test win by a Lions team and, bizarrely, we had been just 3–0 up at half-time. But what a second half we had – the tries and points flew in. That Wallaby side had beaten the All Blacks and Springboks that season and would go on to beat Wales in Cardiff a few months later. That wrapped up an Australian leg of seven wins and one draw, a proud achievement.

So one can see why we headed to New Zealand with a lot of confidence, although that confidence turned out to be misplaced, unfortunately. We got to New Zealand and it was a whole different ball game. This was a country with wall-to-wall rugby, with carnivals in the streets of every town because the Lions were there.

Controversy blew up around our manager, Des O'Brien, the former Ireland number 8 and captain of the late 1940s and early 1950s. Some of the press suggested he had left the squad for a holiday in Fiji, others said he'd been forced to take time away because he was on the brink of a nervous breakdown. The truth was much simpler but I will let Des – who has lived in Lasswade, near Edinburgh, for many years now – tell the story himself.

'We had actually been hoping to set up a match with Fiji on that tour, because they were very enthusiastic about developing links with rugby-playing nations at that time and were desperate to see the Lions. The New Zealand Rugby Union [NZRU] were our hosts and they said they couldn't squeeze it into the itinerary but suggested that I go to Fiji when I had a chance and meet with their officials.

'It was difficult finding the time but I felt we owed it to the Lions' relations with other countries to make an effort. It was reported that I went off on holiday and left the boys in the lurch, that I was suffering from stress and that the NZRU sent me away to prevent me suffering a nervous breakdown, but that was all nonsense. Nobody from the NZRU seemed to have explained to the media why I was away and so I was widely criticised when I returned. But I was only away a few days and it did not impact at all on our match plans.'

There was no doubt that it was a stressful tour, which is why people perhaps jumped to those kinds of conclusions, but the players never reacted to Des's trip in a negative way as far as I can remember. We knew the management was under pressure – Campbell-Lamerton lost two stones in weight during the tour through worry, he was such a conscientious chap – and believed that may have been the reason.

Our coach, John Robins, also had his problems. He refereed a charity match in Wellington to raise money for the family of Brian Ford, a local player who had died, and ended up tearing his knee ligaments. Des, who was 47 at the time, played in the game and scored a try, thankfully emerging unscathed. John had to go about in plaster for a while. A lot went on during that tour and probably more off the field than on!

New Zealand was where the intensity really got to you but I only really felt it as a positive indication of how good a game rugby was and could be and how much we in Scotland could learn from New Zealand. I have been criticised many times for being obsessed with New Zealand and supposedly wanting to replicate their rugby in Scotland but there is a difference between being obsessed in a negative way with something and being impressed and wanting to extract its good qualities. It was simply the fact that I saw and felt raw rugby out there, and knew there were aspects of it, not all of it, but aspects, we could learn from.

You cannot compare the structures we have in Scotland with those in New Zealand, so you could never replicate New Zealand rugby here. I actually used to wonder how twin boys would develop as rugby players had they been separated at birth and one brought up in Scotland, one in New Zealand. If you brought them back together at the age of 21, what difference would there be?

The New Zealand player would have come through a far more competitive system; because rugby is the number-one sport there, there is a far greater number of players at every age level. So his skills level would be high and his knowledge of the game more rounded.

The Scottish player would have established himself more easily at each age level and not had to strengthen his skills or physique to anything like the same degree to win selection for teams. The standard of competition would have been much lower at every age group, so he would have been challenged less from 11 to 18, the key years of development. If he pursued the game, he might step up into a Scotland jersey and full Test status at 21, and then he would be found out, his skills shown to be vulnerable and far behind those of his New Zealand twin. And by then, there would be very little he could do about it.

It was the appreciation of that – that no matter how hard players worked latterly, they wouldn't match up – which drove me in the years after I toured to try and bring the best of what I learned back to my home country, to try and make our younger players better. It wasn't because I wanted little New Zealanders everywhere but because I wanted Scottish players one day to be a match for them.

So, what could Scottish rugby learn from New Zealand? I remember my very first lesson on the fields of New Zealand as if it were yesterday, and it was a painful one. It was in my first game of the New Zealand leg of the tour, the Lions' second, against a combined South Canterbury, Mid Canterbury and North Otago team at Timaru. I remember doing my usual thing and attacking a loose ball, getting there first. But instead of my teammates coming in behind and forming a ruck as I'd hoped, there was this almighty whoosh and I was kicked and rucked off the ball by four or five local forwards coming across it.

I always tried to pride myself on getting to the ball first but there I was discovering that that wasn't good enough and that the opposition was waiting and happy to make mincemeat of me before my teammates got there. The forward technique, of the All Blacks especially, was awesome – the leg speed, the driving and tightness – and, in my opinion, from the coalface, that was what won them that 1966 series.

Players like Colin and Stan Meads, Brian Lochore, Kel Tremain, Ken Gray and Waka Nathan were just incredible. Stan Meads was a very good footballer but his brother Colin, operating from the second row, played like a back row on pure instinct. I remember Hughie McLeod coming home after the 1959 Lions tour and raving about this new young player who could run all day – that player was Colin Meads.

I would rate him as the best rugby player that I've ever seen. He was not unlike the Scotland and Lions flanker Finlay Calder in shape, the sort of bow-legged style of running, handing people off as he went, but at 6 ft 4 in. and over 16 st. – which was a lot back then – he was a bigger, more ferocious version.

For those who remember Fin in full flight, at his best, that should provide quite an awesome picture. Like Fin, Colin had a high knee action, and took big strides, which made him a tricky proposition when he was charging towards you. He was almost impossible to tackle. He was so fast at getting to the loose ball and so strong when he got there; you often see pictures of him running with two or three people trying to pull him down and not being able to.

In fact, pictures of New Zealand forwards at that time tend to show contorted faces straining to get to the ball carrier; they're all girning (a good Scots term) whereas Scottish forwards at the time would be standing, waiting, turning the wrong way, whatever. When I first began to coach the Scottish forwards, I got them pointing in the right direction to start with, because some turned their back when they got the ball or went sideways – I'd say two words: go forward. The All Blacks certainly taught me the importance of getting that basic skill right.

Intriguingly, many of our backs ran across the field until Sean Lineen arrived from New Zealand in the late 1980s. Sean was the first of the modern 'kilted Kiwis', eligible to play for Scotland because he had a Scottish grandparent. He came here initially to play club rugby but went on to be a great player for Scotland. He took the ball and went straight, and showed them how successful that could be. Even John Leslie, who came from Otago to play for Scotland in 1998, was a revelation, because he did the simple things well – he cut straight lines, found gaps, got in behind defences and sparked attacks in ways Scottish players didn't seem able to do.

We lost the first New Zealand game of the '66 tour against Southland 14–8 and that should have been a serious wake-up call. Sadly, it wasn't, as despite midweek wins, we then lost the big Saturday matches against Otago and Wellington. We were criticised for not playing enough expansive rugby. Wilson Whineray, the former All Blacks captain, was later quoted in the New Zealand press as saying:

It is clear in retrospect that the Lions' decision, made early on in the tour, to play the All Blacks up front, was wrong. They suffered from battling to narrow wins, or not winning at all, and the spectators suffered from watching dreary rugby.

In truth, we had started trying to develop our back play as early as the third game, against Otago in Dunedin, but we made mistakes which were costly in that defeat as we tried more things. Whineray was convinced our backs were our real strength and there is no doubt that we did have great players there – David and Stuart Watkins, Mike Gibson, Colin McFadyean, Sandy Hinshelwood, Dewi Bebb and Stewart Wilson, to name just some. And, traditionally, British teams have done well when they've thrown the ball about against the All Blacks. They did that in 1971, so maybe Carwyn James learned from our experience – you could have 25 per cent possession and still win.

Along with Gareth Edwards, Gibson, the Irish fly-half-cum-centre, was probably the best player I ever shared a team with. He was the best Lion on that tour, mainly operating at inside-centre. His full name is Cameron Michael Henderson Gibson and I believe his ancestors were Scottish, so we might have had him. Imagine that.

However, we did have some very good forwards as well, when you consider the likes of Willie John McBride, Noel Murphy, Ray McLoughlin, Derrick Grant, Ronnie Lamont, Denzil Williams and Alun Pask, and some other strong, experienced characters in that squad. Though the All Blacks at that time perhaps didn't have the world's greatest back division, their forwards were formidable and there was a widespread belief among our management and players that we had no chance if we couldn't compete with that pack for the ball. That was the challenge we had to meet and defeat if we were to have a chance.

We went into that First Test in Dunedin not particularly confident, having lost to Southland, Otago and Wellington and drawn with Bay of Plenty, only winning five games. The great hope we'd had as we travelled across from Australia had been brought crashing down to earth. You often find that the away team does well in the First Test before the hosts get themselves organised but the All Blacks' forward play was just too strong.

The first half finished 8–3 to New Zealand, despite being very even. The All Blacks scored through their hooker, Bruce McLeod, and Mick Williment, the full-back, converted. Stewart Wilson scored a penalty and Mac Herewini struck a drop-goal. But they completely overran us in the second half, scoring tries through Williment and Brian Lochore, their number 8 and captain, and made the Lions look like a rabble. We were spared an even worse beating than 20–3 because although Mick Williment scored two penalties, he missed six kicks at goal in the game.

Something that first appeared in that match was 'second-phase possession'. We now talk about third, fourth, fifth phase, but back then the concept was quite new. The All Blacks revealed their second five-eighth (inside-centre) idea in the shape of Ian MacRae. He would run straight off the scrum-half or fly-half into traffic and either fall, setting up a ruck, or turn and his support would maul it. But the ball invariably came back quickly and you had a situation of forwards running at backs and backs at forwards.

It was clever, and typical of the All Blacks, always looking for something new. Some players in this country might remember running a move called the 'Rangi'. Gregor Townsend used to like it as a schoolboy and when playing for Scotland. Well, that was named after Ron Rangi, a Maori outside-centre from Auckland who used to come inside on a scissors against us on that tour and cause havoc.

After the Test, one of the local newspaper reports summed it up by stating, 'Here endeth the first lesson.' It was actually our second, after the Southland defeat in our opening game.

It wasn't long before I made the headlines with some words that, while said with honesty, I perhaps should not have bothered with. As I've said, when in New Zealand, you couldn't escape the atmosphere and when you were losing games, you maybe could have done with a quiet spot but there wasn't one. From the moment we arrived in New Zealand, there was a feeling of intimidation, not off the field, where it was very sociable and people were very hospitable, but on it, where players in the provinces were determined to do whatever they could to bring the Lions down. We simply weren't a match for that; I accept that. But much of it was dirty and we were maybe a bit naive trying to strive for good Lions rugby all the time while being drawn into real wars on the field. It was frustrating.

We knew, of course, that you always had to win the physical battle before you could play rugby, so we were committed to being physical from the start. But in most of the games, we never did get on top and so never got to the rugby. I was picked to be captain in the 12th match, against Canterbury, and it all blew up. We had beaten West Coast-Buller, not a great side, 25–6 to help wipe away the First Test disappointment and then arrived in Christchurch to face Canterbury.

It was a Saturday game and it was tough right from the kick-off, with punches being thrown at the first scrum. It was a dour battle from start to finish and we made sure we stood toe-to-toe with Canterbury.

While it didn't make for a great game of rugby, we came out 8–6 winners with a late try from Dewi Bebb, the Welsh left-wing, and in front of nearly 50,000 supporters baying for the formidable home team, it was a great victory. Canterbury has a great history (they went on, of course, to become the dominant team in Super 12) and the win was a great achievement for the Lions. I was very proud to captain the team to it. We had, by that stage in the tour, grown accustomed to the games not opening up into the entertaining matches we had hoped for.

Now, if I had followed protocol at the dinner under the Lancaster Park stand afterwards, I would just have thanked lots of people and sat down, because if anything else was to be said, it was the responsibility of the tour captain or manager, and theirs alone. Des O'Brien, our manager, had been in the dressing-room and was unhappy at the number of injuries which had resulted from dirty play, Colin McFadyean, for one, having suffered a broken nose. It was clear he was not going to stick to pleasantries. In his speech, he said he was not happy with the dirty tactics in the game and made it clear we had had enough. I was still angry about the game when I had to stand up and give the captain's speech.

As you can see from the transcript at the start of this chapter, I was quite honest and to the point. I can still clearly remember saying, 'I wouldn't say today's game was dirty because every match I've played in on this tour has been dirty,' and it just went on from there. I got to the point where I didn't know how or when I was going to finish; as I spoke, I was trying to convince myself to leave it at that and sit down. I remembered I had to thank the officials but then I realised the referee was partly to blame for the way the game had become a battle and said so before saying I hoped he had a safe journey home.

What annoyed me, though, about that was the way in which a number of New Zealand reporters came up to me afterwards, shook my hand, told me what I'd said was the truth and it had been needing to be said for a long time, only for them to then lambast me the next day in the papers and call for me to be sent home in disgrace.

The possibility of me being sent home was never discussed as far as I'm aware. No one in the Lions party said anything about it to me. But I never captained the Lions again on that tour, quite obviously because of what I said that night. I have had some regrets because it showed a lack of control which was not befitting of a Lions captain. The media loved it, of course, and it made big headlines back home, but I found it interesting to note the reaction in New Zealand, where a lot of local papers seemed to have been inundated with letters which criticised Canterbury and their club officials for trying to pretend they didn't play dirty. I think I won more support from people on the street in New Zealand than anywhere else!

But though it made the matter a big issue, it didn't change the provinces' approach. A week later, when England were winning football's World Cup in London, we were beating Auckland in a game of absolute thuggery. It was reported at the time that it was as bad a game of rugby as the Lions had ever experienced and I take no pride in having been involved in it. There were meetings at a high level after that as the New Zealand authorities tried to calm things down but, luckily, we never had the same kind of problems in the Test matches because the All Blacks were better, more disciplined players.

The wins over Canterbury and Auckland were part of a run of five successive victories between the First and Second Tests, a period when we made up our minds simply not to accept any more stick. When you're on a tour like that, with strong characters, you pull together and we definitely got stronger after that First Test. I think when it goes badly, you quickly sort out the men from the boys, and we then went on that run where we didn't lose and had ample opportunity to pull it back together.

The management was using those games to rearrange the team and you could see they had changes in mind for the Second Test. When the team was announced, Sandy Hinshelwood and Alun Lewis came in and out went Ken Jones and Roger Young from the back line. There were four changes in the forwards, with Alun Pask, Ken Kennedy, Brian Price and Michael Campbell-Lamerton, our captain, being dropped and Frank Laidlaw, my Melrose and Scotland teammate, coming in alongside Willie John McBride, Delme Thomas and Noel Murphy.

It was a real shame for Mike at the time because he wasn't really playing well and the press there gave him a very hard time. He was a great, tireless character who would do everything he could for the squad. But he was under pressure from the other selectors – of whom I was one – and he decided that he should step aside. That was a gesture which merely enhanced his reputation among the players.

As a result of the changes, the new team seemed rejuvenated and went a long way to proving the First Test display was an aberration. We so nearly did it, losing 16–12. It was a real case of 'if only' for the Lions. The All Blacks played against the wind in the first half and we had three chances to score tries but fluffed them all through forward passes or knock-ons.

We still went in at half-time 9–8 up, David Watkins having dropped a goal and Wilson kicking two penalties. But the All Blacks had scored a try through Tremain, converted by Williment, into the wind. With the wind at their backs, they grabbed their chances, Meads scoring quickly on the restart and Steel scoring with minutes to go. Stewart Wilson scored a late penalty but it was not enough. Playing the All Blacks was very different to taking on the provincial sides. They were much cleaner and more precise, and the intensity was far greater, so the Tests were largely incident-free, which made a pleasant change.

Test rugby hasn't changed much: when you play at that rarefied level, little mistakes can cost you Test series and immortality. It can come down to one poor pass or catch dropped, which is something I think many players don't realise until it's too late.

That was the case in that Second Test. Many believed us to have been the better team but guilty of missing chances.

We went from that Test defeat into facing the Meads brothers in their own back yard, Wanganui-King Country at Spriggens Park, and they showed how they could dish it out as well. For some of us, the midweek games were part of building towards the Tests, whereas every single match for the provincial players was about their one chance of glory, probably the one opportunity in their lifetime to bring down the Lions and go into history, and so there were some fierce buggers in these games.

We hadn't played badly in that Second Test, to be fair, so we were keen to get the show back on the road but the Meads and their mates had other ideas.

Colin was at three in the lineout, against Campbell-Lamerton, and Stan at five, and they were so good, with Stan jumping and tapping the ball down to Colin, that they dominated. I stood behind Stan in the lineout and decided to upset things a bit by pulling him down by his jersey as he went to jump. He turned and belted me a cracker across the face, so I thought, 'OK, I'll just leave it at that.'

We played poorly in that game, losing 12–6, but we never tasted defeat again, apart from the remaining Test matches. We went straight into the New Zealand Maori match, which was almost like playing another All Blacks side, and we won it 16–14.

What I remember of that, however, was the first appearance of Terry Price, the great white hope who turned out to be the great white let-down. He was brought out as a replacement for Don Rutherford, who had had his right shoulder smashed in the game against Manawatu-Horowhenua, just after the Canterbury match, after stopping a certain try. Don, who was slight but a very tidy footballer, later became the technical director of the RFU and was a big influence on England's domination in the early 1990s.

His injury opened the door for Price, who had been rushed back from the injury which had prevented him from starting the tour. We were all looking forward to him getting out but we couldn't believe it when he turned up at training. He was obviously out of condition and limped every time he ran. He had difficulty getting to high balls before they bounced – and this was the guy brought out to help salvage the tour?

The Welsh players rallied round him but, after he played against the Maori, it was reported in the local papers that he was 'an embarrassment to the Lions'. There was a lesson in that for all future Lions selectors: you have to be very sure before taking a player recovering from injury.

We beat East Coast-Poverty Bay and Hawke's Bay before the Third Test but when that team was announced, I was dropped amidst another flurry of changes. Sandy Hinshelwood was also left out. Up front, the selectors thought they'd bulk up the pack so they put Delme Thomas, a 6 ft 3 in. lock, up at prop, which let Campbell-Lamerton return at second row while Pask came back for me at number 8.

It was a cold and wet Christchurch when the team ran out onto Lancaster Park but the Lions again did well in the first half. The scores sat tied 6–6 at half-time, the Lions scoring tries through Ronnie Lamont and David Watkins, while the All Blacks had penalties from Williment to thank for still being in touch. Ronnie was a great forward, probably the best on that tour. But he suffered such a bad shoulder injury early on that he wore a harness to protect it when he was playing. I'd be surprised if his shoulder wasn't knackered now.

The Lions legs started to go a bit in the second half and we lost that one 19–6. It was a major disappointment for us, as it signalled the end of our hopes of winning or even drawing the series. And yet the New Zealand backs were still criticised for not impressing enough.

Journalists accompanying the Lions certainly admitted they felt for us. The renowned Welsh rugby writer J.B.G. 'Bryn' Thomas reported in the *Sunday Times*:

> No one present at Lancaster Park today will agree that the Lions deserved to lose this exciting Test match by 13 points. The bad luck that has dogged them throughout the tour was with them again and time after time they were just denied scores.

Another journalist of the time, Tremayne Rodd, a former Scotland internationalist, wrote in *The Observer*:

The score could and should have been in reverse order. At half-time with two most wonderful tries the Lions fought back . . . and it seemed that the All Blacks had lost their grip on the game and themselves.

It was the fault of the Lions backs that victory slipped away. After brilliantly setting up scoring positions, one after the other, they made the final and oh so costly mistakes.

By the time we got to the Fourth Test in Auckland, we were very weary. The All Blacks had a formidable record there and many of the Lions were virtually hanging together with sticking plaster. It is different now because they have far fewer games, only three Test matches and bigger squads to cover the injuries. But even as recently as the 1997 Lions tour, the team in the Third Test was almost unrecognisable from the one in the First because of the number of injuries sustained by the end of the tour.

That 1966 tour was the longest ever. It matched the 35 games of the first British Isles tour of 1888 and it was incredibly arduous. It's no surprise that it hasn't been repeated since.

For the Fourth Test, it was all change again as we tried to get a fit side out, and I returned along with Sandy Hinshelwood, Brian Price, Ken Kennedy, Denzil Williams and Ray McLoughlin, who was the best prop there but had spent most of the tour injured. Campbell-Lamerton was dropped again, replaced by Brian Price, and I took the place of Noel Murphy this time. Injuries remained a major concern, however, as Alun Pask was carried off and we were forced to play with a seven-man pack. There were no substitutes then, of course, and so we had to play for around an hour against what was termed 'the world's best pack' without him.

We were ten points down at that point. I moved to number 8 in the scrums, striving to lead the pack and regain some pride. We showed a lot of spirit then, though, with the tour coming to an end, and Sandy Hinshelwood and Colin McFadyean, the talented England centre, scored tries to pull us back into the game. Still, we couldn't get the scores in the second half to make it close and we ended up losing 24–11. The reports in the local press that this was New Zealand's hardest Test provided no consolation.

There is no doubt the tour was a disappointment but I left New Zealand believing that it wouldn't be the last time I would be there and that I would take a lot more away from the country for the future than I would leave behind.

As something of a strange postscript to that tour, however, we duly turned up in Canada and lost a game to British Columbia because we'd been out sunbathing! On the way home from New Zealand, we stopped off at Honolulu before arriving in Canada for two matches.

Some players – myself included – couldn't play in the first game against British Columbia in Vancouver, which we lost, because of too much sun. We felt the tour was over, to be honest, because it had been a horrendously hard four months, so we'd enjoyed a bit of sunbathing.

The climate in Honolulu was a complete change from the New Zealand winter, so we soaked it up and ended up looking like lobsters. I remember I couldn't put my rugby jersey on. It was embarrassing, but we felt that whoever played for the Lions would win and it wouldn't matter much. It wasn't too great when we lost the game 8–3.

We took on virtually the same side, as Canada, the following week in Toronto and won 19–8 to set the record straight; but being ruled out of a Lions match by sunburn just completed an unwanted series of firsts uncovered in 1966.

If you looked through that squad, I would say that a number of those Lions, if they looked themselves in the mirror, would have to accept that they could have played better. In all honesty, I don't think I could include myself in that, because I gave my all on that tour and played as well as I possibly could. In fact, early on in New Zealand, John Robins ordered me not to train because I'd taken such a battering. He told me to go off and lose myself for a while. I eventually played in 22 games out of 35 and missed one game through sunburn.

There was the time, of course, when I slept in, which I have to mention. I put it down to the time gap in the travel because it was when we went from Perth across Australia! I had fallen asleep in my room during the day and when I got downstairs, there was nobody there. Nobody thought to check on me and I missed training – but I didn't even get a row!

I don't look back on that tour with any real negative feelings. The social side was fantastic. Every player was adopted by a school, whose pupils enthusiastically produced scrapbooks of the tour for us. Mine was Papakura High School, south of Auckland, and the lad who presented my scrapbook to me, Bob Lendrum, went on to play for the All Blacks in 1973 against England. It remains a great memento. The rugby master, I recall, was Mr F.J. Graham, a great artist – I still have one of his Maori drawings on my wall at home. Scots are always welcome in New Zealand and everywhere we went, from Bluff in Southland to Whangarei in Northland, there were Scots there to entertain us. In Whangarei, a few of us went out to dinner with Dr Norman Davidson, who played for Hawick and Scotland in the early 1950s. I also spent a lot of time in the company of Dr Gibby Abercrombie, who also played for Scotland, in 1949 and 1950, out of Edinburgh University. One of his sons was a very good player as well, and understudied Sean Fitzpatrick, while another became the physio to the All Blacks.

I was actually offered a job in a school in Lower Hutt, near Wellington, the birthplace of the Leslie brothers and Tana Umaga, the current All Blacks captain. I did consider it but eventually turned it down, as I wanted to continue to play for Scotland and it was a bit too far to commute!

I came back from that tour tougher and perhaps more ruthless in the way I played and approached the game. We used to think Borders rugby was tough but it wasn't a patch on New Zealand rugby. It may have been over-robust, even dirty at times – it got to a point where parents didn't want their children to play it – but, typically of New Zealand, they then changed it.

The team, I believe, which adapts most quickly to what is happening around them on the pitch is the All Blacks. There was an instance in the Fourth Test when the All Blacks scored a try and it was too quick for the TV cameras to catch. The ball had been kicked into the corner by Herewini, the All Blacks first five-eighth, and Dewi Bebb took the ball out of play. Meads ran up, picked up the ball quickly, threw it in underhand to Waka Nathan and he scored. Because it was so quick, the cameras had to show a still of Nathan.

Now, you will often see the All Blacks in dire straits when

suddenly someone has the presence of mind to do something different, to take a quick throw-in or whatever, and they counter-attack. The French are similar. Many might remember the famous 'try from the ends of the Earth' France scored in 1994, I think, when they beat the All Blacks twice in New Zealand. That try was started from their own corner – which is why people say it started 'at the South Pole' – by Philippe Saint-André and finished with Jean-Luc Sadourny scoring at the other end after the ball had gone through lots of hands.

And so the lessons had begun: New Zealanders were winners; they were among the quickest to adapt in order to reverse losing situations; and they commanded respect for the way they approached their rugby. If only Scottish rugby could be like that. It was a thought which grew inside me over the next few years.

7

A Kipper's Life for Me!

Gareth Edwards
Wales (53 caps)
British and Irish Lions (1968, 1971, 1974)

There is no doubt in my mind that the 1968 tour to South Africa laid the foundations for the successes of the Lions in 1971 and 1974.

It was a great apprenticeship for my Lions career and those of others at the core of later triumphs, and that was in no small way down to the senior figures like Jim Telfer. I had been aware of Jim from 1966, really, when I was a schoolboy desperate to follow the progress of the Lions in New Zealand. It was obvious then that he was a really tough, abrasive, no-nonsense back-row forward and someone the Lions were better having in their team than in the opposition.

I remember the reverberations of the well-documented speech in which he was highly critical of the New Zealanders. It was national news in Wales because it was very unusual for rugby players to say anything out of the ordinary, so I was intrigued to meet this character in 1968.

By then, he was clearly a man with great experience and was a great player to have alongside you. I got injured halfway through the tour and didn't play much towards the end, so my game-time with him was limited, but I had enjoyed playing with Jim. He was a real workhorse, very committed and a good link player, excellent at killing the ball. He thought nothing of putting his body on the line and so was hugely valued by his teammates.

There was great respect for Jim – no doubt about that. No frills, no compromising, he just got on with the job.

And it wasn't much fun putting your body on the line out there. I was thrown down on the ground and scraped my whole face on what was a bone-hard cricket square in the middle of the pitch at Loftus. The medic came on and asked if he could help me, and I told him, 'Yes, you could dig up that bloody cricket square!'

The 1968 trip became known as the 'wreckers and kippers tour' but that was more a high-spirited thing than any real division between players – I fell into both camps! It wasn't far from being a successful tour: we had lots of injuries, drew one Test, should have won another and lost only one provincial game out of twenty-three. The 1971 and 1974 tours attract all the attention, naturally enough, but the 1968 players helped guide many of us towards those successes.

It was fascinating to return to South Africa in 1968 with the Lions, but I had had a lot more to go through that year before I could contemplate becoming a Lion again.

The knee cartilage injury I suffered in October 1967 meant I was out of action until February of that season. I went through nearly the whole season not playing for Scotland, until we faced England at the end of the 1968 Championship. Scotland had lost to the All Blacks and then to France, Wales and Ireland in that season before I had been able to return. To get some match fitness, I played in a Thirds match for Melrose – I had to ask Stuart Henderson, the late legendary secretary of the club, who was Thirds captain then, for permission to play – and then I was picked for Scotland. I remember John Reason, the *Daily Telegraph* rugby writer, saying in his book *The 1968 Lions* that it seemed the Lions selectors were waiting for me to come back so they could pick me for the tour, even though he didn't think I was all that good.

It was not unlike the situation Scotland's current number 8, Simon Taylor, found himself in this year, having to return from a long time out injured and trying to get games to prove his fitness. He went to play for Saracens for a week rather than Melrose Thirds, which is a sign of the times, but it was enough to get him into the Scotland squad in time to show he was fit for the Lions.

I played against England and though we lost 8–6 – which made it a whitewash and the worst season for Scotland for 14 years – the Monday after that, the Lions squad was chosen and I was in.

But with the concerns over fitness, I hadn't even asked my boss for time off, so I had to go and see him, which was a bit worrying. I remember saying to my head of department, 'By the way, I've been asked to go on the Lions tour, which will mean a few months away,' and he wasn't too chuffed. Thankfully, the headmaster at Gala Academy, Jim McIlwraith, was very supportive, so I was given permission to go on tour. Once again, it cost me a lot of money, being away for three months, because my wages were stopped for the duration. Frances would send money out to keep me going.

But things were done a bit differently in those days in many ways. I was chosen in 1968 as the only number 8 and there were only five back-row forwards picked, which proved to be a problem as the tour progressed. The 2005 squad had three number 8s and eight back-rows among the twenty-three forwards – we had fifteen, and fifteen backs. We were also given one pair of trousers, two blazers, one voucher to buy rugby boots, two red towels and a kitbag to carry our training gear. We had to provide our own training kit – rugby jerseys, shorts, tracksuits, and other clothes. Our daily allowance was 10 shillings per day (50 pence). The IRB turned down a request for an increase to 30 shillings per day!

It was great to be involved in another Lions tour and this one was completely different from the 1966 trip. The results did not look good on the South African tour either – we were beaten three Tests to one draw – but the games were a lot closer than the scores suggest. However, the 1968 squad will forever be remembered as 'the kippers and the wreckers' because of the way many of the squad socialised, duly wrecking a hotel.

There was actually a very good group of players on that tour – Syd Millar and Willie John McBride were on their third Lions tour, the captain Tom Kiernan was on his second to South Africa, and others, namely Bob Hiller, Mike Gibson, Gareth Edwards, Barry John, Delme Thomas, Gerald Davies, John Taylor, John Pullin and Willie John, would go on to use the experience to good effect, winning in New Zealand in 1971. Then there were also good players who came back and went to rugby league: Keri Jones, Mike Coulman and Maurice Richards.

Ronnie Dawson, who had captained the Lions in 1959, was a very good coach and he worked us hard. He was actually fitter than some of the players. The manager was David Brooks, an experienced figure who had already toured South Africa with Harlequins the year before, and after a game there was always what you might call a 'happy hour' as David encouraged players to sit around in a circle with a drink.

I remember him coming up to me early in the tour when we were having a night out and saying, 'You know, Jim, when we picked this squad, I knew there would be three or four who would be different and wouldn't approve of this kind of thing, who might not enjoy seeing all these shenanigans going on, and you would be one of them.'

I said, 'Yes, I understand what you're trying to do, just as long as the focus of the tour is to win the Tests.'

I have sometimes acquired a reputation for working too hard on my rugby or being too serious about it to the detriment of all else but that is exaggerated. I'm not a monk. I enjoyed going out for a drink, and I occasionally got drunk, but I liked to think players would make sure it didn't affect their performance on the pitch. Later, we'll return to how the 'wreckers' lost control in Cape Town.

South Africa has always been a very different place to tour from anywhere else and couldn't be more different to New Zealand in terms of the countryside and the weather. In New Zealand, different races mix without any real problems, while the first time I went to South Africa, in 1967, apartheid was very strong.

As you might expect, I looked on apartheid with quite a bit of displeasure. I remember being struck by how it was an accepted part of life – black people would walk with their heads down as if embarrassed and not make eye contact with you. If you met a black man walking along the street, he would often cross the road to stay away from you. Clearly that wasn't what we would see in the media, with coverage of riots and the ANC campaigns, but there on the ground I saw this deference by black people to whites, which was unsettling.

With apartheid now gone and rugby having played a part in bringing the 'Rainbow Nation' together, with the World Cup success there in 1995, there is obviously more equality and hope shared across the country now. But I have to say that some things haven't changed a great deal. I was back in 1999 and 2003 with Scotland and still black people appear to do and be expected to do the menial jobs – the waiters, handymen, cleaners were still mostly black; I didn't see any white people doing these jobs.

I admired South African rugby but, as a coach, I was never really influenced by the way they played, mainly because they were out of international rugby for such a long time and because the conditions in South Africa are so different to those we play under in Scotland.

Tours to South Africa are unique because of the altitude differences. You have to be more careful with training and rest. Unfortunately, the itinerary was organised in such a way that we were regularly travelling up and down to the high veld, between sea level and high altitude, which was tough to cope with.

We played 20 games and won every match apart from the Tests and one midweek game against Transvaal. We started the tour at Potchefstroom against Western Transvaal and it was a good start to my second Lions tour. I scored after snaffling a loose lineout ball close to the home line and though we turned around 6–3 down, Jock Turner, my Scotland teammate and a good friend, then scored. It was quite a try, considering what he had already gone through.

In the first half, Jock was injured and he admitted afterwards that he thought he had broken his neck at the time, suffering an injury similar to Danny Hearn, the England centre injured against the All Blacks the year before. Jock stooped to get a ball and his head connected with a South African and his mouth snapped shut; he broke two teeth, chipped his jawbone and jarred the top of his spine. He stayed on the field and started the comeback with his second-half try.

I then took a pass from Gareth Edwards to score another try and we eventually won the game 17–9. But we finished it with Jock, Gareth (hamstring), Mike Gibson (suspected broken ankle) and Keith Jarrett (tonsillitis) all ruled out; we were down to 26 men with 24 matches still to come.

We then moved down to sea level to play Western Province and a few of us went to watch them train. I remember not being all that impressed. But we were keen to see a number of aspects of their play. Two areas which we had problems with on that tour, right from the start, and which seriously hampered our chances, were in the refereeing of lineouts and scrums.

The South Africans had different interpretations of hooking, scrum feeding and using men in and beside the lineout: their hookers were allowed to swing their legs about before the ball came in, which was outlawed in Britain; the scrum-halfs' feed to the scrum was different from our way of doing it; and in the lineout they were permitted to 'double-bank', which means having a forward standing outside the lineout and receiving a tapped ball off the top, which was illegal at home.

The number of penalties awarded against us in the scrums was very high and it meant we struggled for some time to form good platforms. Our hookers John Pullin and Jeff Young were penalised at every turn; Jeff was left out the team for the Fourth Test because of the penalty count against him and John had to get out of his sickbed to play. Roger Young, the scrum-half, became so demoralised by being penalised at virtually every scrum put-in we had, he didn't know what to do.

It emerged later that Dr Danie Craven had used his influence to tell the referees to watch for these particular areas and keep the Lions in check. He had also had a hand in drawing up the itinerary, I understand, which ensured gruelling trips back and forth to the high veld.

My own tour hit a low point in only the second game. I injured the medial ligaments in my right knee (not the same knee as I'd had cartilage removed from the year before) and although it was quite serious, the South African doctor looked at it and sent me back on. I was forced to limp for the rest of the game, and until the end of my career, I played with my knee strapped to strengthen the ligaments around it. There is little doubt that it was foolish to send me back on in that state.

John Taylor was also limping, after a knee and ankle injury, then Gerald Davies injured an ankle and the doctor sent him back onto the field as well. We won 10–6 but John, Gerald and I joined Jock Turner and Mike Gibson in being ruled out for a while and we didn't travel to Mossel Bay for the next match.

I remember being treated at Groote Schuur Hospital in Cape Town, the hospital where Christiaan Barnard performed the first heart transplant operation. Some of the team met him and the second heart transplant patient, Dr Philip Blaiberg, who had been a keen rugby player. I was quite shocked to see how the hospital was divided into two distinct mirror images of each other, one for black people and one for white people.

The squad beat South Western Districts 24–6, and myself and the other injured players rejoined them at Port Elizabeth, where we beat Eastern Province 23–14 and then moved on to defeat Natal 17–5 in Durban.

In Rhodesia (now Zimbabwe), we met Ian Smith, the country's last white prime minister, and I was struck by the beauty of the city of Salisbury, now called Harare. Mike Gibson and Gerald Davies made their returns from injury and we beat Rhodesia 32–6. As it was the first game at altitude for a while, it was good preparation for the First Test at Pretoria.

I was selected at number 8 for the Test but I didn't recover from the injury in time and had to call off on the morning of the match. It was frustrating both to sit out and to watch us lose. Barry John suffered a broken collar bone after a high tackle from Jan Ellis and at that time replacements had to remain in their blazers in the stand, not primed ready at the side of the pitch. It took around ten minutes for Mike Gibson to get down out of the stand, into the dressing-room and changed to replace him.

The Springboks were a formidable side, with great players like Jannie Engelbrecht, Dis Nomis, Dawie de Villiers, Hannes Marais, Mof Myburgh, Frik du Preez, Jan Ellis and Tommy Bedford. They scored six points in the time we were down to fourteen men and another five points just after he got on, while we were still getting organised – Bob Taylor, the English number 8, had been filling in at centre during that time. We ended up losing 25–20 and the players were pretty disappointed because we felt we could have won.

We then moved to a small place in the country, Upington, and I returned and captained the team for the first time on tour, against North West Cape. I had to play with a bandage around my head as well as on my knee because I'd been injured in training and had stitches in a cut, but we won the game 25–5.

Top left: The Telfers – mum Peggy, dad Willie, Sheila (left),
Elma and a reluctant four-year-old James.

Top right: Aged 12 at Wester Housebyres, having
clearly put too much air in my rugby ball.

Above left: Elma (left), Sheila and me, ready for a night out in 1957.

Above right: Frances and I make a quick getaway
on our wedding day in 1967.

Top left: The Jubilee Cup-winners from Darnick in 1953.

Top right: Galashiels Academy 1st XV in 1957 – I'm between rector Mr Forbes and 1st XV coach Mr Shearer.

Above: Winning the Gala Sevens trophy with Melrose five years later in 1962. (©The Tweeddale Press Ltd)

Captaining Melrose at the Greenyards (left) and the Scottish Border Club in South Africa (right) were great honours, but my Scotland debut against France on 4 January 1964 was beyond compare. The team was: back row (l–r): R.C. Williams (referee, Ireland), S. Wilson, R.H. Thomson, J.W. Telfer, W.J. Hunter, P.C. Brown, B.C. Henderson, T.O. Grant, D.M.D. Rollo, D. Hill (touch judge, Hawick); front row (l–r): J.A.T. Rodd, I.H.P. Laughland, C. Elliot, J.B. Neill, N.S. Bruce, J.P. Fisher, G. Sharp. (© E.R. Yerbury & Co.)

Top: My debut Scotland try, against England, sparked the first pitch invasion at Murrayfield.

Above left: Scotland's Melrose quartet – Alex Hastie, Frank Laidlaw (back), me and David Chisholm (with president Geoff Rutherford) – never lost playing together in 1966–67.

Above right: My second Test match, with the All Blacks at a misty Murrayfield, ended in a 0–0 draw. Tremayne Rodd breaks, I (left) support and Peter Brown keeps Colin Meads grounded (right).

Top: The 1966 British and Irish Lions: back row (l–r): D.
A.R. Lewis, D.K. Jones, D.I. Powell, K.W. Kennedy, S.J. Watkins, D. Grant,
C.M.H. Gibson, C.W. McFadyean, S. Wilson, F.A.I. Laidlaw;
middle row (l–r): K.F. Savage, H. Norris, D Williams, R.A. Lamont,
W.J. McBride, B. Price, W. D. Thomas, F. P. K. Bresnihan, G. Prothero,
A. J. W. Hinshelwood; front row (l–r): D. Watkins, D.I. Bebb,
R.J. McLoughlin, J.W. Telfer, D.J. O'Brien (manager), M.J. Campbell-
Lamerton (captain), J.D. Robins (coach), A.E.I. Pask, M.P. Weston,
N.A. Murphy, R.M. Young; insets: J.C. Walsh and T.G. Price.
(courtesy Duncan Campbell)

Above: Howard Norris waits for my pass as the Lions protect me from
Colin and Stan Meads and Jack Hazlett in the second Test in
Wellington. (© *Wellington Evening Post*)

The Lions overcome the Junior All Blacks and the mud of Wellington's Athletic Park . . . but jet-boating with Roger Young, Ken Kennedy, Colin McFadyean and Barry Bresnihan provides a good wash!
(both © *Wellington Evening Post*)

By day a studious chemistry teacher at Galashiels Academy and by night let loose in the Folies Bergère with Sandy Carmichael, Douglas Jackson and Rodger Arneil – we were celebrating Scotland's 1969 win in Paris. (below right © Associated Press)

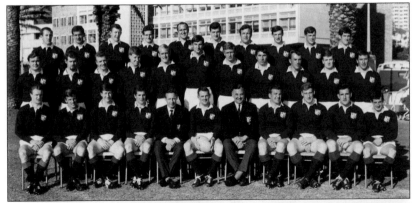

Top: The 1968 British and Irish Lions squad: back row (l–r): W.K. Jones, R.M. Young, M.G.M. Doyle, W.H. Raybould, J. Young, K.S. Jarrett, A.L. Horton, J.W.C. Turner, B. John, T.G.R. Davies; middle row (l–r): J.P. O'Shea, J. Taylor, F.P.K. Bresnihan, R.B. Taylor, R.J. Arneil, P.K. Stagg, P.J. Larter, R. Hiller, M.J. Coulman, M.C.R. Richards, J.V. Pullin; front row (l–r): C.M.H. Gibson, K.F. Savage, J.W. Telfer, A.J.W. Hinshelwood, A.R. Dawson (coach), T.J. Kieran (captain), D.K. Brooks (manager), S. Millar, W.J. McBride, W.D. Thomas, G.O. Edwards. (courtesy of Akkersdyk Studios, Cape Town)

Above left: Bob Taylor goes for Dawie de Villiers in a 1968 Lions Test, so I get Springbok lock Frik du Preez!

Above right: Trying to be impressed by our manager David Brooks' first 'kill' of the tour. (© *Die Transvaler*)

John Taylor also returned then. Because of injuries, it became a case of all hands to the pump – we had started the tour with only five back-row forwards and Willie John McBride had already been forced to play in the back row against Eastern Province because of the shortage. We then had games against South West Africa in Windhoek, where the captain was the Springbok number 7, Jan Ellis, and against Transvaal at Ellis Park, Johannesburg.

Strangely enough, after the Windhoek game, Ireland number 8 Ken Goodall came out to replace Welsh fly-half Barry John – work that one out! Ken had not been available at the start of the tour due to university exams. The management wouldn't allow him to postpone coming out for three weeks but when Barry John had to go home, it was a chance to strengthen the back row.

Unfortunately, we lost our first provincial game to Transvaal, 14–6. The game had been scheduled for the Wednesday before the second Test match, which would mean another move from high altitude down to Port Elizabeth at sea level, but we managed to get it brought forward by a day. Transvaal were one of the strongest provinces and we had to field a strong team; we picked ten of the Test team and I was playing my third game in a row.

It was a frustrating game, as every time we got near to their line, the referee would penalise us for a scrum infringement or something else. It was reported that our scrum-half, Roger Young, was penalised for standing to one side of the tunnel, for not putting it in straight, for dummying, for not letting the ball bounce, not putting it in at the right speed and anything else you could care to dream up! As well as penalties in their half, Transvaal had ten kicks at goal while we had two in the game.

We too had chances to win it, but we didn't take them, so we were not best pleased heading towards the Second Test. Ten inches of rain had fallen in the preceding eighteen days – as much as Port Elizabeth would usually have in a year – and that made the pitch a bit less rock-hard but it turned out to be a fairly drab game and ended in a 6–6 draw, two penalties for each side.

We then had a bit of a break. We went to the Kruger National Park and it was great to get away from the rugby for a few days. We flew to Johannesburg and then went by train to Nelspruit, dropping 4,000 feet overnight, and that was where the wreckers started tipping anyone who wanted to sleep out of bed. When we started off, there were only about eight or so enthusiastic wreckers, led by the captain and manager, and more than twenty kippers, but many realised that kipping was a self-defeating exercise because as soon as you got your head down to sleep the wreckers would come roaring down the corridor shouting, 'The wreckers are coming, hurrah, hurrah!' to the tune of 'The Campbells Are Coming'.

Bob 'Boss' Hiller was the leader of the kippers, I recall, and I was a kipper as well – our nickname because we liked to sleep during the night when others seemed more interested in running around and having a laugh at our expense. There was little you could do about it and you just accepted that you'd be woken up if you tried to sleep. But it actually helped team spirit and, as well as being tipped out of bed, we had some great sing-songs, barbecues and games of rounders.

The wreckers-and-kippers issue wasn't bad-tempered but a good laugh, really. John 'Tess' O'Shea was a great entertainer and would lead the singing – he did a great impromptu comedy act while we flew from Windhoek to Jo'burg – and Jock Turner and Rodger Arneil introduced 'Wild Mountain Thyme' to the group, which became a tour favourite.

The team had also started growing moustaches and beards after Windhoek and some had agreed not to shave until we'd won a Test or beaten a provincial side by 50 points. However, we never managed either and the resolve did not last long. But it was an example of the camaraderie on the tour.

Unfortunately, big Tess was unable to laugh his way out of a situation in Springs, where he was sent off against Eastern Transvaal. There had been flare-ups early in the game, with the front rows going at each other. Jeff Young, our hooker, got upset with his opposite number waving his striking leg about in the tunnel. Fists flew and then there was some head-butting.

In the second half, we were leading 23–6 when an Eastern Transvaal forward went to knock Roger Young out of the way and Tess stepped in and held the South African back. He duly received a punch for his efforts and Tess hit back. Blows then rained down on him from all sides. As this was going on, their scrum-half was scoring a try – it was very dubious, but I don't think the referee knew which way to look.

He called Tess over and sent him off but the drama was not over. Tess had to walk across a very wide running track and, as he did so, he was pelted by missiles. A spectator then jumped down from the stand and tried to attack him. The Lions leapt in and Willie John hit his attacker a couple of times; we had a farcical situation where Tess was restraining Willie John! McBride had already injured himself by cutting his leg on glass outside the team room in the hotel after the First Test and while the cut initially healed, it kept opening up again and at one point turned septic. So he was no doubt pretty wound up after spending some time sitting in the stand.

I remember going in to see O'Shea in the dressing-room and he was crying because he felt he had let the team down. O'Shea apologised to the powers that be and he was let off with a reprimand at a hearing the next day, which meant he was clear to continue playing. Ironically, O'Shea was the judge of the players' court and it later emerged that the referee, Bert Woolley, had written to him saying he regretted being forced to take the action he did – and Tess gave him two tickets for the Third Test!

The next big game for us was against Northern Transvaal, which was termed the 'Fifth Test' – they had four Springboks in their pack – but there was another bad blow for me personally. Ken Goodall had come out and played one game but he had broken his thumb, so he was out of the tour and we were back to meagre back-row rations.

It was a lovely day at Loftus Versfeld and the match was close, but we were behind 16–13 when I had to be carried off on a stretcher with a bad head wound. The ball went over the tail of the lineout and I body-checked Gys Pitzer, the hooker, as he went for the ball. I fell to the ground and, as I fell, he went over the top of me and back-heeled me in the face. I was taken off with blood spurting out of a cut just above my nose and I was led into the treatment room. The famous Springbok forward Dr Ernst Dinkelmann, who had toured with South Africa in 1951 and played in the infamous 44–0 defeat of Scotland at Murrayfield, quickly set to work putting stitches in.

I thought that I would be unable to continue but he kept saying, 'There you go, you're fine, get back on again,' and made me go out. I thought, 'Here we go again,' after being forced to play with ligament damage at Western Province. It was only a cut this time and we had to play with seven forwards while I was off; I could see the players' relief when I got back on and we took control of the game. We then drew level and Tom Kiernan kicked another two penalties to put us 22–16 clear. Of course, this was South Africa and the referee gave them two kickable penalties late on, which were both reported to be very dubious. They only got one, thankfully, and we hung on for what many believed to be our best win of the tour, 22–19.

The following day, I was one of the walking wounded, with my head stitched and my knee injury having been aggravated by the game. I didn't play again until the Third Test.

We will come to the game in a moment but first we have to note one incident which brought shame on the Lions on that tour and had the word 'wreckers' splashed all over the papers in South Africa and at home. It basically only involved three or four Lions, including the manager, and was nothing to do with the 'kippers and wreckers' fun of the train to and from Kruger Park. Their behaviour was disgraceful. We were in a hotel owned by Jeff Reynolds, a Lion of 1938, and a small group took advantage of his great hospitality.

It was not that some Lions were enjoying themselves, it was their behaviour and attitude that brought disgrace on the Lions. It seemed to start with high jinks after the Griqualand West game in Kimberley, which we won 11–3, and continued on the flight back to Cape Town and then at Jeff Reynold's hotel in Rondebosch. The men involved were drunk and they were emptying their glasses and smashing them on the ground so that the whole carpet in the bar was an inch deep in broken glass by the time they had finished. This went on in front of other hotel guests and that annoyed me because these few Lions seemed to show little respect for other people and the hotel we were in, or the fact that somebody had to clear up their mess. It did not show the British and Irish Lions in a good light.

Jeff reluctantly handed over a bill for damages to the Lions management. He was reported to have halved the true cost and then halved it again before giving them a bill for £900. Our manager, David Brooks, did not seem too concerned; he was reported to have said, 'Huh, it couldn't have been a very good party!' He probably didn't remember much.

It wasn't finished yet, either. We played and beat Boland 14–0 and that night some of the Lions had fun tearing each other's shirts to pieces and setting them on fire, although by this time they had learned something and did it outside the hotel entrance rather than in the bar. This, and the bar damage of the weekend, was widely reported in the local and UK press, and the wreckers became infamous.

It took away some of the lustre of the Lions ethos, I think, and the incident certainly seemed to affect our display in the Third Test at the end of that week. To be honest, we should still have won that Test match.

We threw away three good scoring chances which, had they been taken, would have won us the game and put us back in the running for the series. Both Rodger Arneil and I were stopped driving near the Springbok line. From the subsequent lineout, Mike Gibson went for a drop-goal and missed. The second chance occurred when Rodger seemed certain to score but was distracted by a shout from Keith Savage. He was caught in two minds with the line beckoning and the chance was lost.

The third good chance fell to Bob Taylor. Dawie de Villiers had been tackled into touch three metres from the Springbok line and Maurice Richards, the wing, spotted Bob unmarked at the back of the lineout. Bob only had to catch the ball and fall over the line to score but he lost the ball in the sun coming down behind Table Mountain and dropped it.

We were beaten 11–6 and again I had the sinking feeling of a series which had seemed within reach being lost. I had captained the Lions at Upington and twice more I was given the honour of leading the team, against Border at East London and against North East Cape at Cradock. We won both games convincingly, 26–6 and 40–12, which pleased me.

There was still a tremendous amount of interest in the final Test, even though the Springboks were leading two Test wins to a draw. The supporters were convinced that the Boks would abandon their cautious defensive game and play attacking rugby, and we sensed they wanted to be there for the final kill.

It proved to be something of a damp squib and though it was tight at 6–3 to the Springboks at half-time, they pulled away in the second half. The game came nearly four months after we'd first arrived in South Africa, and fatigue, injuries and simply wanting to be home were inevitably catching up with the players.

It was very disappointing to lose a Test series again but this was very different to New Zealand. We did not play badly and actually produced a lot of good displays; we surpassed the feats of previous tours, losing only one provincial match; and we should have won at least one Test, and would have done, had the refereeing not been so much against us. To think that, at that level, we couldn't pick a fit hooker (Jeff Young) for the last Test and had to get John Pullin to play with the flu simply because the referees were penalising Jeff off the park is incredible.

Injuries right through the 30-man squad, some to crucial players – Mike Gibson, Gareth Edwards, Barry John, Roger Young, Gerald Davies, John Taylor and Willie John McBride – also undermined our efforts. Gareth, Barry and Gerald, however, played very well on their first Lions tours and there is little doubt that the experience they gained was invaluable to the success they enjoyed in becoming the first Lions squad to win in New Zealand, three years later.

Of the Scots, Rodger Arneil was another player who really stood up well in South Africa, especially as he arrived as a replacement. He had been called up when Bryan West pulled out after training with us at Eastbourne. Bryan had to hand over all his kit to Rodger before leaving us!

Where we fell down on that tour was in the lack of tries in the Test matches and the backs were criticised for that. Thinking about it now, I wonder whether it was not unlike the situation when I coached the Lions in 1983, in that we only had one coach and he was a forward. Ronnie Dawson worked extremely hard but perhaps our back play was not well enough developed.

It was a happy tour, however, and the management deserved credit for creating that harmony and bringing the players from four nations together. The only thing missing was the Test results. But, sadly, we cannot rewrite history and we returned to the UK the gallant losers of another Test series in the southern hemisphere.

8

Chemical Reactions

Terry Christie
Ex-Headmaster, Musselburgh Grammar School
Manager, Alloa Athletic FC

After Jim followed me down from Forrester High to Portobello High, we worked together for three years, sharing an office, and we had some great times in that school.

Jim and I were both chemistry teachers and assistant heads to John Baggeley, the head teacher, who encouraged staff and pupils to be involved in sport. Jim played in the staff football team and he was a great centre-half, as competitive as hell. He would always shout at me, 'C'mon, Terry, get them going!' He was an uncompromising centre-half and if he'd lived in the Central Belt and not Melrose, there is no doubt in my mind he would have been a professional footballer; he was strong and fit, he attacked the ball like hell and put the fear of death into people. How could he have failed?

As a teacher, he was actually quite gentle and obviously cared for the children but I watched him frightening folk with his low voice. He would say, 'Do you understand what I mean?' I added that to my repertoire! He could be stern and strict but he had a soft side too. He was dedicated to his pupils and had a lovely sense of humour, which didn't always show. They really respected and liked him. It was a pleasure to teach alongside him.

Of course, Jim had this burning ambition as a rugby coach and I was as ambitious in football; we used to share a lot of ideas and talk a lot about Scottish sport. We would also laugh at each other's sports: I used to tell him footballers were more skilful and he would just go on about Jim Renwick or Keith Robertson. 'But your guys get a clap if you kick it into the crowd – at least we keep the ball on the park!' I would say.

He opened a guest house, as well, and I remember Jim working as a part-time barman in a Newington pub to learn the licensed trade because he wanted to own a pub. I also recall that, in the time we were there, the school was inspected and our teaching was inspected.

The head teacher said the inspector had made the same comment about the two of us: 'They are good teachers but a bit old-fashioned.' And we were only in our 30s at the time!

My teaching career had begun in earnest in 1964, when I joined the new Galashiels Academy. It was opened as a large new school adjacent to the Scott Park, the old Academy where I had been a pupil later becoming the Borders College campus on the north side of Galashiels.

It was a purpose-built school on four floors, and within the seven years I was there, an extension had been built. The school needed every square inch because the roll quickly rattled up past 1,200.

I enjoyed teaching there – there were a lot of good pupils – and although I mainly taught science, I also took rugby. To help the PE department, some enthusiastic general teachers were timetabled to take an afternoon of rugby once a week, when a whole year group would go down to Netherdale. Because I was the least experienced rugby teacher, I had the dubious pleasure of taking the bottom 30 pupils, those who had very little interest in sport. That was a tough introduction to teaching rugby, I can tell you.

Among my pupils at the school – though not in that rugby group, I would add – were the Scotland international Kenny Lawrie, whose son Andy has played professional football for Falkirk for many years; and Rob Moffat, later my assistant coach at Melrose and now Scotland's sevens coach, who started as a number 8 but later moved to the wing. I assume he must have found the number 8 position too demanding, or maybe it was because he had brains and speed! He toured Japan with Scotland in 1977. There was also current Peebles High School PE head Jim Henderson, who played for Melrose and toured France with Scotland in 1980. Ex-Gala captain and coach Bruce Rutherford and Robin Wood, a Melrose boy who played for Currie, are others I remember.

My enthusiasm for science was also growing and new courses on integrated science were being introduced at that time. Teachers from all over the Borders met regularly to share ideas and discuss new methods of teaching. Chemistry is a fascinating subject and I enjoyed starting my day by explaining to the children how chemicals and chemical reactions were all around them and made the world tick, from the breakfast cereals they ate to the beds they slept on.

The subject also granted me the freedom to be a bit of an actor and experiments brought excitement to the lesson. I would work on my intonation, being quiet and then louder, to keep youngsters interested. I found it enjoyable pushing them and seeking high standards. Insisting the children should do as well as they possibly could, I never felt anyone would leave my class bored. Later, it was an approach I tried to bring to my rugby coaching.

As in rugby, my natural desire to organise came to the fore in school and I wanted to run my own department, so when I got the chance to be a guidance teacher and housemaster, it was an opportunity to take on more responsibility. As master of Ellwyn House, I was determined that it was going to be the best in the school.

Teaching was central to my life and when I was dropped by Scotland, it made me assess what the future held for me. Rugby, and playing for Scotland, may have helped steer me into teaching, which I am thankful for, but it was time to look for new challenges. Being tied to the Borders was no longer a priority and, though I never wanted to play for any club other than Melrose, the chance of moving to a new school was on my horizon.

In 1971, I applied for a variety of more senior posts and got one as principal teacher of science at Williamwood High School in Clarkston, Glasgow, which, although at the time its best pupils went to Eastwood High after second year, was still a good school. I note it is now among the top-performing schools in Scotland.

At first, Frances thought her whole world was falling apart, because she hadn't known anything other than the Borders. I hadn't lived anywhere else either but I suppose I had seen more, thanks to my rugby career and tours abroad. Moving didn't worry me – I relished it. Frances soon settled into our new home in Victoria Crescent, Clarkston, and life became quite special when Louise arrived to join her brother Mark. I was still travelling to Melrose to play while making my first steps up the ladder in the world of education, in an area of Scotland that was new to us all, and it was exciting.

Those two years in Clarkston were also struck by tragedy, however. Only months after we'd arrived, I was in the school when we heard news that there had been a gas explosion in a local shop. We didn't know at the time how serious it was but it wasn't long before we discovered that 22 people had been killed and over 100 injured as the explosion ripped through shops and brought the car park over the shops tumbling down into them. The explosion even killed some people in passing buses.

It was a midweek afternoon and my first thought was of Frances, who liked to walk to the shops with the children. It was some relief when I phoned home and she was there and all right. But I'll never forget the headmaster, Sandy Thain, calling the pupils into the main school hall and telling them some people had been killed. Looking at the faces of the children at that assembly, knowing that some of them would have lost mothers in those shops, was a harrowing experience.

That was a terrible thing that happened and it obviously had a big effect on the school, the pupils and the staff. I was only at Williamwood for two years but that memory still haunts me.

I left Williamwood in 1973 to take over as principal teacher of chemistry at Forrester High School in Broomhouse, to the west of Edinburgh. I had continued to take rugby at Williamwood and often wondered what happened to the youngsters after I left and whether they kept up an interest. But I was pretty busy myself, training at Hutchesons' Grammar School FP during the week and travelling back every weekend to Melrose with my family in the car, winding through the Clyde Valley and down the Borders roads.

We moved to Balerno, on the outskirts of Edinburgh. Forrester was the perfect working-class comprehensive, with some clever children from council estates like Stenhouse, Longstone and Carrick Knowe, and some not so clever. It reminded me of Galashiels in the way that many parents, although not well off, were enthusiastic about education and pushed their children to achieve.

There was a less exciting story at the school about one pupil who went on to great things. Les McKeown, later of the Bay City Rollers, was a Broomhouse boy and he was infamous for using a school lift as a toilet on one occasion. I won't go into detail, as it was before I arrived at the school and one trusts his toilet habits improved as he 'shang-a-langed' to the top of the charts.

I took a rugby team at Forrester as well and enjoyed working with the PE staff, particularly Arthur Ross, Colin McLean and Dave Blamire.

The headmaster, Peter Hollis, was a real old-fashioned type who stayed in his office most of the time and was seldom seen around the school. When I went down to say goodbye to him when I left in 1975, he told me the reason he had been waiting on the steps of the Dean Teaching Centre on the day two years before when I'd gone for my interview was that the other two candidates on the leet hadn't shown up, and he was just relieved to see me. 'That's the only reason you got the job, Telfer,' he said. Thanks, sir.

That area of Edinburgh was growing all the time, with the Wester Hailes estate expanding, and we had up to 2,000 pupils over two sites while St Augustine's, the Roman Catholic school next door, had over 1,000. Interestingly, there were over 3,000 children going home from these two schools of different denominations every afternoon and I don't remember any sectarian trouble.

My next move, in 1975, took me to Portobello High School and that was another huge school – over 1,500 pupils, again split over two buildings. The rugby was great there as well, though that's not why I went. It was another challenge for me, stepping up to an assistant head's role. I seemed to follow Terry Christie, an exceptionally gifted man who made a successful career in teaching and football coaching.

Terry and I shared some great times and the fact that we were both sports coaches probably had a lot to do with it. He had been principal teacher of chemistry at Forrester before me and then I got the same level of job as him, assistant head, at Portobello. There was a great tradition of sport at Portobello and rugby was part of that under Alistair Cuthbertson, who everybody in Scottish rugby knew. He was an art teacher and also a housemaster and he would use his 'house' room, miles from the art department, to talk rugby with his pupils. If there was any art taught in that room, it was by accident!

All boys had to play rugby in their first year and I've since heard the likes of Chris Robertson, the former Rangers player, his brother John, the ex-Hearts manager, and Dave Bowman, the former Dundee United and Hearts footballer, talking about how they were made to play rugby. That was just a rule of the head teacher's and I think it was aimed at ensuring all the youngsters, who tended to play football non-stop, tasted something else for one year. Not a bad idea. But I actually played a lot of football then, with Terry and other staff members – centre-half, the stopper, I think.

It was a quality school but latterly I began to feel that it was just too big. It was difficult to get to know the pupils, which is something most teachers like to try and achieve, and I left in 1978 thinking Portobello was more like a factory than a school.

My next move was to Livingston. Three schools in six years? I was either a very good teacher or a very bad one. I write earlier in the book that my move as a child to Wester Housebyres was the making of me as a rugby player; this was the equivalent for me as a teacher. Arriving at the newly built Deans Community High School in 1978 was a move to a totally different world.

The school was part of a pioneering approach to education by Lothian Regional Council led by the education committee convener, George Foulkes, who later became the MP for Carrick, Cumnock and Doon Valley, and recently returned to Edinburgh as chairman of Heart of Midlothian FC. The Wester Hailes Education Centre in Edinburgh, and Deans and Inveralmond in Livingston were the first of these new schools.

The post of depute head at the new Deans attracted me because I was enthusiastic about the new ideas for education they had, and I was delighted to get the job. The head, Stewart Wilson, was something else. He was a real left-wing Scot, an eccentric with long, flowing hair and light-coloured suits, and boundless energy. He had been head in a community school in Nottinghamshire and, though he was the complete opposite to me, we had a similar excitement about the new school and hit it off really well.

The whole design of the school was different: it was built both for the pupils and the community, and was the brainchild of John Carsewell, the architect, and Bob Ferguson, the assistant director of the West Lothian division of Lothian Regional Council. The PE department, theatre, squash courts, swimming pool, and home economics, art and technical departments were all near to the front door, with the more academic areas like the English, history and geography departments further away. The idea behind that was to enable the public to come in and use the facilities, practical subjects being the preferred options for adults.

There were carpets in the classrooms, a new idea then, to soften the noise of feet around the school, and no bells sounded; there were coffee areas where children could mix with staff; and a lovely library for school and community use. The school was open seven days a week and there was a distinctly relaxed atmosphere. All teaching staff were contracted to work at least one evening a week and the senior management had to run the school during weekends and holidays.

It was very innovative. We ran mixed classes, with adults in with children, and there were also night classes purely for adults. The integration of children and adults was more effective in some subjects than others – it was particularly good in the fifth- and sixth-year Higher classes. The adults always seemed to have a calming influence on the children, which was fascinating to watch. Not everything worked but when it worked well, it was invigorating.

Livingston itself was one of Scotland's innovative new towns, so we had a lot of families who had recently moved from Glasgow and Edinburgh in our catchment area and the school, with so many amenities, became a natural meeting place.

Although one of the requirements of the job was that I would live in the area – to which I agreed at my interview – I never actually moved. I started off travelling out from Edinburgh but by the end of my time at Deans I was living in Selkirk and driving over an hour to get there. I still tried to make sure I was always in before most of the staff, so it meant early starts and sometimes overnight stays in Bathgate. Despite all my efforts, I could never beat Stewart, who would be in by seven in the morning and often still there at ten at night.

While the school was a great idea in my opinion, I have to say that in practice some ideas were not an overwhelming success, not because of Stewart but largely because they were so new and different. We had to work hard to encourage parents and other adults from the area to feel the school was for them too and not, as their own schools probably were, purely for the children.

Some parents took their children away to Bathgate, which was considered more academic, and we attracted the label of being too modern for people. I felt then, as I have done in Scottish rugby many times, that Scots have a problem with adapting to change and that many don't even give new ideas a chance before damning them, which is a real shame.

Some of the staff didn't take to it brilliantly either. It was made clear at our interviews that we were coming into something quite different: this wasn't your normal school and it was up to us whether we wanted to be involved or not. We were paid more than the usual rate for being part of the new community ethos but we also had to work outwith normal school hours more. It required different teaching methods as well, because we had only two periods a day to begin with – one in the morning and one in the afternoon.

I could see the idea behind this: to cut out the disruption caused by short periods, where children spend so much time moving between classes that there's less time for actual learning. It also contributed to the quiet, relaxed air about the school, with less movement than other schools. But long periods require quite a variety of teaching methods. Primary teachers are very adept at this kind of teaching but some secondary teachers had not developed in this regard because they had not needed to. I admire primary teachers and the way they can hold children's interest for up to two or three hours without a break. That demands very good organisation and a variety of skills, and some of our teachers at Deans found it very difficult.

Stewart was very supportive of his staff. At that time, I was starting to become more involved with Scotland and the Lions, and he and Lothian Regional Council supported me going on tour – with a salary, which was new to me. But that was typical of the relationship we struck up. When you have a groundbreaking educational approach, it's imperative that everyone buys into it – pupils, staff, parents and community – and Stewart and I tried to lead that.

Along with the PE department, mainly through the efforts of Ian Hanlin, we started rugby at the school and I was allowed to choose the colours, so the teams played in a very attractive yellow and black striped jersey, not dissimilar to a certain club in the Borders. I was six years there and many of the youngsters from the school teams graduated to Livingston Rugby Club, where they were always well looked after.

Deans Community School certainly brought me out of myself a great deal. Senior members of staff had responsibilities as duty officers and that involved liaising with the community and dealing with the interaction between adults, pupils and other professionals. I also had to take school assemblies, lead meetings and speak in public, which taught me a lot.

In truth, I loved the whole approach, the sweeping away of the cobwebs which Stewart strived for. He was a great influence on me and my educational beliefs: the encouragement not to fear new ideas, to try, to think of adults working with youngsters. He had a philosophy that education lasted from 8 years old to 80 and he played a big part in my development not only as a teacher but also as a person, which would extend into my rugby coaching.

I will write later in the book about how I tried to bring some new ideas to the more traditional Hawick High School in my next move, and how my friendship with HRH The Princess Royal helped cap a satisfying achievement for me in that Borders school. But by this stage, rugby coaching was really pulling at me and there was much to achieve with Scotland before I returned as a teacher to the Borders.

9

Born to Coach

Richie Dixon
Scotland B captain (1978–80)
SRU head of coach development

Coaching was a recognised part of rugby throughout the world long before Scotland appointed its first national coach. When the new coaching advisory panel was set up by the Scottish Rugby Union in the 1970s, however, it moved forward at a fair lick.

I was still a player when I first came across Jim Telfer and it was his coaching with the Scotland B team, which I captained, that gave him his first taste of working at an international level. He had been known as a club coach for some time, but then most of us coached with our clubs, bringing ideas back from the representative levels.

Jim and I had a similar way of thinking about rugby even then and developed a very good rapport. I remember after we had beaten Ireland in a B game for the first time, he said afterwards that he had been sitting there thinking about how to change the lineout when I changed it on the field.

There were a lot of good rugby thinkers around the Scotland team in the 1970s and innovative thinking has been a trademark of coaching in Scotland. There are problems to do with resources and a simple lack of playing numbers which can make it tougher than elsewhere, but that hasn't stopped coaching from developing over the last 30 years and we owe a lot to those men who put the art and skills of coaching on to a firmer, more sound base in the 1970s.

Coaching may have had an inauspicious start in Scottish rugby but we have always had an innovative approach to playing the game and, having studied it in some detail, it was natural for me to move into coaching when it became an accepted part of the sport.

But when do you start to coach? Is coaching offering words of advice, cajoling fellow players, or does it only begin when you sit down to work out tactics or a style of game? Clearly, coaching brings together a wide range of tasks and talents, and I was already on the road to being a coach when I was playing.

My first steps were probably at Melrose in 1964, in my first season as captain, where I would lead fitness training and skills development. There weren't any coaches in those days, other than teachers coaching rugby in schools and sometimes helping in clubs. We had other Scotland players at the club at that time but for some reason they did not take the lead in training, whereas I was happy to try to organise things and bring back the international ideas to my teammates at the Greenyards. I was not alone, as many internationalists were similarly returning to their clubs with new ideas inspired by the way Scotland and other nations played.

But it was after the Lions tour in 1966 that my coaching began to take off. There, I had learned a lot from John Robins, the Lions coach, and from speaking to coaches in New Zealand. At Melrose, I had six seasons as captain in three two-year blocks, and I was also captain of the South of Scotland; along with that responsibility, I was happy to take training too.

One of my eccentricities, even at that time, was to make notes for all the coaching sessions I conducted, which I would write in science lab books 'borrowed' from the school. I now use A4 sheets, which can be kept in folders – an idea pinched from Ian McGeechan. The concept of note-making came from my experience of having to prepare lessons in school, where it was vital to ensure you had enough material to fill a full lesson. Some coaches frowned on my using notes, as if only poor coaches couldn't retain everything in their head, but it didn't bother me. I still produce new notes for every session I take, at whatever school or club I go along to. Preparation is vital.

That was a theme from my early days. When I became captain

of Scotland in 1968, I felt the players needed to prepare in the week before the game as well as the few days leading up to it, so I suggested to the SRU that the team be given the chance to meet on the Sunday before an international. This was met with approval by the committee and the players, even though some were playing in London, like Stewart Wilson, Sandy Hinshelwood, Ian Robertson and Pringle Fisher, or in Neath, as was the case with Wilson Lauder.

At the time, it seemed a novel idea here to have some form of coach, but I had learned that southern-hemisphere countries had used coaches at all levels of the game for some time. Someone like Fred Allen, who brought the All Blacks to Scotland in 1967, was widely recognised as the head coach and main selector of the New Zealand team.

Yet it was only in 1971 that the SRU appointed its first coach, Bill Dickinson, and even then he was only termed 'an adviser to the captain'. It is worth stating, however, that the SRU's attitude to coaching merely reflected that of Scottish clubs at the time, who viewed coaching with some disgust. Even today, intriguingly, you'll see the names of the captains and presidents on boards in clubhouses but you will not see the names of the coaches.

Despite this, there was a lot of good coaching going on in schools in the 1960s and '70s; most of the first rugby coaches came from teaching backgrounds. Well-respected teachers like Adam Robson, Arthur Ross, Donald Scott, Donald Mitchell, Tom Pearson and Jim Shearer were doing sterling work under the guiding influence of the tremendously enthusiastic 'father of coaching' in Scotland, George Thomson, a member of the SRU committee and later president. We lost a great man when George died in 2005. It was his enthusiasm for developing a professional, cutting-edge approach to rugby coaching that inspired me. Intriguingly, he was fanatical about the development of the ruck as a part of the Scottish armoury and, believe it or not, I occasionally had to dampen down his enthusiasm!

George was chairman of the SRU's first coaching sub-committee in 1968 and he set up their first coaching advisory panel in 1970. The panel was chaired by Lyn Tatham and consisted of Bill Dickinson, Adam Robson, Arthur Ross, Jim Shearer and Tom Pearson. It was, therefore, the drive of these individuals which brought Scottish rugby into the modern coaching world and, without doubt, we owe them a great debt of gratitude.

Each of the districts appointed a number of advisory coaches and I remember Les Allan, another ex-internationalist at Melrose and a South district advisory coach, said to me, 'The Union want to put someone on the new panel but he's still playing and they worry in case he feels he has to retire from playing.' In other words, a player could not get onto the august new panel. The player he was talking about was me. I was honoured when I was asked to join the panel.

I recall one of the first big coaching courses was organised at Murrayfield in the summer of 1970 and over 200 participants stayed at the Pollock Halls, the Edinburgh University halls of residence. It remains a vivid memory because the Commonwealth Games had just taken place in Edinburgh and all the athletes had stayed at the Halls, so we had a fantastic choice of food. But these annual courses, organised by the advisory panel and run by volunteers, were excellent. Suited to various levels of coach education, they set the trend for many years.

Coaching was in its infancy in the other countries of the four Home Unions, too, and we all shared ideas. A key motivation for us all was to uncover methods of beating the All Blacks – some things don't change! I remember in the summer of 1971 driving home through the night to Glasgow from a week's coaching course at Aberystwyth organised by Ray Williams, the technical administrator of the Welsh Rugby Union. As I drove, I listened on the radio to the whole Lions First Test in New Zealand.

This is my memory: '. . . and the All Blacks have it, and it's back to Going and he chips it and there is a ruck formed and the All Blacks have it and it is back to Going and it is out to Burgess, he kicks and the ruck is formed and the All Blacks have it.' It just seemed to be a litany of 'the All Blacks have it'.

The Lions won that Test match 9–3 – despite the All Blacks being all over them like a rash during the whole game – thanks largely to an Ian McLauchlan try when he charged down a kick by the New Zealand number 8 Alan Sutherland near the All Blacks line. The Lions went on to win the series and remain legendary as the first, and so far only, British Isles team to win a series in the Land of the Long White Cloud.

Willie John McBride was a player in 1971 and I remember him 12 years later as manager on the 1983 tour telling the players, 'You may have been told how great we were in 1971 but I can tell you we were bloody lucky. We won the Test matches sometimes on 25 per cent possession, so if you can do as well if not better, you have a chance of winning.'

By 1973, my playing career was coming to an end and I decided to retire . . . for the first time! The Scottish club season opened with new official leagues in 1973–74 but, having retired, I was shopping with Frances on George Street in Edinburgh on the first Saturday. I remember thinking, 'This is great, free from rugby, no problems – I've retired.' Then I went to look for the results in the sports paper. Melrose had been beaten by Glasgow High School by 41 points to 3 . . . I spent the weekend trying to pluck up the courage to tell Frances I was going back to play and try to help them stay in the First Division.

I agreed to go back for one season and Melrose managed to stay up, so I felt it had been worthwhile. I played my last league match against Edinburgh Wanderers in March 1974 and then signed off by playing for an old crocks XV in a traditional match on the eve of the Melrose Sevens the next month.

Coaching was to take over my thoughts from 1974. I began to study the game more and compare Scottish rugby with that in leading rugby nations around the world. Having played in South Africa, Argentina, Australia and New Zealand, and having tried to learn as I had gone, my philosophies on coaching were fairly well developed. I was already coaching the Scotland B team and was able to put some of my ideas into operation when the coaching panel asked me to produce a paper on Scottish forward play. That gave me my opportunity to research areas of the game in much more detail. I knew we mirrored some countries more closely than others and, as I worked on it, I found myself beginning to be drawn more towards New Zealand. Scotland and New Zealand have a number of similarities: weather, terrain and the physical characteristics of players our respective countries produce.

The two countries are also quite similar in size and population – we both have four big cities and lots of small towns with plenty of small communities and local rivalries. Actually, in 1978 when the All Blacks came on their tour to Great Britain, 26 of the 30 players were of Scottish ancestry – names like McKechnie, Robertson and Bruce spring to mind. In fact, in the 1979 team that came, Eddie Dunn was the stand-off and his grandmother had emigrated from Hawick, so there was perhaps no surprise that I found Scotland and New Zealand closely linked.

I then developed my philosophy, based on dynamic and aggressive forwards with ball in hand who would, when stopped, form a tight, low driving ruck. Size and weight were not that important if the attitude and the techniques of the players were correct. Of course, some critics in recent years have stated that I am obsessed with the ruck – I am obsessed by a lot of things, if you believe everything written about me – but I have always said that the formation of the ruck is indicative of a failure. Players should do their utmost to stay on their feet in the tackle. But when contact on the ground is inevitable, as it is in rugby, it is important that players know how to ruck properly and maintain quick possession.

The whole essence of rucking at that time was to play the game in Scotland at a faster pace than our competitors. Rucking was developed by the Vic Cavanaghs (father and son) in the 1930s and '40s in Otago on the South Island of New Zealand, a very Scottish part of the country – Otago Highlanders, the Super 12 side, take their name from their Scottish ancestry. In fact the ruck was developed to combat the physical superiority of their opponents and rugby supporters will recall that in the Lions tour of 1993, the touring team were completely outplayed by the speed and dynamic forward play of Otago, resulting in a comfortable win for a home team which included John Leslie, who later played for Scotland, and Gordon Macpherson who came to play and coach in Glasgow.

Rucking was only part of my coaching but, to be fair, it never really disappeared, because I felt it did suit the Scottish style of play – we still don't have massive men who can power through tackles. Others have shared my thoughts on this. The 1970s were a good time to be involved in Scottish coaching because there was little rugby politics and people like myself, Derrick Grant at Hawick and Johnny Gray at Gala were all developing a similar game aimed at improving Borders and Scottish players.

As I said, I started coaching the Scotland B team in 1974. My first game was at Bayonne and the captain was Richie Dixon, who also became a devotee of our playing philosophy. In some ways, the SRU can be very innovative and the setting up of two B-level matches each year against France and Ireland proved to be a very successful preparation for players from clubs and districts before they made the transition to international rugby.

I learned a lot which shaped my coaching approach in those early days. Coaching to me has always been about looking at the individual player and trying to make him better before looking at the team performance. I have always said that rugby is an individual's game first and a team game second. I think of myself as a teacher first and a coach second.

I have no doubt that I have made mistakes in my coaching career but I am pleased to be able to look back on more than 40 years in the game during which I learned much, passed on a lot and enjoyed a good share of success as well as having a hand in players improving their game.

I find it interesting to look at the careers of other Scottish coaches who have been involved at the highest level of their sport, people like Bill Shankly, Jock Stein and Sir Alex Ferguson. I've been compared to Ferguson on occasions and while we're from quite different backgrounds – he's from Govan in Glasgow and I'm the son of a Borders shepherd – we do seem to have similar socialist tendencies and a strong sense of discipline. We're both loyal to our players and I think, if we were ever to meet, we would have a fascinating discussion on Scottish sport and sportsmen.

During my early period of coaching, I worked with Melrose and had spells with the South and the B team before I took over coaching Scotland in 1980, and each experience helped provide me with a good grounding. It was not all successful. I was in charge of Melrose when the team was relegated in 1977, the club's centenary year, but luckily for me, we bounced back into Division One the following season.

I remember saying to some of the press at the time, 'If I had been a football manager, I would probably have got the sack.' Coaching at Melrose was a godsend for me because, with fewer resources than existed in some of the larger clubs, I had to make a little go a long way. That was perhaps the biggest single lesson I took with me when I moved to the next level – returning to the international arena, but this time as coach of my country, not a player.

10

Leading the Nation

Andy Irvine
Scotland (51 caps)
British and Irish Lions (1974, 1977, 1980)
SRU President (2005)

All successes have foundations and those which took Scotland
to the 1984 Grand Slam – the first in 59 years – were laid by Jim
Telfer. I was fortunate to be playing during that building period in
the early 1980s and, having played in teams capable of some
great rugby in the 1970s, it was fascinating to see how Scotland
were transformed from entertainers to winners.

The story really began on the 1981 tour to New Zealand and
then carried on through the 1982 tour to Australia. It was in those
faraway places that Jim brought the players through who would
become heroes. I have to say, when I look back on Jim's
introduction as Scotland coach, there are a few painful
memories!

He wasn't everyone's cup of tea, because he was a very hard
taskmaster; but he introduced a structure to the coaching set-up
and brought a definite mental hardness to Scottish rugby. He
was a very good forwards coach. I've heard people comment
since that he was very conservative in his approach and only
interested in forwards. That is completely wrong.

Jim had great ideas on back play as well, but he would never
overstep the mark – he would not tell me how to play full-back
or John Rutherford how to play stand-off. He relied a lot on Colin
Telfer, his assistant coach, and would give the players their head

119

but help, guide and offer alternatives, clearly having studied different methods of attack. He was never as dogmatic as some people seem to think and was a better listener than he's given credit for. He would ask others' opinions to develop his research but he was decisive and once he'd done his research, he didn't waver; he gave us leadership.

Jim made some enemies in that first spell as a result of his strong belief in fitness. The game in 1980 was very much amateur and there was a great deal of variation in the fitness of rugby players. The Border teams were generally fitter than city teams, and Scotland a bit fitter than the other home nations. Jim brought that discipline but he possibly drove the players too hard early on – we would do a long session on the Thursday and another one on the Friday, on top of our club training. The guys were used to only two or three sessions a week, so they struggled. But Jim was still learning and he was right in believing more work had to be done if Scotland were going to be winners.

I also noticed then how good a selector and judge of a player he was and that is half the problem with some coaches. Matt Williams, Scotland's first foreign coach, for example, had good ideas but he was not great at getting the best XV on the park. We had good players and a good captain in Jim Aitken in the 1984 Grand Slam, but Telfer made the most of them. One of his strengths was helping players to be the best they could be, Jim and Fin Calder in particular, and David Leslie he helped shape into the world-class flanker he became.

You had to admire Jim's integrity. He was absolutely dedicated to his team and that became clear in 1980 when he took over as Scotland coach and we began a journey which was to make legends of some Scottish players.

I had not set out with the dream of one day coaching Scotland but after I was passed over for the job in 1977, I was determined to make the most of the opportunity when it came my way in 1980. I wanted to build a Scottish team which would be a credit to the nation.

The first 'adviser to the captain' was Bill Dickinson and he coached the team from 1971 to 1977. Having been the Scotland B coach for three years, I thought I stood a good chance of being asked to become the Scotland coach, so I was a little disappointed when Nairn MacEwen was given the job; the feeling was that he had fresh ideas, coming from his playing career. I quickly got over my disappointment, however, and remained B coach and became a selector for the top team. Again, that was quite a revolutionary change for the Scottish Rugby Union, as up to that point national selectors had always been committeemen, so it was quite a coup when a coach became a selector.

Nairn and I got on very well as management colleagues. He was different to me in that he preferred mauling to rucking, but I thought he was a good coach. I think he found it difficult to adjust to giving orders to players he had played with only the year before, and the relationships off the field needed to be adjusted. Unfortunately, during his tenure, Nairn developed a heart condition which affected his coaching and became quite serious during 1979 and 1980. He used to make light of his condition but I know that Donald McLeod, the SRU doctor at the time, was never far from his side and Nairn had to have major surgery just after the 1980 season finished. Fortunately, he made a full recovery.

The late 1970s proved to be a key moment for player development in Scottish rugby. Although the Scottish team contained lots of talented players, there seemed to be a lack of consistency in their play at international level. The management team decided to do something different to lift the standard of the best players. So in 1980, we began to look at how we could prepare players to make them better at international level. The SRU agreed that we should send players away on regular short but meaningful tours.

Five Scottish players went away with the Lions in 1980 – Bruce Hay, Andy Irvine, Jim Renwick, John Beattie and Alan Tomes – and whilst they were away, a short three-match tour to France was organised. France was chosen because of the high quality of opposition we could get in provincial areas there.

We took a small group of players, some of whom had played for Scotland and others who had played for the B team. We lost the first game 20–6 against a provincial team in Bordeaux and then played the French Grand Slam side of 1977 – Fouroux, Rives et al., under the guise of the French Barbarians – in Agen. We lost that game 26–22 and then finished the tour with a 6–6 draw in Brive, against another provincial side. I was not pleased at losing but, more importantly, that trip proved to us that Scots players on tour could improve dramatically given the right incentives.

It is important to emphasise that we went there to make the players battle-hardened because we felt that the domestic competition, even at that time, did not prepare our players adequately for international rugby. Scotland had gone on tour before that of course, in 1975 to New Zealand and to Japan in 1977, but there had not been the same level of concentration and attention to planning of venues that took place as we started the '80s. Over that decade, we set up more tours, to New Zealand, Australia, Romania, Canada and the USA, France and Spain, Zimbabwe, and Japan. Later, the IRB took over the organisation of all major international tours as everyone realised how beneficial they could be.

My first game in charge of the full national side was in the 1981 Five Nations Championship. Colin Telfer, no relation of mine, was chosen as the first assistant coach, another milestone in the evolution of coaching in Scotland. Colin was one of the most astute players ever to represent Scotland but he had many injury problems and so he did not get as many caps as his talent deserved (he gained 17). His family came from Hawick – he is Hugh McLeod's nephew – and, although he was brought up in Edinburgh and a former pupil of the Royal High School, he played all his senior rugby for the Borders club.

He made his Scotland debut in the win over Australia in 1968 and he played his last game in 1976. At that time, Scotland, unusually, had quite a number of quality stand-offs – Colin, Ian Robertson, Jock Turner and, latterly, Ian McGeechan – but Colin, if fit, always got the nod over the others, with McGeechan and Turner versatile enough to play in the centre. We lost our first game in charge of Scotland, 16–9 away to France, and I remember Jim Renwick telling me before the game he was getting his 36th cap and that he had never won away from home – he didn't break his duck until his 47th cap away to Wales in 1982, just five games before he retired – so it wasn't a huge surprise that we didn't start winning all of a sudden.

In Paris on that day, Jim actually scored a try under the posts which was disallowed for an alleged forward pass. The referee was Ken Rowlands and years later he wrote to me apologising for the mistake. But we didn't have too bad a Championship that season, starting with John Rutherford scoring a great try in that defeat in Paris and then beating Wales – with, incidentally, Andy Irvine converting the first-ever penalty try in a Championship match after he had had his jersey pulled by Gareth Davies as he went for a loose ball over the try-line. We just lost to England, 23–17 at Twickenham, with each team scoring three tries, and then narrowly beat Ireland.

After that, we were due to set off to New Zealand, my second tour in a year, with eight games, including two Test matches, to be played. A significant incident occurred before we left, however. At one of our last training sessions, we lost John Beattie when, on the back pitches at Murrayfield, he sustained one of the most sickening injuries I have ever seen. Near the end of the session, we were doing a rucking drill where the forwards, standing in a bunch, were asked to react to a ball thrown to one of them.

I threw the ball to John and, unfortunately, the first person he encountered was Iain Milne who was bent down on one knee, ready to tackle him. John drove with his knee into Iain's shoulder and the kneecap was moved back. The pain must have been excruciating and John fell to the ground. Selfishly, I thought, 'Oh no, one of my best forwards is out of the tour,' but then I felt guilt because I realised that it had been my fault. That was certainly the end of the practice and there was a very gloomy atmosphere around the camp.

John took a long time to recover from that injury but was selected for the Lions tour in 1983. To make things worse, we lost our second number 8, Peter Lillington, about the same time, due to exams, and so we had to find two replacement number 8s. Iain Paxton and Derek White were called in. Derek would be part of the 1990 Grand Slam team, and this was only 1981, so he was still young. I didn't know Derek very well at that stage but I had taken him for a couple of sessions when he played for the Edinburgh Under 21s.

I phoned Derek up and said there had been a call-off, how would he fancy going to New Zealand? Considering the importance of the tour, I thought he would be delighted, but all he said in his laid-back, nonchalant way was, and I quote, 'Do you think it will be worth my while?' I don't know what I replied but he went and the rest is history, as they say.

We had Ken Smith as manager with us and he was good; he'd been there in 1959 with the Lions, so he knew a fair amount about New Zealand. One of the problems of taking players to countries like New Zealand is that, however much you tell them about how intense the rugby will be, they have to witness it themselves before they appreciate what is going on. It may not be true now but I always felt that we had more chance of beating southern-hemisphere countries when we were touring. Scottish players responded well to full-time rugby on tour; their concentrated preparation often put them at a slight advantage over their hosts, especially in the first Test match when their opponents may have been a bit rusty.

When you tour New Zealand, it is like opening the door on a roaring fire. We walked into a huge jamboree in which the whole country seemed to be involved and you could never escape it – the atmosphere, the pressure – not that you'd want to, and certainly I was awestruck once again. There really is nowhere like it.

However, before we reached New Zealand, we had some excitement. We stopped over in Singapore for a couple of days and I thought it would be a good idea to do a bit of training, so we found a park close to the hotel and did some running. Suddenly, Tom Smith, the Gala second row, collapsed with exhaustion and lay under the shade of a big tree to recover. I can still see the expressions of disbelief at our antics on the faces of the locals. You see, it was 12 o'clock midday and the sun was beating down (mad dogs and Scotsmen go out in the midday sun came to mind!).

Once in New Zealand, we won five of the six provincial games and Scotland gave one of the best displays I've seen outwith a Test match when they played Canterbury, coached by the famous All Black Alex 'Grizz' Wyllie. The team won 23–12 and, as a reminder of my speech-making history in those parts in 1966, I was asked to make the speech after the match instead of Ken. The speech went down very well!

We had started the tour by beating Colin Meads' King Country team – he was coach then – 39–13, having spent a week in preparation at Tauramanui. I remember in that first week I got into a fairly heated political discussion in the dining room of the hotel with Andy Irvine and David Leslie about the merits and demerits of state and private education. After a while, there was a big crowd of players and locals around us listening attentively and egging us on.

Andy was making the valid point that he had been given his chance in rugby by gaining a scholarship to George Heriot's School, whilst his elder brothers had gone to state schools in Edinburgh and played soccer. David maintained he had been given the same chance as a result of going to the private Glenalmond School.

I pointed out that my school, Gala Academy, and my club, Melrose, had given me the same opportunities in rugby, so both systems were to be recommended, as all three of us had represented our country. However, I learned a salutary lesson – that you can lose friends very easily when you mix rugby with politics. Despite that temporary fall-out, the three of us have done many things together in Scottish rugby since and continue to enjoy each other's company.

It was a typically tough tour and we lost the second game to Wellington but, in fairness, just getting there had caused quite a stir! While we were travelling down by bus from Tauramanui to Wellington, a tyre burst and the tour party had a worrying ten seconds or so whilst the driver wrestled to keep the bus under control. Luckily, no traffic was coming in the opposite direction or it could have been messy. When the bus eventually came to a halt, there were a few white faces and brown trousers!

We were 'marooned' in the middle of nowhere, so big Tom Smith, a qualified HGV driver, got out and organised the changing of the wheel. It was quite a different scenario to him scoring the winning try at Twickenham in 1983, but he came to our rescue on both occasions.

With that excitement and the defeat behind us, we then beat Wairarapa Bush, coached by former internationalist Brian Lochore. It was amazing how many famous All Blacks were returning to provincial coaching at that time. When we played at Ashburton, Derek White received a very bad injury when he twisted his knee. He tried to play on but was eventually brought off on a stretcher.

I remember him lying on the table in the dressing-room and his leg could swing from side to side with no control – how he had played on with snapped ligaments, I'll never know! But a well-planned network of medical care, organised by Donald McLeod, our team doctor, kicked in and Derek was immediately transferred by ambulance to Christchurch and operated on by Dr Bill Gillespie, a Watsonian. That efficiency and the use of good local contacts were features of Donald's very professional approach, which was in evidence again when he returned as Lions doctor in 1983.

In rugby terms, certain countries are very knowledgeable – Wales and New Zealand come to mind – and one thing that struck me on that tour was how hero-worshipped Andy Irvine was. Very few Scots have had such an impact in countries like New Zealand; Ken Scotland, with the 1959 Lions, is the only other player who springs to mind. Wherever he went, Andy was instantly recognised. I remember as part of the marketing of the Second Test, the two captains' photos were displayed on billboards. The caption read 'This is possibly your last chance to see this legend' and it wasn't Graham Mourie they were talking about, it was Andy. It was so rare to have a Scot so highly respected in New Zealand – he was looked on as an icon, mainly because of his deeds with the Lions in 1974, 1977 and 1980.

Of course, there's no mystery as to why. Andy was the best player I've ever seen in a Scotland jersey and he was an absolute joy to coach. A little-known fact is that we almost had him at Melrose. He was a George Heriot's pupil but had come to play with Melrose Colts because George Elliot at Gala Academy, a Scottish Schools teammate, had invited him down. Andy was actually picked for the Melrose senior seven but Heriot's FP got wind of it and by the end of the week he was back up at Goldenacre. He will never know what he missed, not playing for a Borders club!

That New Zealand tour in 1981 was very good for us, though. Our dynamic rucking game had begun to attract widespread interest and although we lost both Test matches, it was by just 11–4 in the first one in Dunedin and the improvement we'd made was clear. In the Second Test, in Auckland, the scoreline (a 40–15 defeat) did not reflect how well we played. We were behind just 10–6 at half-time and had two good try-scoring chances early in the second half. Steve Munro, the Ayr wing, intercepted a pass on the halfway line but he had been suffering with the flu all week; he got out of his sickbed to play and it showed, because he couldn't run away from Bernie Fraser to score.

Bruce Hay scored a great try, coming in off his left wing, and though the All Blacks went 22–15 up, Jim Calder looked to have scored to peg them back again. But the referee disallowed the try due to a forward pass and New Zealand then ran away with it, scoring three tries in overlaps out wide.

What pleased me most about the tour was the strengthening resolve of the Scottish players. They knew they had come close to beating the All Blacks in the First Test and in fact the pack and half-backs in those Tests were the same as in the 1984 Grand Slam. The players had improved by 20 to 25 per cent – their mental toughness was a significant factor, as was their ability to take on a side like the All Blacks physically.

The team started the new season by beating Romania and then Australia 24–15 at Murrayfield, and there was a feeling in the squad that things were beginning to build. Colin and I were confident that we could beat any team at Murrayfield and that we could give a good account of ourselves at any away venue. There was a significant tactic in that game with Australia which led to our winning try. At lineouts, Australia defended in the backs by putting the blind-side winger in at stand-off and moving all the backs one space out. Rugby coaches, certainly in Scotland, will recognise that formation, because it was known later as the Queensland or Australian defence. It meant that the full-back had to cover a wider area than normal and John Rutherford used that vulnerability to the full.

On the halfway line, John received the ball from the lineout and put up a garryowen in front of the posts. Roger Gould, the Wallaby full-back, not too sure of his position, missed it, the ball bounced and Jim Renwick followed up, caught it and scored a try which was the turning point of the game. It was our only try. Australia scored three and were suitably aggrieved.

At the beginning of 1982, we drew with England and lost to

Ireland but beat France and Wales. The last game ended a Cardiff hoodoo stretching back to 1962, as well as Wales's impressive run of 27 home games unbeaten since 1968. It might be a bit harsh on him but I felt I had Gareth Davies to thank for that – he sent a kick straight to Roger Baird and the Kelso winger sparked one of the best counter-attacking tries I've ever seen, finished by Jim Calder. We scored four more and won 34–18, which remains a record for tries scored against the Welsh by a Scotland team and a margin of victory no Scottish side has matched in Cardiff.

I always liked to have a theme for my team talks and I've been reminded by players of what I said before that Wales game. Apparently, I told them, 'We're like the SAS: we're going into Cardiff to kill the bastards and come straight out again, almost without them knowing we've been there.' Crazy stuff, perhaps, but then I liked the imagery, the idea of creating something as we went into battle to focus the players. Who knows how much difference it made?

We finished the Championship just a point off champions France in the end, so we headed off to Australia with some confidence that summer. That was our next tour stop. It was intended to be a challenging one, but I could hardly imagine how far off the pace we'd be when we got down under.

I will talk more about specific coaching highlights later in the book, from the 1984 and 1990 Grand Slams to the 1997 Lions success in South Africa and the 1999 Five Nations, and in the next chapter we'll look at the lowest point in my whole career, the 1983 Lions tour to New Zealand. But I want to tackle more of the unwarranted criticism I've received in my time, largely from players for whom I seem to have become the worst coach in history some time after we finished working together. There are some things that I feel need to be put right.

In my latter years, I think it must have been the white hair or increasing number of wrinkles on the forehead, but I became a target for 'ageism'. The criticism tended to be along the lines that I was out of date and an old stick-in-the-mud, either unaware of or unwilling to embrace modern coaching techniques. Of course, the age-old one is that I can't see past New Zealand and believe that everything they do is fantastic and must be copied. I have already tried to explain why I developed great respect for New

Zealand rugby and why I tried to develop facets of it that I felt, after much study, would work here, but I have drawn inspiration for my coaching philosophy from elsewhere, not purely from the Land of the Long White Cloud.

This might surprise some but it is Australia that provided my biggest influence in terms of backs coaching and player development. That stemmed from what I saw on tour in 1982. It was a good tour for Scotland in general. Though we went there with confidence, it had been a tough season physically because, with the tour, we stepped up to eight Test matches in ten months. The training was also increased as I tried to push the players to new heights and I felt it paid off, with us beating Australia in December and then again in July.

We did very well to win the First Test out in Australia, at Ballymore in Brisbane; that remains our only win against one of the big three southern-hemisphere nations down under. We lost the Second Test, unfortunately, but the way we had forced Australia to change their team and tactics for that match showed we were on to something.

From early on in the tour, we knew we would be up against it because of the incredible style of Australian back play, especially the sleight of hand and the accuracy of passing. It was eye-opening for all of us and left an indelible mark on me. We had won the opening tour game in Mount Isa, a coal-mining town in the middle of Queensland, but then played and lost 18–7 to Queensland in Brisbane in our second game. They were so far ahead of us in the way they moved the ball that they could shift it to the wing and back in again before we'd moved! We were an international side, so we came back well and were not beaten by a big margin, but in actual fact we were totally outplayed.

We then suffered a real going-over from Sydney, losing 22–13 in our third game, and we decided if we were to survive on the tour, we had to learn quickly. So when we got down to Melbourne, a group of players – Andy Irvine, the captain, John Rutherford, Roy Laidlaw and Jim Calder, the open-side flanker, were involved – and I tried to work out a system of defence to ensure we were not beaten on the outside as easily as we had been in Sydney. The key was to use Jim Calder, at scrum and lineout, to mark Mark Ella, the Australian stand-off, and allow our backs to mark one out.

We did not actually use that tactic in the next game, against Victoria, because we were confident of winning that game, but we brought it out when we returned to Sydney to play New South Wales, which was practically the same team as we'd played a week earlier. We also changed tactics in the lineout; we shortened it and brought forwards round in peels to further tie in their backs and make sure we had plenty of forwards running at their backs. The team played really well and won easily, 44–3, which set us up nicely for the First Test match in Brisbane.

We had been able to work together to change our game plan and that was a good example of how important it is to have players on the same wavelength as the coach. It certainly helped to build up a mutual confidence in discussing tactics in the lead-up towards the players' performances in the Grand Slam year.

Iain Paxton's height in the lineout was critical as well. He had been injured early in the tour and we didn't have a doctor with us, just David McLean, the physiotherapist. I remember David phoning Donald McLeod in Scotland to ask how to treat Iain and he got him fit for the New South Wales game. David was a key member of the management team. I relied on his expertise on fitness and rehabilitation, and I would sit down with him every night to discuss the next day's training sessions.

When Iain was injured, we called out John Calder as cover. There was some rivalry in that Calder family. I can tell you, Fin, not yet capped, wasn't delighted at the prospect of his big brother John arriving and possibly getting a cap before he did! As it was, Iain recovered, John didn't get a cap and his time passed.

On the lighter side, two incidents off the field proved quite funny at the time, although they could have had serious repercussions. Our hotel on the Gold Coast was close to the beach and some of the players had gone for a dip in the sea. After a little while, most of the players had come in but we noticed one, Bill Cuthbertson, quite far out, waving his arms above his head. We all waved back, not realising that the current had taken him further out than he had wanted and he was actually calling for help. I only discovered later that he could not swim!

The second incident involved Derek White. On the evening

after the New South Wales game, the tour party was about to go out to the function when Derek suddenly took cramp in the foyer of the hotel where we were staying. He was lying rigid on the carpet, not able to move, and he was whiter than ever! I can tell you that Ian McGregor, the tour manager, was panicking, knowing we had no doctor on tour with us. But David McLean looked after him and he eventually came back to normal!

We went into the First Test feeling there was a chance of beating Australia in Brisbane. It wasn't a great Test match, but it was good for us because Jim Calder policed Ella very well and we won it 12–7. Keith Robertson scored in the corner. That was also the occasion of Andy Irvine's 50th cap – quite fitting, I thought. He was to finish his career on 51 a week later.

We were crucified in the Second Test at Sydney Cricket Ground, where, I recall, there was a hard wicket in the middle of the park and players didn't want to get tackled there. But Australia had not been happy at how we'd nullified them in the First Test, so they dropped Ella and took us on physically in the backs with Peter Grigg, the right-winger, leading bruising charges through the middle.

I remember Ian McGregor turning to me after about 20 minutes, with the Australians having scored at a rate of a run a minute, and saying, 'I hope it's not going to be a massacre, Jim.' Thankfully, there was a downpour not long after that and the scoring ended at 33–9.

But that tour meant so much more to me than merely a handful of results. I admired a lot of French backs rugby then but the Aussies blew me away, especially when we had come up against the Ella brothers, Mark, Glen and Gary, in Sydney. This is where I got more of my coaching ideas from and is something on which I have been at odds with almost every backs coach in Scotland ever since.

Mark Ella was the chief architect of their back play. He had beautiful hands and was a sublime passer, as well as a lovely runner, and I've heard him say that if he was involved three times in the same attack, he would score. It was done with such precision. He took the pass at hip level and passed it straight to the next player, short or long, without the ball rising or falling from that straight line. That was how I felt we should pass across the backs.

Had it only been Mark Ella whose passing was so precise, I would not necessarily have been as taken by it; but when we were training at Queensland University later, I watched the Queensland Under-21 team going through their paces on a pitch beside us. They were doing exactly the same kind of passing, taking the ball at hip level and firing it along the line. I later discovered that the Under-21s fly-half was Michael Lynagh, who passed the same way as Ella. It was clearly ingrained into Australian backs from an early age.

I'll give you an instance of how that back play worked. In the World Cup quarter-final at Lansdowne Road in 1991, Gordon Hamilton grabbed an interception and scored for Ireland with a few minutes to go. Everyone thought Australia were beaten. But they got a scrum on the left-hand side of the posts on the Irish 22, and moved the ball swiftly with that type of passing for Lynagh to loop and score in the right-hand corner. That showed great mental toughness, relying on your skills to score when it really mattered, and I remember thinking that it was a credit to the way the Australians passed and looped round. It was so clinical. It took them into the semi-final, where they defeated the All Blacks, and they went on to beat England in the final.

At that time, the Australians didn't always use the full width of the field; they would pass in short, tight spaces, drawing men in and then outflanking defences. I have admired since then the clinical nature of Australians in their ability to finish off a set-piece move, especially from left to right, be it Ella, Hawker, O'Connor and Campese in the early '80s or, in the '90s, through Lynagh, Horan, Little, Tune or Roff. I realise that in the modern game players use a variety of passing techniques to move the ball wider, and that short, quick passes are not the be-all and end-all. The balls are far more aerodynamic now and that helps with passing over longer distances. But watching the Australians back then made me wonder how many times I had seen Scottish teams create glorious opportunities but fail to finish off because a pass was too high, too low or delayed. That continues to frustrate me today.

We have never been renowned in Scotland for good combined back play. We have been able to produce some great players – Jim Renwick, Andy Irvine, John Rutherford, Gavin Hastings, Keith

Robertson and Chris Paterson, to name a few – but their individual exploits have masked deficiencies in the ability of our back divisions to perform clinically under pressure.

I was not an expert in back play, in handling and passing, but I tried to find answers. We placed great emphasis on handling in the 1990s and I thought we were getting somewhere. Graham Shiel and Gregor Townsend were products of that push and both of them had spent summers in Australia. We worked to take the ball early, with an emphasis on the pendulum pass, and I believe the skills of Scottish players improved more than people in the street probably realised. However, defences are now a lot better organised, which can conceal any genuine improvement.

Since that tour to Australia, I have put the case to backs coaches in Scotland that we in this country should adopt a similar kind of passing. I have not necessarily convinced the top coaches but healthy debate is good. Some of them might think I am naive, and I do realise that other techniques can be used. But watching Mark Ella passing made me see that he must have been taught that skill at an early stage in his development.

I also suggested to my colleagues at Murrayfield a few years ago that we should use the name 'rugby teacher' for those working with youngsters in their formative years and 'rugby coach' for those responsible for older players. To me, there is a subtle difference between the two roles. Put in simplistic terms, a teacher looks at development, a coach looks at performance. There is a saying in rugby: 'Get the little things right and the big things will fall into place.' Those words have been my guiding principle all through my teaching/coaching career.

It is even more important nowadays in the professional era – rugby is now a profession, just like being a doctor or an accountant – that all the individual skills are properly taught at a young age. It is also important that youngsters should be taught these essential skills under the best conditions, for example in good weather. Most of the parents I met during my teaching days wanted the best for their children in academic subjects – good teaching in a good working environment – so why should rugby be any different?

I feel Scottish rugby should be seriously considering moving the development aspect of our game, the youth game, to the months when the better weather is with us, when players would improve so much more quickly. Playing all rugby in better weather would be great for our sport and our players, and while obstacles exist in the senior game, there is no reason why we cannot allow our youngsters the chance to develop like their southern-hemisphere counterparts by training and playing at a time of year more suitable to rugby skills than our midwinter.

If we continue to practise in winter, during the worst weather, then we must accept lower standards compared to countries where the players practise in good weather. Gregor commented, after his first week with Natal Sharks in the Super 12 when he moved there in 2004, that he was amazed to see the passing skills of the players around him and felt he had a bit of catching up to do. He remarked that he believed it owed a great deal to the weather, which encouraged players to train and practise skills. He is a devout campaigner for playing rugby in Scotland in the better weather, because of his experiences around the world.

However, I arrived back home in July 1982 suitably encouraged by the progress made by the squad and looking forward to my next big challenge, which was something quite different – coaching the British and Irish Lions in New Zealand.

11

Gripping the Lions' Lead

Willie John McBride
Ireland (63 caps)
British and Irish Lions manager (1983)
British and Irish Lions (1962, 1966, 1968, 1971 and 1974)

Tours to New Zealand are incredibly difficult; winning in New Zealand is even harder. I have won and lost there, and people may only remember the winners, but the difference between the two tours was a lot smaller than many realise.

In 1971, we had a great squad, we had luck at times and we came out on top. In 1983, we didn't have the same quality, we had incredible bad luck with injuries and we lost close games.

Ireland shared the Championship with France in 1983 but, in all honesty, it wasn't a great Championship. England won the wooden spoon – they were struggling to make the most of their great resources. Jim and I watched players in the months preceding the Lions tour and had to keep changing our selection plans because of injuries.

We eventually took some players whom we hoped would become fit by the time the games started in New Zealand. While Ollie Campbell got over a blood virus and was fully fit, he was not the same Ollie who dazzled at Lansdowne Road before that. Terry Holmes, the best scrum-half in the British Isles at that time, also got fit for the tour but he suffered injuries early on. The second one, during the First Test, ruled him out altogether.

135

And yet the efforts of the players, and of Jim Telfer in particular, took that squad to the brink of victory. One pass cost us one Test and similar little things swung other Tests. I knew Jim as a teammate from the 1966 and 1968 tours, and knew he would be a good coach, so it didn't surprise me in the slightest that he went on to great success with Scotland the year after and with the Lions in 1997.

I never did get him to relax and party a bit on any of the tours we were on – though, by God, I tried. He just wasn't that sort of guy but he was a great tourist. I remember him on the 1966 tour speaking after the Canterbury match, having really exhorted the team as captain to a good win in that game, and he ripped into New Zealand rugby. I can see him yet standing there telling it like it was and it was exactly what the Lions wanted to hear. He may have got stick locally, but we felt there was too much diplomacy sometimes and he earned lots of pats on the back from his players that night.

That was another difficult tour to New Zealand – but is there any other kind? The tour squad, Jim and I took a lot of flak in 1983 but you have to expect that in New Zealand because they are very good at the old psychological stuff, through their media and the public. Few saw the problems we had to deal with internally. I even had to scrummage in a Lions training session because we ran out of fit forwards, and I hadn't played for nearly ten years!

But one constant was Jim Telfer. He is a very intense sort of guy, a 100 per cent man, and nobody gave that tour more than he did in his thinking and preparation; nobody worked harder. There was no question he was the right man for the job, and it was not through any of his doing that we were not successful.

He sometimes worked the players too hard but that was just a coach striving to get his team up to the required level to beat the All Blacks. We simply did not have a squad good enough to reach that level and it was incredible that we came close.

That was a very tough tour, and Jim and others suffered mentally and physically as a result. But there is often a very, very small margin between winning and losing, and if you have been beaten by a better team, there's not a great deal you can do.

The feelings I had when I was asked to coach the British and Irish Lions in May 1982 were pride and anxiety. They contrasted sharply with my feelings when the tour came to an end in July 1983. I started that period of my life believing I was being given the chance to show I could coach with the best in the world and finished it wondering if I had the ability to coach ever again.

I had started out full of hope and enthusiasm. Willie John McBride had been put forward by Ireland for both coach and manager, and he was chosen to be team manager. I think the home unions felt that he and I would work well as a partnership, as we'd been Lions players together in New Zealand in 1966 and in South Africa in 1968, and we did get on very well. I liked the way he handled the off-field business.

He put me at ease as soon as we met by saying he would take care of the speaking and socialising demands, which were many in those days. We had engagements planned for us from the day we arrived, often on nights before games, and I was concerned they would get in the way of the tour. But Willie John said, 'Leave it to me,' and he was very good at handling that. He received some criticism for speaking out against referees on that tour and though I agreed with what he said, I had learned by then that that was not the way to win people over. On a tour, particularly with the Lions, you have to rise above that and we did, most of the time.

As had been the custom since 1966, the Lions management was appointed a year before the tour. I was given a sabbatical from the Scotland coach's position to prepare for the trip.

I travelled all over the British Isles that year watching players, taking my role very seriously, as anyone who knows me would expect. We had time to formulate the kind of game we felt could take on the All Blacks, who were a formidable side then and who, we knew, would save their best for the visit of the Lions. We wanted the best players, of course, but we also tried to use the year to find players who would fit well into the patterns we wanted to create and our draft XV changed often.

Selection for that tour ultimately became a huge issue in the media and we were criticised for some of the players we took. While there were one or two choices which I might now regret, including the decision to name Ciaran Fitzgerald as the tour captain, getting the right combinations and bringing them together in a short space of time is the key to success and that is never an easy thing to achieve.

It was widely reported at the time that we settled on big, strong midfield players, men with stamina, and that was true. According to Bill Beaumont, the captain of the Lions in 1980 and manager in 2005, we should have taken Paul Dodge, the England centre, whom he believed to be the best inside-centre. He was close to being picked and we might have chosen Keith Robertson, the Scotland wing/centre, but he was injured shortly before the squad announcement. The management – remember, Willie John and I had witnessed first-hand how tours can be ruined by injuries – were of the belief that players had to be physical enough to stand up to a real battle out there.

For example, Nigel Melville, the England scrum-half, wasn't taken initially and when he did come out, he played one midweek game against Southland and then lasted three minutes against North Auckland. He was taken out wickedly in a blindside attack and had to be carried off. That was perhaps simply unfortunate but it provides an indication of how hard that tour became.

From having all 30 players fit and available for the first game in Wanganui, we started losing men quickly and had to cope at times without forwards Bob Norster, John O'Driscoll, Iain Paxton, John Beattie and Jim Calder, and backs Hugo MacNeill, Dusty Hare, John Rutherford, Clive Woodward, Ollie Campbell and Roger Baird, on top of losing Terry Holmes, Ian Stephens and Jeff Squire from the tour altogether. We had to call up six more to cover and in fact Willie John, at the age of 43, even packed down for a vital scrummaging session. Donal Lenihan we'd lost at the airport before we left – he discovered he had a hernia and had to stay at home, though he did come out later – and maybe that was an omen.

Now, all these injuries happened despite the facts that New Zealand had cleaned their act up considerably since I'd toured as a Lion in 1966 (there was a lot more rugby on television by then and international rugby was being seen around the world more) and that this was a tour of only 18 games, less than half the number of the 1966 tour.

But there were undoubtedly tough calls on selection, as there inevitably are when you are dealing with the best players from four nations. One decision which I found very hard was that of leaving behind David Leslie, the Scotland flanker who would go on to become one of my best-ever Scotland forwards. In truth, he was not yet at his peak, which was a factor, but there was another key reason for my choosing others in 1983.

On Scotland's 1981 tour to New Zealand, David had come off second-best to the All Blacks flanker Graham Mourie and, while Mourie was so good that many probably would, the Tests stuck in my mind when it came to selection. Mourie was the openside flanker in 1981 and David was the openside for us, although we tended to play left and right because Jim Calder was equally adept at getting out of the scrum. Later, David became very adept at the back of the lineout and really came into his own, but in 1981 Mourie was much quicker and had a higher work rate than David, and I felt that if that was the standard being set in New Zealand then, while I rated him highly in a Scottish context, David might be shown up on such a demanding tour. The irony, of course, was that when we came up against the All Blacks, Mourie was gone – he'd taken a surprising early retirement from rugby and gone to live in France.

I went instead for Jim Calder, whose work rate was very high and who was also a very intelligent player. He was completely different to his brother Finlay, as a player and a person. He was a bit like Richard Hill, a veteran of three Lions tours between 1997 and 2005. Richard is the kind of guy whose name goes down first on the team sheet. Jim was like that – he was like the oil in the machine.

Famously, the tough selections didn't end when we got to New Zealand, either. The captaincy and hookers had been controversial from the start. Ciaran Fitzgerald was an army officer and I couldn't fault his courage or endeavour. But when you go with the Lions, you have to lift your game to be a Test player and he struggled with that. He had, however, been an outstanding captain in Five Nations rugby: he had pulled Ireland up by their bootstraps, leading them to the top of the table in two successive Championships and to a Triple Crown. Then, Lions captaincy tended to go with the most successful team of the time, so he was chosen.

Colin Deans was the outstanding hooker during the Five

Nations that year. There was also a strong argument for taking Peter Wheeler, the former Lions and England hooker, and, had we, he would probably have been my captain; but England were not on form at the time and it was thought that, at 34, he was getting on a bit. We went instead with Ciaran and Colin, whom we believed to be the best players at that point. Looking back, we probably should have taken Wheeler and used his experience as a double Lions tourist but that would have meant leaving the best hooker or the most successful captain of the Championship behind.

As it was, we ended up in a scenario very similar to 1966, when Mike Campbell-Lamerton, the captain, stood down for the Second Test because he didn't feel he deserved his place. He returned and then stood down again on that tour and I've said before how courageous I thought he was. Similarly, Ciaran was not playing well in 1983; despite a poor First Test, however, he wouldn't take the same course of action. I voted for Colin to replace Ciaran after the First Test and was outvoted by Willie John and Ciaran. I accepted the decision but it was difficult to have to bite my lip as Willie John stuck by Ciaran through all four Tests.

I remember Colin coming to my room after the Third Test team was announced and his actual words were, 'Right, Jim, what's the score?' He knew he was playing better than Ciaran. I said I could tell him nothing, that the decision had been taken and Ciaran had been chosen. I felt for Colin but there was nothing I could do; it had been a private selection and it had to stay that way.

There was a funny story about that afterwards which shows how much my rugby filtered through to the family. When I came home from the three months away, I got back to the Glen Hotel in Selkirk, which we owned, and Frances took me up to our living quarters. I thought, 'Great – lot of time away to make up for,' and she took me into our bedroom and locked the door. Then she said, 'Right, before anything happens, tell me why Colin Deans wasn't in the team.'

Nothing happened that night, anyway, because I refused to tell her as well. She was as angry as Colin had been, though she got quite used to me not telling her about selections – walls have ears, you know, and wives have tongues! It's only recently that I've admitted to Frances that I did want Colin in the team, because I felt that, unless Ciaran or Willie John wanted to discuss it, then it wasn't my place to talk about it. They haven't said anything as far as I'm aware but perhaps the new Freedom of Information Act allows me to reveal the truth now! I've taken criticism for the decision for long enough.

It doesn't alter the fact that I liked Ciaran and still have respect for him. That tour was very hard for him, constantly having to justify his position to the media. We've spoken a few times since – he was the Ireland coach for a while – and remain friends but that episode taught me that you can't compromise on selection.

The tour had a number of problems, one of which was that the Lions were going back there for the first time since the 1977 tour, which hadn't been a very happy one and had left a sour taste in the mouths of many New Zealanders. They had a very good squad, with players like Phil Bennett (the captain), Andy Irvine, J.J. Williams, Steve Fenwick, Ian McGeechan, Peter Wheeler, Fran Cotton, Bill Beaumont and Gordon Brown. But there were splits in the camp, problems with homesickness, atrocious weather followed them wherever they went and they suffered from some adverse press.

We were keen to restore better relations but were disappointed with the itinerary as soon as we saw it. We had games with the strongest provinces – Auckland, Wellington and Canterbury – in midweek, the latter just days before a Test match, and we were to drive or fly about between the North and South islands with no rhyme or reason. But the itinerary wasn't changed and we had to get on with it.

Personally, however, my chief problem was that I was the only coach. Our management consisted of Willie John, myself, Dr Donald McLeod and our physio, Kevin Murphy – a bit different to the 29-strong management party on Sir Clive Woodward's recent tour! It was hard work having to split my time between forwards and backs, though I did enjoy the challenge of working on back play.

I was aware when we travelled out that many players might not respect me as a backs coach. That was something I anticipated, so I spent a long time beforehand researching and planning the coaching sessions, particularly with the backs, and I like to think I won the respect of a lot of them.

With Scotland, I had introduced the idea of inside- and outside-centres. Jim Renwick wasn't much in favour of it, I remember, but while players might be able to play in both positions, I'd long felt the skills each required were different. That feeling stemmed from New Zealand, where they called them second five-eighth and centre, and always played specialists in those positions. The man who had the most pressure put on him was the outside-centre, who had the opposition backs coming to fell him. He had to have particularly quick hands: Jason Little was such a star for Australia, and Bruce Robertson for New Zealand, because they were very good distributors under pressure.

The style of passing I'd learned in 1982 – short passes in front of the man, never deviating from a low straight line – was what I tried to preach. We used small parts of the field and I used players to loop others in order to open up attacks. But as I found later with Gregor Townsend, who came back from Australia having learned the southern-hemisphere style, you need everybody to be on the same wavelength, reading the angles with quick, flat passes, or it doesn't work. It took time to develop on that tour and we didn't have a lot of that.

I was criticised at the time for not being very precise and letting mistakes go unpunished, which surprised me, and I was glad to read the account of the tour by the journalist David Frost in his book *Lions 83: The New Zealand Tour*, which said I had 'confounded' the sceptics with my backs sessions and that 'everyone was impressed' by the early coaching. Our physio, Kevin Murphy, helped out with warm-ups and Dr Donald McLeod, the team doctor, was on hand to ensure the players were well looked after medically.

We opened the tour with a stirring 47–15 defeat of Wanganui on a glorious sunny day and the media were intrigued by my playing Rob Ackerman as inside-centre with Michael Kiernan outside, instead of the straightforward two-centres teams they were used to at home. Robert did very well, with straight, direct running, and our loose forwards, Peter Winterbottom, Jeff Squire and John Beattie, were excellent at developing profitable phases.

The second match, against the national champions Auckland, was a different matter and resulted in one of our two provincial defeats. The weather was strange, with sunshine, rain and wind.

We were leading 12–6 at half-time and I thought we were doing quite well. But a try early in the second half and then an injury-time drop-goal from Grant Fox handed them a 13–12 win. We had started to suffer injury problems already but, in truth, our scrummage wasn't consistent, Auckland did well at the tail of the lineout and we deserved to lose. The Auckland coach was John Hart, who would become All Blacks coach some time later, and he was very gracious in saying that we probably weren't fully recovered from the journey out.

Interestingly, fitness experts told me some years later that teams should be given more than ten days to recover from the journey on long trips to the southern hemisphere – we'd flown via Los Angeles on that tour – as the tenth day was when the worst effects often hit. The Auckland match came ten days after we'd arrived.

We did pick up and, while the injuries started to mount up, we also started collecting tries. We beat Bay of Plenty (in a game which featured a massive 30-man punch-up), Wellington, Manawatu and Mid Canterbury before the First Test came along, scoring over 170 points in 6 games.

We had had another distraction to deal with when it broke in the media the day before the Manawatu match – just a week before the First Test – that 20 of our 30 players had supposedly signed up for a new professional 'circus' run by a chap called David Lord. He apparently had 200 players ready to break away and form a new professional league. Nothing ever came of it, but it was a destabilising distraction on the eve of another very tough Saturday match.

It was quite bizarre but the more I thought about it, the less I was worried, because it was clearly a circus which didn't have the support of the unions, hence the need to break away. Even when the issue reared its head again just after the 1995 World Cup, I didn't feel that this kind of thing would last without the support of the unions. It would have been the same men playing each other time after time, isolated from the rest of world rugby, and while it might be exciting at first, I felt sure that the public and media would become sick of watching that pretty quickly. The strength of rugby, I feel, has always been its unpredictability – different teams and different players succeeding, the appearance of new stars and disappearance of others – and a circus doesn't have that.

The media talk was an irritation but it didn't take long to return the focus to the very much live rugby in front of us. We had tried to use those first six games to find good blends of players and to give everyone the chance to wear the Lions jersey, to push their cases, and we had a good spirit going into the First Test.

The All Blacks brought Jock Hobbs, a Canterbury flanker and now chairman of the NZRU, in for his First Test, Mourie having now departed for sunnier climes. It was a lovely day in Christchurch and I arrived at Lancaster Park confident that we could win. When the score sat at 13–12 to the All Blacks with just over five minutes of a cracking game to go, I felt it was still in our hands.

We had really taken on the All Blacks pack, and played well in the scrum and lineout. While we relied on three penalty kicks from Ollie Campbell, our back play wasn't poor either. We were sound in defence and twice came close to tries, with Ackerman held very close to the line on one occasion. As the game neared the finish, we were forcing New Zealand under pressure close to their own line and when we rucked well and the ball came back in front of the posts for Hugo MacNeill, our full-back, I envisaged a winning drop-goal. Unfortunately, he slipped on the moist grass and the chance was lost.

With two minutes remaining, Allan Hewson, having only just recovered from glandular fever in time to play, sealed it for the All Blacks when he took a loose kick from Campbell and dropped an excellent goal. Andy Dalton, the All Blacks captain, when asked what his feelings were at having won, replied with one word: 'Relief.'

We scored a lot of points – 150 to be precise – in beating West Coast, Southland and Wairarapa Bush before the Second Test but we were beginning to really suffer from injury problems by then. Terry Holmes, the Welsh prop Ian Stephens and Jeff Squire were all out, and we had the headache over whether to swap Ciaran Fitzgerald.

Intriguingly, the All Blacks made only one change to their side, restoring fly-half Wayne Smith, who would later coach the All Blacks with a good friend of mine, Tony Gilbert. There were also some contemporaries of mine in action with the 1967 All Blacks team, who staged a reunion to play a charity benefit game the day after the Test.

The Second Test itself, played at Wellington, might have been close in that we lost just 9–0, but the All Blacks gave us a lesson in how to play the elements that day. There was a strong gale blowing down Athletic Park which had the posts swaying. Andy Dalton won the toss and chose to play with the wind in the first half. When we turned around only nine points down, we thought we had a real chance but they dominated possession in the second half, keeping the ball from us and simply outsmarting us. Dave Loveridge, their scrum-half, was outstanding that day.

Again, we had injuries, with Iain Paxton and Bob Norster struggling, and we thought we had scored when Ciaran got over in the corner only to be pulled back for a Lions scrum! Drop-goals and penalty kicks drifted wide. In truth, the All Blacks were sharper, quicker and more intelligent. The fact that they gave us very few penalties underlined their discipline and to hear them scolding themselves in the media afterwards about how their performance hadn't been good enough was quite worrying.

We beat North Auckland, but then lost to a formidable Canterbury side – narrowly, 22–20 – in a game which, crazily, was scheduled on the Tuesday night before the Third Test. We had had a long journey from Whangarei near the top of the North Island to Christchurch midway down the South Island on the Sunday and we were struggling to get a team out in training due to injuries. But that gave us another tough call: do we play the strongest side, risk more injuries and give them just three days recovery, or play a second XV and run the risk of a morale-sapping defeat?

New Zealand allowed Canterbury to field their five All Blacks, so we were in no doubt that the game was potentially our toughest on tour apart from the Test matches. We also still had question marks about our best team for the Third Test – the series was gone but we could draw it and the aim still had to be to beat the All Blacks, a task which traditionally becomes harder as a tour progresses. Hugo MacNeill and Gwyn Evans were now contesting the full-back berth, so we decided to take another look at Hugo.

The problem was that he was not the best goal-kicker and his failure to convert more than two from seven in the Canterbury game – in contrast with Robbie Deans, another All Black who was to become an international coach, who kicked five from seven in a personal tally of eighteen points – was clearly a factor in the defeat, as we lost by just two points in the end.

The mood of the squad was understandably down after that, and the wind, hail, sleet and snow which greeted us in Dunedin ahead of the Third Test didn't help matters. Gwyn Evans, John Rutherford at centre, Steve Bainbridge and Jim Calder were given starts this time, and the boys dug in and were sharper and harder in this match. We outscored the All Blacks two tries to one, Rutherford capping a fine game with what the local press described as the try of the series and Roger Baird scoring the other. It was a great game despite the conditions and I felt the Lions deserved more from it, but Stu Wilson's try and 11 points from Hewson ensured the All Blacks emerged the winners 15–8 to claim the series.

It was at this point that I began to realise that, no matter how our boys played or how much effort they put in, they were simply not going to match New Zealand, and that was very depressing. We went on to score another 90 points in provincial matches, defeating Hawke's Bay, Counties and Waikato, but, despite my exhorting the Lions to just go out and enjoy the game, salvage some pride for the great efforts they had put in, the combination of the All Blacks, with the pressure of the series off, wanting to play great 15-man rugby and fatigue in our camp made for a desperate finale. We lost 38–6, still the worst margin of defeat in a Lions Test match, ensuring another 4–0 series defeat for me after the tour in 1966.

There have been many theories passed around as to why we were whitewashed, from poor selection to poor form, injuries to key men to lack of leadership, but it was more simple than that in my opinion: we simply struggled to find a winning game. I had tried to work on developing the rucking game which was lifting Scotland to new heights and causing problems for other sides but we had a lot of players in the squad more used to mauling – Maurice Colclough, for example, was a very upright player – and it took a lot of time to get them to change, as Grizz Wyllie, the Canterbury coach, brazenly pointed out after our defeat there.

Some said I should have changed my style to fit them more, and I did think about that on tour; but my conclusion was that I had been selected as the Lions coach ahead of people like Mike Davis, the England coach who had led his side to the 1980 Grand Slam, because of my style and I had a duty to stick to that, to try to make it work.

It was tough being the only coach – the Lions had always had only one – but that was one of several lessons we learned from 1983. The Lions have never again toured with just one coach and on the next tour, to Australia in 1989, Ian McGeechan had Roger Uttley as his assistant.

Willie John told the media at one stage, after the Second Test, I think, 'This party has worked harder day by day than the 1971 or 1974 Lions I was with as a player and they deserve better than they've got.' I had good chats with him about that and it brought home to me the fact that luck can play a bigger part in successes, and in miserable disappointments, than I liked to believe.

But there was an underlying, significant difference between us and New Zealand which I felt strongly about. It was in the way we prepared players for international rugby and, to my mind, this had to change in Britain and Ireland before we could hope to compete with the All Blacks.

While the southern hemisphere was pushing forward with new ideas and structures, with the Super 10 and 12 coming on top of the National Provincial Championship (NPC) and Currie Cup competitions, we, in Britain and Ireland, rested on our laurels after the Lions did well in the 1970s and didn't move forward like the southern hemisphere did. We saw the results of that in 1983.

All the cajoling, the great spirit you might have as the battling underdogs, the psyching-up in dressing-rooms will get you maybe 10 points in a game, but that's it. You need a solid structure right through the system from early teens to adulthood to produce great players, to test them and push them and, sadly, we didn't have that.

I believe that has changed in the last 10 years and that the right structures are now in place in the home nations, with a competitive Premiership and an improving Celtic League lifting the quality of competition for the other nations. The Heineken Cup is like our Super 12 in that it takes the standard up another

147

notch; but, as we witnessed in New Zealand recently, it is still not high enough. Scottish teams are still not yet competitive in the European tournament, in terms of being real contenders for the latter stages never mind the title, and that remains a major issue in Scotland as the SRU try to create a brighter future.

However, in 1983, no amount of reasoning could lift my personal feelings of failure. My overriding thought when that tour finished was that I had believed I was ready to be a Lions coach but that the tour had shown me I wasn't. I failed to find a game that would beat the All Blacks, who were always better than us technically and tactically. People asked me at the end of the tour whether I feared facing the Scottish media on our return. I said, 'No, I am more worried about hearing the comments as I walk along the street in Selkirk, where I live.'

I could not fault the players, because they had come through a system that wasn't good enough to beat the All Blacks. I failed and maybe I wasn't the right person to coach them. Saturday, 16 July 1983 – the date of the Fourth Test – remains one of the saddest days in my life. A 38–6 defeat, a 4–0 series loss: there was no coming back from that. The dreams I had held three or four months earlier were in tatters.

I was very disillusioned with coaching and with rugby, and I was also totally against the whole Lions concept by this stage: it was so difficult to get the team together and prepared properly before going into the biggest Test matches these players would ever experience; and though the media was supportive to begin with, the national papers in England, Wales, Scotland and Ireland quickly descended into cheering on only their own compatriots and pulling the Lions ethos apart.

Willie John spoke to the press at the end of the tour and said he hoped the Lions would pick me to coach the next tour, as this experience would have been invaluable. But I remember my own response to the media. In reply to one question on my future involvement, I asked them, 'Is there life after death?' It summed up how I was feeling.

Roy Laidlaw and John Rutherford worked hard to keep my spirits up on the way home. They could clearly see I was at my lowest ebb. That pair had been like blood brothers to me and we had been through a lot together. I'll always remember what they said. It was along the lines of, 'We may have lost this tour but we will return to Scotland and win the Grand Slam next season because we have learned about the weaknesses of the other teams in the last few months.' And how prophetic that proved to be.

12

Grand Slam Fever –
The Best Birthday Yet!

John Rutherford
Scotland (42 caps)
British and Irish Lions (1983)

There is nothing players like better than to reflect on great achievements and the 1984 Grand Slam squad have something no one can ever take away from us – we ended 59 years of waiting in Scotland for that ultimate prize.

Scottish players generally have an inferiority complex but tours to Australia and New Zealand in 1981 and 1982, and then with the Lions in 1983, gave a core of that squad an understanding of the level the top players were at and also a belief that, with hard work, we could get there. That confidence grew with the Lions because we discovered we were fitter, better and mentally stronger than some of the best players from England, Wales and Ireland.

Coming back from New Zealand, we knew we had a real chance in the Five Nations the next year. We were all at the top of our game; we weren't young lads, but experienced, hardened internationals and, with confidence, we'd be hard to beat at Murrayfield. The 1984 Championship had France and England coming to us. Perhaps our biggest problem was keeping Jim. He was so depressed after the Lions tour that we had to persuade him to continue – we didn't believe we could reach the highest level without him.

Thankfully, he agreed to stay on and, after drawing with the

All Blacks in the autumn, we beat Wales in Cardiff, then England at home and had the Triple Crown won by half-time in Dublin. Suddenly, we started to think about the Grand Slam for the first time.

Jim stressed to us that the French game would be twice as hard as anything we had come up against so far and he was right. There were times when I thought we might not do it but after Jim Calder's try, I knew we couldn't be stopped. So did the crowd – the noise was incredible.

It was a bit surreal at the end and it took a long time to sink in. But I'll never forget that our captain, Jim Aitken, asked us all up to Edinburgh for lunch and Roy Laidlaw couldn't get there because he had a job on in Jedburgh – he was rewiring the public toilets!

In 1984, Jim was the best coach in the world. Tactically, he knew how to win and knew the opposition inside out but, crucially, he also knew his own players and how to get the best out of them. His team talks were masterpieces – he knew what to say and who to say it to: some needed shouting at; others, like me, maybe, didn't need that. Jim's part was awesome – we couldn't have done it without him.

Roy Laidlaw
Scotland (47 caps)
British and Irish Lions (1983)

Jim, in my opinion, has influenced most of the successes of Scottish rugby. His achievements latterly as director of rugby at the SRU, where we worked closely together, were hugely undervalued. He knows better than anybody what it takes to make Scotland win at international level and how far behind the leading nations we are.

The Grand Slam success didn't just happen overnight. Jim was the B-team coach from 1975 to 1980 and he brought through a lot of players, including myself and John, who were at the core of the 1984 Grand Slam team. He also knew that domestic rugby wasn't at a high enough standard to prepare us for real success, so he organised tours to New Zealand in 1981 and Australia in

1982, and drove the players further than they had ever been driven – the win over Australia in the First Test in Brisbane remains our only win in the southern hemisphere.

In 1984, we had good players but he tipped the balance. He was ruthless and hard, and he left no stone unturned in terms of his knowledge of the opposition. We got to a stage where we believed we could take on and beat anybody. I beat Australia home and away, drew with New Zealand, and in ten meetings with France in my Scotland career, I beat them five times at home, lost four times away and drew with them on neutral ground in the World Cup in 1987. It was a great time to play for Scotland.

There is no doubt in my mind that the 1984 Grand Slam was the biggest achievement in my time with Scotland, and that Championship title I would place higher than the 1990 one, mainly because it ended a wait of 59 years in Scottish rugby.

It is strange to think of the emotions I went through in 1983 and 1984. I returned from the Lions tour very disillusioned and was considering quitting coaching, to be honest, fearing that I didn't have the ability to be successful at the highest level.

I was a bit surprised that it seemed to be taken as read that I would return from my year's sabbatical with the Lions to the coaching helm with Scotland. I half-expected to find someone else in my place. Colin Telfer and Derrick Grant had been the national coaches during 1983 and they had had a hard time of it, losing three games before beating England 22–12 at Twickenham to leave the English with the wooden spoon.

However, once back in the Scotland tracksuit, I discovered that the enthusiasm that had been generated in the players on our tours in the early 1980s was still there and they were a very committed, determined bunch who wanted to be successful. Colin remained with me as my assistant and he was a great support. I inherited Jim Aitken as captain, as he had taken over from Roy Laidlaw at the end of the 1983 season, and I thought he was a good captain. He was very good at encouraging players, that was his skipper, and he led from the front, carrying out the instructions Colin and I gave to the letter.

My first game back was against the All Blacks. They came

because their tour to Argentina had been cancelled as a result of animosity after the Falklands War and they agreed to play Test matches in England and Scotland. They came with a weakened group: Gary Knight, Andy Dalton, John Ashworth, Andy Haden, Gary Whetton and Dave Loveridge were notable absentees.

Before we played them at Murrayfield, they had already beaten the South of Scotland by 30 points to 9 and quite a number of Scotland players had been part of that team. In fact, I feared then that we were seeing the demise of Borders rugby, as the team included 11 internationalists, including Lions Colin Deans, Iain Paxton, Roy Laidlaw and John Rutherford, as well as David Leslie, Alan Tomes and Tom Smith. Jim Aitken called off with flu. The South then went on to win the Inter-district Championship without breaking sweat and a South official was quoted as saying that, apart from the 'blip against the All Blacks', South rugby was in the best of health.

That angered me, as that defeat should have been taken seriously as a wake-up call to Scottish rugby, an indication of how far behind we were slipping. It underlined for me the fact that Colin and I had to work even harder to try and lift the group we had to a much higher level merely to compete.

In the Test match with New Zealand, who were captained by Stu Wilson, David Leslie was missing because of the injury he sustained playing in the South game, as was Keith Robertson. Euan Kennedy won his first cap and John Beattie played on the flank in place of Leslie.

Scotland played very well and scored in the last minute through Jim Pollock to tie the match. Peter Dods had a very difficult conversion from the touch-line, which he didn't get. But there was still some controversy to come after that. The All Blacks were pressing near our line and Bernie Fraser was allegedly taken out of play by Pollock chasing the ball. Play went on and New Zealand were awarded a penalty near the line for offside but Fraser had by then swung a punch at Pollock, which the touch judge saw. The referee reversed the decision and we were able to clear and save a draw – 25 points each.

The All Blacks manager, Paul Mitchell, was quoted afterwards as saying it was nice to see Jim Telfer smile, as he'd been their manager during the Lions series the year before and obviously saw me looking pretty disappointed most of the time.

We went into 1984 quite confident because we had had a great win against Wales in Cardiff two years before and then, as is the case now, the feeling was always that our best chance of winning the Grand Slam was when we had France and England at home and Wales and Ireland away. Some might think that, as we had not won a Grand Slam for 59 years, we might not have been bothered any more but that wasn't the case at all. Every year that went by when the Grand Slam didn't come to Scotland, there was more pressure on the shoulders of the players.

Wales chose a running scrum-half, Mark Douglas from Llanelli, as Terry Holmes was injured, and I remember reading that our players had 266 caps to their 60 that day. They played a big second row, Richard Moriarty, at the tail of the lineout to combat David Leslie, and a specialist openside, David Pickering, further down the line. Ironically, it turned out to be 'David Leslie's game' because he completely dominated the tail of the lineout, cleverly dropping back behind Moriarty to take Colin Deans' long throws.

We didn't play particularly well but we scored two decisive tries. The first came from Iain Paxton, who took what looked like a forward pass from Leslie at a planned free-kick move in the first half; the second was the result of a drive at the tail of the lineout after the break which ended with Jim Aitken being shunted over by Leslie. We won 15–9, our third win in five games against Wales, having previously won only three times in fifty-seven years.

Next in our sights was England at Murrayfield. Already, the press were talking of a first Triple Crown since 1938 and, worse, a first Grand Slam since 1925 but we had to ignore that kind of talk because we still had three big games to play. This was the 100th match between the two auld enemies and England came up having beaten New Zealand in the autumn but without having played for 11 weeks. Dick Greenwood, the father of recent Lion Will, was the England coach.

The game was a classic example of the different philosophies of ruck and maul, and on that day ruck came out on top. At that time, England were quite predictable, with big forwards Maurice Colclough, Steve Bainbridge and Peter Simpson, and a scrum-half, Nick Youngs, who did a lot of running from mauls. Clive Woodward was also in their team.

Steve Munro was injured and his place on the team was taken

by Keith Robertson. We planned to play a fast, wide game but when I went to the pitch on the morning of the match, it was raining and the pitch was slippery, so we changed our tactics.

We decided to use Roy and John to kick on to Dusty Hare, their full-back, and recognised that our scrummaging would be the key in the wet. We played with the normal south-westerly wind at Murrayfield in the first half and the first try was the result of a ball over the top of the lineout. Paxton hacked it on and David Johnston dribbled on and scored. The tactic of putting pressure on Hare obviously worked, because he missed six penalty goals out of eight.

The second try is one of those that sticks out clearly in my mind, because it was an occasion when everything just came together perfectly. England took a 22 drop-out and Scotland caught it, drove and rucked, then Roy chipped over the ruck and Dusty was caught in possession. Jim Calder ripped the ball from him and the Scottish forwards, with David Leslie and Alan Tomes in the van, rucked perfectly, laid it back, and Roy passed to John, who took it off his toes, drew Woodward and gave a short pass on the burst to Euan Kennedy, who went in at the posts. We won 18–6, but unfortunately Euan and Bill Cuthbertson were both injured, to be replaced by Jim Pollock – he came and played on the wing, while Keith Robertson moved to centre – and John Beattie. Sadly, neither Euan nor Bill made it back in that Championship.

So, on to Dublin for what would be the Triple Crown. There was now real fervour around the squad and TV crews were appearing all over the place; Jim Aitken was being asked to speak and appear at dinners around the country as well. We tried to play the hype down in the squad because Scotland had played for five Triple Crowns since 1938 and lost them all, usually to England at Twickenham.

The custom at that time was to stay in Dublin before the match. We used to stay in the same hotel as the Irish but we had decided before the Championship to be different this time and we stayed ten miles out in the foothills. There had been a month between the England and Ireland games, so I'd gone to watch those two meet at Twickenham, and Ireland were beaten 12–9 and didn't play well.

They made quite a number of changes to the side which had

shared the Championship with France in 1983: Fergus Slattery, Ollie Campbell and David Irwin were dropped; Ciaran Fitzgerald was injured; and they included a new cap, Derek McGrath, the current Heineken Cup chief executive. We brought in Alastair Campbell for his first cap, replacing Cuthbertson, and Pollock and Robertson retained the positions they'd taken up after the switch when Kennedy was injured against England.

The pressure was on both teams, because they were facing the wooden spoon if they lost this Dublin encounter. We trained at Palmerston RUC on the Friday before the game and the weather was vile. I remember at the team talk on the Friday night before the game, I decided to show them a video. It wasn't of the games against Wales or England, but of the South against the All Blacks. This was for two reasons: first, ten of them had played and had been beaten; and second, the referee had been Fred Howard, the Englishman who was to take charge of our Triple Crown match in his first international.

Showing the players not a victory but a defeat was carefully thought-out reverse psychology. I left them to watch it on their own in the team room. That was how I worked – I brought them down to earth with a bump and then lifted them – but it is only effective with honest players. As a result, they came out bursting to show what they could do, with real commitment.

It is always windy in Dublin and you have to decide beforehand what to do if you win the toss, and not be swithering. We had played against the wind when we'd lost two years before, so we decided this time we'd play with it if we won the toss. But Willie Duggan, the Irish captain, actually won the toss and gave us the wind.

For 30 minutes, the game was like a dream – the tries and the points just kept coming. Roy scored two great tries in the same corner of the ground. The first came from a lineout peel deep in the Irish 22, where he swept blind and sidestepped four Irish players to score. He scored a second on the half-hour straight from a quick channel-one ball in the scrum, outflanking the Irish back row. As a result, that part of the ground has become known to Scots supporters as 'Laidlaw's Corner'.

In between, the referee made a brave decision to give us a penalty try. Our scrum near the Irish line was wheeled and

Duggan was deemed to have illegally prevented us from scoring. It was a soft penalty try but it was great to see Howard running across towards the posts with his arm aloft.

We went in at half-time 22–0 up but Roy had taken a knock to his head. Gordon Hunter, the Selkirk scrum-half, came in for his first cap and played well after giving away a penalty early on through over-exuberance. We scored two more tries in the second half: Hunter made a fine diagonal break which resulted in Keith Robertson cutting in to score near the posts; and the second came from a glorious sweeping movement when Peter Dods ran outside Roger Baird to score in the corner. We beat Ireland 32–9 and the mythical Triple Crown was won.

The drama wasn't over, though, because Gordon Hunter broke his cheekbone when he collided with a supporter as he ran off the pitch. It was the third time he'd broken his cheekbone – he had done the same in New Zealand in 1981 – and he knew straight away that he was going to miss the next game. He was indeed ruled out for six weeks.

Winning something felt tremendous. I believed the Triple Crown was very special – I had been trying to win it as a player and as a coach since 1964 – and I never even thought about the Grand Slam. The BBC broadcast the festivities in Dublin late into the night and we were singing songs in the studio, which I think delighted Dougie Donnelly and Bill McLaren. Bill always went straight home to Hawick after games, so the fact that he stayed on showed how special the occasion was.

Roy spent the night in hospital but returned to Scotland with us the next day. Obviously, we were very worried about him, especially with Gordon injured as well. With the France game just a fortnight away, we had to look at a completely new set of scrum-halfs. We actually asked Dougie Morgan, who wasn't playing much rugby and had last played for Scotland in 1978, if he would be available. We also looked at David Johnston's brother, Stuart, and Dave Bryson, the Gala scrum-half, who had sat on the bench before. We went for Stuart, who was playing well for Watsonians.

But we decided to announce an unchanged side, with a vacancy left at scrum-half. Roy had undergone several tests and the medics said it wasn't concussion, which we were glad of because that would have brought a mandatory three-week lay-off. Apparently, he had suffered from bad migraines in the past, which impaired his vision at times, and the symptoms seemed more connected to that history than the actual knock in the game. It was a bit bizarre but the good news for Roy and for us was that the medics passed him fit to play.

There was frenzy in Edinburgh as the game approached, the French arriving in the Scottish capital as favourites for the Grand Slam. They had played better and scored more points in victory than we had. Peter Wheeler, the influential England hooker, had described them as 'unbeatable'.

France started well and outplayed us in the first half but they got on the wrong side of the referee, Winston Jones from Wales. At one point, they had had nine penalties given against them to our none. One of their star players, Jerome Gallion, the scrum-half, scored a superb try, very similar to the second one that Roy scored at Lansdowne Road. We were trailing 6–3 when we went in, Peter Dods having kicked a penalty, and shortly after half-time, Jean-Patrick Lescarboura put them 9–3 up with a penalty.

But early in the second half, Gallion was injured and that proved to be a defining moment in the game. France had a move from a short lineout where the ball was thrown over the tail and Gallion was to run onto it. We had a plan for this situation: we would put a forward beside John Rutherford at stand-off; when he saw the ball being thrown, he would run flat out to get it. We normally used Colin Deans for this because he was quick and it left the back row free. On this occasion, however, David Leslie was in the position. He ran up and hit Gallion as he went for the ball and laid him out, quite legally!

Gallion had to be carried off and he was replaced by Pierre Berbizier, who recently took over as Italy's national coach. We drew strength from that, the French, Jean-Pierre Rives in particular, started arguing more with the referee and they started to lose the place. Twice this resulted in penalties being moved nearer their line and Dods kicked them to level the scores.

There then came another key moment in the game when Serge Blanco, the mercurial French full-back, was caught under a high ball and driven some way back downfield. The impetus that gave us was crucial and we scored from more or less the next lineout. That was a planned move as well. When Colin Deans threw the ball to the tail and Iain Paxton won it, Alastair Campbell would come round from the front, sweeping to take a tap-down. But if the opposition won it, then the man in front of Paxton would go through the lineout.

On this occasion, Deans threw the ball to Paxton. It was deflected by Jean-Luc Joinel onto his side and Jim Calder was already on his way through when it fell. He grabbed it and fell over the line, and many felt it was a fluke score – it was no fluke. Dods then kicked the conversion and even added a fifth penalty goal with just one eye open, the other having swollen up badly.

I did not actually feel great elation at the whistle, because I had felt all that in Ireland two weeks before. But then it began to dawn on us all, I think, that we'd made history. It had been 59 years in coming, so it was difficult to take in the significance. There was also a personal celebration for me, in that the day we beat France to win the first Grand Slam in so long was also my 44th birthday. It was a happy coincidence and I received quite a number of cakes from all quarters – including my friends in the press – but it paled against the achievement of the players on the field. They had provided me, however, with my best birthday present.

Afterwards, unusually for me, I singled out one player, Iain Milne, for special praise, because of the way he had held the scrum up. Thinking back now, Peter Dods deserved a tremendous amount of credit, because his five penalty goals and conversion kept us in the game and took us away from France at the finish, and he had to play with one eye almost fully closed towards the end.

A lot of the players went on to greater things and became legends; but one player who might not have been capped in other countries, Bill Cuthbertson, was absolutely pivotal to what we achieved. This was not a one-year thing but a four-year project and Bill was Scotland's unsung hero through much of that time.

We enjoyed great support from the SRU at that time – 11 clubs were represented in that squad – and I believe the key to that success was our ability to take players away on tour to play at a consistently high level. We actually built up a club atmosphere within the Scotland team. In fact, Robin Charters, who was later a selection convener, put forward the suggestion that Scotland should take away the top 50 or 60 players and prepare them for international rugby, leaving the clubs to do what they were best at – running a competitive club game. Robin, a former Hawick and Scotland centre and SRU President in 1992–93, has a very good rugby brain and knows the club mentality.

Two very important individuals off the field in that Grand Slam era were Ian McGregor, who had been the convener of selectors for four years, a manager in Australia and one of the most knowledgeable people you could come across in rugby terms; and Adam Robson, the SRU president that year, whom the players related to because he had played 22 times for Scotland and was a very approachable person.

But one other unsung hero, and just as crucial a character to that success, was Colin Telfer. It is a great shame that his picture doesn't even appear in Ronnie Browne's famous portrait 'The Turning Point', commissioned by the Royal Bank of Scotland. Colin, my assistant, had just retired from playing, so he had a good grasp of the modern game; he was a good communicator. A coach for four years, he deserves his place among the rest of us as an integral part of that famous time in Scotland's history.

Jim Aitken has said that this was a greater triumph than the 1990 Grand Slam and I agree with him, because the yolk was finally removed from the backs of Scottish players after 59 years. It had been a heavy burden for many to bear.

One last thing: sadly, Andy Irvine had hamstring problems and didn't play in the Grand Slam year; neither did Jim Renwick, who also had injury worries. That was a shame for two players who had been great servants of Scottish rugby for many years. They were excellent men to have involved and were enthusiastic, very positive about helping younger players, even though they were at the ends of their careers.

The 1984 Grand Slam remains my proudest memory, even lthough the Lions tour to South Africa in 1997 took my coaching to another level altogether.

13

Saying Goodbye to Rugby

Ian Landles
Principal Teacher of History, Hawick High School
Renowned 'Hawick Man'

There have been some changes in education over the last decade or so and one of them is a deterioration in the standards of discipline.

When Jim Telfer was the head teacher at Hawick High School, discipline was not a great problem and I often wonder how he, with his quite intimidating big frame, would have dealt with the changes in children's behaviour had he still been around.

It was not that the Scotland rugby coach would march about shouting all day but he had a presence, because of both his physical size and his manner, which cowed the most cocky, awkward youngsters a bit. It was interesting as a rugby supporter to follow Jim's career as a coach and then watch him in action in a school environment, where, obviously, his style in dealing with a cheeky wee girl had to be quite different to that used in making grown men cower in an international-team dressing-room. But when he coached school rugby teams, you would be hard pushed to find anything different in his style: he would be as intense on the touch-line at a Hawick school game as he was in South Africa with the Lions in 1997 and he was like a bear with a sore head if we didn't win!

Jim arrived at Hawick High School straight after the Grand Slam of 1984. It must have been difficult for other aspiring heads

161

on the short leet to compete with Scotland's most successful rugby coach for a place at a Borders school! But he was just the same as anyone else inside the school doors. The fact he was from Melrose was never an issue, to be honest, and he was 'the Peche' the same as every head before him.

The term, which I think is unique to Hawick, dates back to a head teacher called Mr A.M. Watters, who was at the school just after the Second World War. There are two explanations I know of for the name. He was a keen fisherman and one story is that some youngsters took the French verb *pêcher*, meaning 'to fish', as a nickname for him. The other is that, because he had this big red face, particularly when wound up, the children thought he looked like a peach, the French for which is *pêche*. They're clever kids in Hawick.

Jim was quite obviously a committed teacher and passionate head, proud of his pupils and staff. We had the added bonus that because Jim was here when the school was extensively refurbished, his friend HRH The Princess Royal, the SRU patron, came along to open the school, which was a great thing for Hawick. It was a pity he left but I could understand his rugby ambitions. I don't know how dealing with Scottish rugby compared with dealing with Hawick schoolchildren but I remember Jim as a firm but fair head who did a good job steering the school through a time of change.

Turning my back on rugby was not easy. I had never seriously contemplated the prospect in the 30-odd years I had been involved in the game as a player and coach, and even when my playing career at Melrose ended, coaching was such a natural progression that moving away from the game was never in my mind.

But, after playing my part in helping Scotland win their first Grand Slam in 59 years, I had a choice: take up what I saw as the ultimate post in my teaching career, headmaster of a large school, or try to keep coaching (without any money, of course, then) while sticking where I was as a deputy head. Staying put would not have been a great problem, as I liked working at Deans, but I was as ambitious in my teaching as I was in rugby and had a strong desire to challenge myself.

The job as rector of Hawick High School was attractive and I was delighted to be offered the post, but I had to be fully committed. It was now rugby or teaching, not both. Though it wasn't a condition of the interview, the Borders director of education at the time, James McLean, expected me to give up coaching Scotland and I agreed that it was the only course of action.

I called off from Scotland's tour to Romania in May and in August 1984 I stepped into my new job as Hawick High School's head teacher. It was a move I was looking forward to and never regretted. I was taken around the town by Ian Landles, a well-known Hawick entertainer and historian. He was the principal teacher of history at the High School when I was there and, as we were walking in towards the school, he showed me the point where you could close off the town and stop invaders.

He pointed to the main road running south to Langholm and said, 'This is the new road, of course, Jim.'

I said, 'Oh, new road, when was it built?'

He replied, 'In the 1850s,' and he was dead serious. But that's a Hawick history teacher for you!

I also remember speaking to my first-year rugby team. The boys were talking about the Five Nations win when one piped up, 'I don't know about the Grand Slam, but my dad's coached the YM, ye ken.' They're a Hawick junior team. In his eyes, not much was better than that.

The job in Hawick was a real challenge and it was quite a culture shock going from the purpose-built Deans to Hawick High School – a traditional school with some Victorian buildings and some newer buildings on the campus – where the whole ethos was different, with no real community involvement.

Having taught in five different schools, I knew how a comprehensive worked and had my ideas on shaping the school. As I endeavoured to lead from the front as a captain on the rugby field, so I did as a head teacher. On my first day, I told the staff that I was a person who wanted to go round the school, go into classrooms, and have an open-door policy whereby staff and pupils could come and see me whenever they wanted. That was quite new for some and it met with suspicion initially.

It was the biggest school in the Borders then, with around 1,200 pupils. I realised quickly that, as in all schools, there was a tremendous amount of talent among the staff and the pupils, and from the start I attempted to maximise their potential. I really enjoyed teaching at Hawick High School and there were some cracking pupils there, many of whom went on to universities across the UK and into great careers.

As a new head teacher, I brought many positive ideas from my previous schools with me, and modernising the head teacher's approach was an early move. Because the buildings were so spread out, there were five or six staffrooms and a tannoy system, with speakers attached to walls inside and outside the school. The headmaster would speak from his office in the morning, giving out the instructions for the day. It reminded me of a commandant in a German prison camp shouting 'Achtung, Achtung'. I used it on the first day but felt completely ill at ease, so I had the contraption taken away and from then on we had a daily paper bulletin.

Another change we made quite early on was to try to improve the school uniform. It was not that the pupils at Hawick were badly dressed; in fact, some of them were very well dressed because of the knitwear industry, and standardising the uniform was a challenge, as girls would wear the fanciest clothes they possibly could. Some pupils could not afford to compete in the fashion stakes, however, and the new uniform, I felt, would help poorer families and also look very smart. We had a competition amongst the pupils for the best design and we were given advice by some of the local knitwear companies – there were plenty of them. I still see pupils wearing the uniform, which makes me quite proud.

If you're not careful, much of your time as a headmaster can be spent talking only to the staff but I always maintained I wanted a teaching commitment. I took a first-year class for six periods of science a week. I tried to ensure that I was not disturbed when teaching, because I felt it would be unfair if the pupils did not get their proper education.

It was my way of keeping in touch with classroom problems and being able to empathise with both staff and pupils. I used to try to get to know the names of all the pupils in the school. I probably never did but I would spend time with the PE staff, who always know names, continually asking who this child was, or that one. It was a great advantage when dealing with problems.

We had difficult times in those early years, not least those caused by the national teachers' strike in 1985, which engulfed schools across the country. There were some changes in the school when the strike hit but most extra-curricular activities, including sport, continued as normal. The unions were very sensible. Jock Houston, now a local councillor, was their leader, and he and I worked on a very amicable basis.

At Hawick High they have a name for the headmaster – he's 'the Peche' (pronounced 'pesh') – and I was considered quite a strict Peche, I think, especially when I was on lunch duty or patrolling the playgrounds.

The school stopped playing 1st XV rugby during my time there, which some people might find surprising. As in most schools, there was great enthusiasm in the first three years for school rugby but by the time pupils turned fifteen, there was a marked difference in the attitude of the ones who wanted to go on to university and those who were planning to stay in the town and get a job. The boys staying were looking at life, and sport, outside the school, so there was a strong pull to play for the youth teams and it was a tug-of-war to get boys to represent the school. Other schools in the Borders experienced similar problems.

Tony Stanger, for example, was an outstanding schoolboy and was picked for the Scottish Schools squad; he was also playing for the Hawick senior team. The Hawick president at the time, Derek Deans, who gained his Scottish cap against England in 1968, came round to tell me Tony would have to play for Hawick and wouldn't be available for the Schools squad. I argued that it was a great opportunity for Tony to play for his country, something he would never get again at that level. Deans told me, 'We have a syphon system here at Hawick and the top is Hawick 1st XV. If a player is good enough, he should be playing for Hawick.' End of story.

However, Tony did play for the Scottish Schools team and I was glad. Many Borders schools have recently resurrected their 1st XVs and now play during the week so as not to clash with the youth teams in each town. A school 1st XV provides many boys with a great focus, something to aspire to, and also gives the whole school a feeling of pride when they do well. The Scottish Schools Cup final attracts over 5,000 spectators, mainly schoolchildren, to Murrayfield now.

As in rugby, I found traditions ran deep in the school and sometimes change was difficult. Once, I tried to get the support of the school board to change a local holiday. It was a Monday holiday in late September and, as the pupils had only been back for a month after the summer holidays, I thought it would a good idea to give them an uninterrupted run in the school up to the October break. I put the suggestion to the board and it agreed, but when I put it to the local community council, I was shot down. I was told it was a traditional holiday; local shopkeepers always took that day, despite the fact that there were as many national chains on the main street as local shops. I accepted the decision, however, and decided just to concentrate on improving the school from within.

There had been talk of a new school but a site could not be found that was flat enough to accommodate it with the required playing fields. So, around 1989, as I recall, the decision was taken that money would be spent on refurbishing and modernising the existing school rather than building a new one.

There was £7 million allocated for the project, a large amount of money then, and a lot of work went into the plan. We had a great architect in charge of it, Glen McMurray, who worked for Borders Regional Council. It was a very difficult time at the school – three years of disruption. After the initial plans were produced, each department was asked for its opinion and many of the ideas were incorporated into the final designs. The staff and pupils were excellent in that they just got on with life. The school actually appealed to the Scottish Education Department to take the disruption – the incessant banging and dusty atmosphere – into account at exam time. But they did not.

For my own part, the project enabled me to make a mark in terms of bringing the school together in a way I hoped would make for a better educational environment. We succeeded in creating one new central staffroom, which I believed would allow the staff to mix better both socially and educationally.

A new music department, a library with a spiral staircase up to the sixth-year common room (an idea I pinched from Deans) and a special education department complete with its own enclosed garden and stream were the major projects, and all other departments were upgraded.

We also had an intriguing incident with a well-known politician. The school's sixth-year pupils had a visit from Liam Fox, then Tory candidate for Roxburgh and Berwickshire, and, in 2005, the shadow Foreign Secretary. Like other Tories before him – Malcolm Rifkind, Teddy Taylor and Michael Ancram, for example – he had to head south to England to win a seat. When he left the common room, there was a little capsule filled with white powder found near where he'd been sitting and we immediately thought of drugs. We took the powder to the police, it was sent to Edinburgh, and the drug squad came and searched the whole room. As far as I'm aware, Dr Fox was never told but it was just as well, because it was discovered that it was actually chalk – a pupil had planted the phial near him as a hoax. I never found out who was responsible!

When it came to opening the newly refurbished school, it was suggested that as I knew HRH The Princess Royal, who was patron of the Scottish Rugby Union, she would be ideal, and I was delighted when she agreed to come.

The week before the opening, Special Branch policemen went through the school with sniffer dogs and things were tied down – unruly children and the like! No, in fact, as it was a normal school day, they were encouraged to play truant the day she was coming, or told it was a public holiday! A piece of ceiling actually fell down on the route she was going to follow just before she came and all the security people had to sweep the school again.

It is a big building but I remember Princess Anne walking at a hell of a pace from one end to the other, and it was difficult keeping up. But she took a great interest in the school and particularly in the new learning support area we had created.

She is an amazing woman and a great patron for Scottish rugby. She is an excellent speaker – usually with no notes – and because she is a sportswoman of some renown and has competed in the Olympic Games, she knows what is required to get to the top level.

The refurbishment was finished as my time as a head teacher at Hawick was coming to an end and I regret not having had the chance to spend more time in the new school. Because, at the end of 1993, I made another major decision in my life: to turn my back on teaching altogether and plough a new furrow in rugby. Of course, I had been involved in another Grand Slam by then, having agreed to return to coaching and link up for the first time with Ian McGeechan.

14

The Second Slamming

Finlay Calder
Scotland captain (34 caps)
British and Irish Lions captain (1989)

We could quite easily have just accepted whoever was appointed as assistant coach when Ian McGeechan was promoted to coach in 1988, and that might have been the Scottish way – take what you get.

People get carried away with how good rugby was in years gone by but the truth of the matter was that we did not have a big squad in the late 1980s. There were maybe only a dozen candidates for the first-team pack and if we had injuries, we really hit the skids. But we had a determined group who wanted to be the best they could and we knew that if we were going to survive and compete, only the best-drilled pack would have a chance.

That meant we needed the unique firebrand coaching of Jim Telfer. The game has moved on light years since we played, but he was a fanatical observer of the New Zealand technique and that style of forward play suited our own – a big strong man at tight-head and seven mobile, athletic and hard-working forwards. That was how we wanted to play.

Myself, Iain Milne and Iain Paxton arranged to go down to Selkirk to meet Jim. Milne and Paxton had been with him through his lowest and highest points, having gone with him to New Zealand in 1983 and then played key roles in the Grand Slam success the following year. They were two of his most

169

respected players and that respect was mutual, so my strategy was that it would take a strong man to turn the two of them down. There was no point in taking people he was indifferent towards. It is quite ironic: Jim has spent his whole life playing on people's emotions and, for once, he had the tables turned on him, and he could do nothing about it.

It was actually a very difficult meeting. He took a lot of persuading and, even as we left, I said to the others, 'I'm not so sure he'll come.' He is tremendously committed to everything he does and I worried that he wasn't going to commit his time and reputation to another cause when he was putting so much effort into his teaching. Also, it had been a life's work for him to pull the squad together for 1984 and I don't think he felt he could go through it all again.

We were obviously delighted when he thought about it and agreed to come back, and there is no doubt he was a central figure in what we went on to achieve. He will probably talk about why I relinquished the captaincy on returning from the Lions tour in 1989, because it surprised him; but I only ever saw myself in a caretaker role, to be honest. I was a bit old-fashioned, I believed that the best player in the team should be captain, and David Sole was the player I felt would best lead Scotland forward. The expression 'world class' is used often and rarely does it fit, but it did with David – he would have played for any of the leading nations in world rugby.

I had made my mind up that I didn't want to captain the side and Jim understood that he couldn't change it. We are very similar in that we're pretty dogmatic, and in other ways, too. I was the luckiest person ever to captain the Lions – I happened to be in the right place with a great squad.

The people we had in charge in 1990, from David to Jim and Ian McGeechan, were all the right men at the right time for Scotland. Jim is a quite remarkable man. His strength was that he could turn some very ordinary players, myself included, into men who could compete at the highest level. He did it with Melrose, with Scotland and with the Lions. His legacy consists of the 1984 and 1990 Grand Slams, and the 1997 Lions win. In each success, he made players believe.

170

Behind every success, there lies hard work and preparation. There may be a slice of luck but, just as the 1984 Grand Slam was founded on a determined effort to create something with new tours abroad, we did not stumble across the achievement of 1990 by accident.

As Grand Slams only come to Scotland very rarely – we have still won only three: 1925, 1984 and 1990 – that start to the last millennium's final decade will live long in the memories of Scottish rugby supporters. It is a matter of great pride to me to have been involved in two of them and yet I might have been watching that third special success like any other supporter had it not been for the compelling persuasion of the players.

On becoming head at Hawick High School in '84, I could no longer work at the level I had in rugby; teaching is something which you have to be entirely committed to, dedicated to pupils and staff, and that is especially the case in the post of head teacher.

My enthusiasm for rugby had never gone away but I was thoroughly enjoying immersing myself in teaching at Hawick when, in 1988, I received a phone call requesting a meeting with some senior Scotland players. For four years, my rugby coaching had gone no further than taking a first-year team at Hawick High School through to the third year and then starting again with another first-year group.

It was Finlay Calder on the phone asking if we could secretly meet up, and such was our relationship that I would never have said no. I had actually called Fin some years before after reading that he was considering retirement without having played international rugby. I felt compelled to phone just to tell him not to, to stick at it. I urged him to switch from number 8 to flanker in order to win selection and I was pleased for him when he won his first cap in 1986. People now may be amazed to learn how close the Fin Calder who led Scotland and the Lions so well was to quitting.

Our relationship went back further than that, however. Finlay had come to the Borders from Haddington when he was 18 to work for a grain merchant and he joined Melrose. I lived in Edinburgh but became something of a mentor to him. He would come up to Edinburgh and I would take him to Meadowbank Sports Centre for weight-training. There were always three other people there: the Scottish field athletes Chris Black and Meg Ritchie (who, as Meg Stone, was the national fitness coach for athletics a few years ago), and Jim Aitken, who was really into his weights. The language in that room was blue, and that included Meg.

Fin hadn't lifted weights before and to begin with he was so knackered after ten minutes of doing exercises with the weights bar that he couldn't actually lift the weights. But he learned and developed physically, and went on to play for Melrose for a few seasons before joining his brothers at Stewart's Melville.

Because of that relationship, I think, Fin called me when Derrick Grant retired as national coach. I knew Derrick very well, having played and coached with him for years, and he had become very disillusioned after a 9–6 defeat to England in a dismal game at Murrayfield in 1988. Scotland had taken part in the first World Cup in 1987, in which the hosts New Zealand began their habit of knocking us out in the quarter-finals, and a difficult following year had got to Derrick.

Ian McGeechan was appointed to take over from Derrick – he'd coached the B team and been Derrick's assistant coach – and Fin came down to see me in Selkirk. We met at the quiet Philipburn Hotel on the weekend of the Selkirk Common Riding. He had with him Iain Paxton and Iain Milne, and they asked if I would consider coming back and coaching alongside Ian.

I had been warned by Bob Munro, the convener of selectors, about why they were coming to see me, but I didn't decide straight away. I listened to them and it was very hard; I was committed to Hawick High School and yet these players wanted me to help them. I had to give it a lot of thought.

A good, positive meeting with the director of education at Borders Regional Council helped me make my mind up and I agreed to do it, but with certain reservations: that I did not have the time to be a selector; and that the commitment could not be allowed to interfere with my work at the school. For the first couple of seasons, that worked quite well. And so the next Grand Slam crusade was born.

My first game back was against Australia in November – Gary Armstrong's first cap – and we got stuffed; David Campese ran riot. I remember the Australians had been training in the Borders earlier in the week and I nipped along to the Greenyards to catch them. Unfortunately, the television cameras caught me and I received a phone call the next day from the assistant director of education, Margaret Acton, wondering why I was at a training session when my job was running Hawick High School. She was a very good boss; headmasters respected her and I knew she was right. It was a rare occasion when my enthusiasm crossed the line.

Confidence started to build in the squad in 1989 as the team beat Wales, drew with England, saw off Ireland, with our highest score to that date against them of 37 points, and then lost in Paris. The team also suffered a 28–24 loss in Japan, though I stayed home to work and missed that match. That season thrust a number of talented Scottish players into the Test arena. After Gary, Sean Lineen, Craig Chalmers, Chris Gray, Kenny Milne and Paul Burnell all stepped up to win their first caps; Tony Stanger followed in October and Finlay was captain for the first time.

After the 12–12 draw with England, the rugby writer Robert Armstrong, a strange sort, termed us 'scavengers' in *The Guardian*. Geoff Cooke was the England coach and Andy Robinson, later England coach and 2005 Lions coach, who was the openside flanker, ran around on his hands and knees all the time, so to call us scavengers was a bit rich.

It was a sign that we were worrying them again. The standard comments on the underdog are a symptom of laziness or ignorance in sports reporting; Scottish scrum-halfs are invariably 'living off scraps', or 'always on the back foot'. It means nothing. You acquire a reputation as a smaller country for always trying to be negative but we weren't negative. It is assumed that the All Blacks or England are always playing the game the right way because they win, and that smaller nations like Scotland or Italy are trying to cheat. Referees sometimes go with that idea too and it can be very harmful to smaller nations trying to succeed and improve the global competition.

After autumn warm-ups with Romania and Fiji, we were looking ahead to 1990 with some enthusiasm. There were only a few selection issues; the biggest dilemma was over who would captain the side. Finlay was the obvious choice, having been our skipper in 1989 and come back from Australia as the triumphant Lions captain, but bizarrely he didn't want to do it any more. I couldn't understand Finlay sometimes – he could be a strange, enigmatic character. He said he wanted David Sole to take his place as Scotland skipper. They had made their international debuts together, against France in 1986, and though they were very different characters, they clearly knew each other well, and our respect for Fin meant that his opinion was taken seriously.

But there was another very good candidate to take over the captaincy at that time – Gavin Hastings – and, behind the scenes, there was a lot of discussion about it. They both had strong personalities (a prerequisite for a good skipper) but they were quite different – with Gavin you got what you saw, whereas David was far more deep-thinking and reserved, quite a different kind of leader. But I was not surprised that both of them went on to prove very good Scotland captains.

I admit I was disappointed when Fin stood down, because he'd had a successful time and played well for the Lions in the Test matches, and we had a very good rapport. When I look back, it's no coincidence that my successes were linked to good relationships with captains – Jim Aitken in 1984, David in 1990, Martin Johnson with the Lions in 1997 and Gary Armstrong in 1999.

David did very well and I had no reason to be concerned, though, interestingly, I believe the famous methodical walk down the tunnel before the Grand Slam decider with England actually came from the preceding Lions tour. Finlay had walked the players slowly out onto the pitch in the First Test . . . but they got beat, so it didn't go down then as a particularly great motivational ploy!

Melrose were also back at the forefront of my mind by then – it was a busy time. About the same time as I had returned to working with Scotland, I was asked back to the Greenyards by my friend Eric Allan, then the coach. I seem to recall that it was merely to help out in some way but, sure as days follow nights, I was in charge of the team by 1988–89. So I was coaching a school team, back with Melrose, and assistant coach to Scotland. I maintain that I didn't take much time off during the day, which was important to me, but for Frances I became a virtual stranger again.

Most of the time, work with Melrose and Scotland was at

weekends and nights. Before an international with Scotland, I would go up on the Thursday for a big day of training, return to work for the Friday, then go back to the Scotland camp on the Friday night. The only deviation from that I can remember was for the World Cup in 1991, when I was given leave of absence from the school altogether for the few weeks of the tournament.

I found that it was far more difficult to take time off as the boss at Hawick than it had been when I was the depute head at Deans and I'm sure some members of staff must have talked about it behind my back, but I had a very good senior staff and they covered for me when I needed time off to work with Scotland.

I was never one to do anything by half, though, and I was determined that Scotland would do well when I joined Ian for the first time. He was crucial to that success. The fact that Ian had been in charge of the British and Irish Lions tour to Australia in 1989, and that there were a good number of Scots on it, had a major bearing on the 1990 triumph.

Fin, David, Gavin and Scott Hastings, Gary Armstrong, Craig Chalmers, John 'J.J.' Jeffrey, Derek White and Peter Dods were all Lions in 1989. I remember after Peter was picked for the Lions, he didn't play again for Gala to make sure he didn't get injured!

But the Lions party was a big plus for us. When you look at the Scottish players who toured with the Lions and returned to us better and more mature, they were very influential in Scotland's improvement. We had the captain of the Lions coming back from Australia, young half-backs returning, our whole back row and, of course, David Sole, our captain.

That might seem a lot of Scots to take on a Lions tour – it was the most ever – and some might believe it was because there was a Scottish coach, but they were definitely there on ability. Only J.J., Gary and Peter didn't play in a Test match, and four or five Scots were involved in each one in a winning series.

But there were also some quality Lions in the English side then: Jeremy Guscott, Rob Andrew, Paul Ackford, Brian Moore, Wade Dooley, Dean Richards, Mike Teague. They had some huge men. There was also Martin Bayfield, who went on the 1993 Lions tour – another huge man.

We launched the 1990 campaign in Dublin, without our head coach. Ian had flu and couldn't travel. I was worried because all of a sudden I was in charge of the team again when I'd been prepared for a role in the background, on the training field mainly, and I knew that if we got beat, it would be blamed on me.

The only thing I remember clearly about that game was that we were ahead at the final whistle. It also marked out one player who hadn't been on the Lions tour but who brought something different to Scottish rugby and was crucial to the Grand Slam success: Sean Lineen. We tended to have a lot of cross-field running in Scottish back play at that point but Sean liked to take short passes from the stand-off, run straight and then look to link up. It seemed so simple when he did it but no one had run straight like he did before and because of how he played, we won that game in Ireland.

He took the ball at an angle, beat the first line of defence behind a lineout and passed to Derek White, who scored. Strangely, there was a forward pass involved just as in the opening win of 1984, over Wales, and again the referee didn't see it; like Roy Laidlaw in 1984, Derek scored twice at Lansdowne Road.

The players came off feeling relieved that they'd got away with it, rather than any delight, and I had to remind them they had actually won. But that was a feature of that team, as it was with the 1984 side – they were very, very honest with each other. I found that when you had players like Fin, David, John Jeffrey and Chris Gray, who were listened to when they spoke, you developed a dynamic that pulled teams upwards.

I actually hadn't worked with J.J. before coming into that group and I found him quite a challenging player to coach. He was often ahead of the ball and he did a lot of unnecessary running. He had a very high work rate but he was often caught in a position where he couldn't be very effective. Derrick Grant and I spent some time trying to turn him into a more disciplined forward who would get behind the ball and work more within the framework of the forwards. J.J. had great skill in the way he unsettled defences, he was quick about the park and he was brave, not unlike another blond-haired flanker, Rodger Arneil, before him.

The team realised they were lucky to have won in Ireland. Our next match was France at Murrayfield. We won that one quite easily; it was a bit of a non-game because we were always in charge and won 21–0. Alain Carminati was sent off for kicking at

Fin's head, which was a rather daft thing to attempt, I always thought. The Welsh game was much more nip and tuck, and we won 13–9 when Damian Cronin scored after Gary Armstrong had broken down the blind side.

After each game, the players wanted a quick debrief before the evening's dinner and, for me, that was another sign of their maturity: their desire to get to the mistakes, be honest and give themselves a clear outlook to move forward from. We needed clear heads going into that last game because Scotland was going crazy.

England had won their three games too and theirs were much more comprehensive victories than ours, so there was a sense of inevitability as we moved into the game that England would be big favourites to win the Grand Slam at Murrayfield. If you like, the 1984 Grand Slam was something of a rehearsal for us in terms of getting the country worked up. Beating France in the Grand Slam is good but beating England at Murrayfield is the way most Scots would want to clinch it. So there was incredible Grand Slam fever and I remember we had to calm the players down a lot.

But I was also involved with Melrose and the week before the Grand Slam, we had the biggest game the club had ever taken part in, certainly in my lifetime – to secure Melrose their first-ever Scottish Division One championship. Having played through league domination by Hawick and Gala, and watched a couple of good city clubs get in on the act, I never thought that Melrose could win the official Division One championship. So when Craig Redpath scored a try at the turnstile end at the Greenyards and we beat Jed-Forest to clinch it, that, for me, was actually bigger than the Grand Slam. I'd won that six years before but my club becoming Scottish champions was something I never believed I would see.

It then became an incredible few days. One thing in our favour was that England were expected to win. They had come up in 1980 and scored five tries to win the Grand Slam. It was a debacle. And so they thought they were coming up to do the same again.

There was quite a poisonous anti-English atmosphere, as Jerry Guscott and others have detailed in books since, but that wasn't generated by the players or management; it obviously came from the media and people of Scotland. Because it was such a great event for Scottish sport, all the media were interested, including the tabloids, for a change, and I even heard that stadium announcers at football matches were interrupting the games to give out score updates from our match, which was unheard of.

On the day, Scotland played well but it wasn't a great game of rugby. The slow walk out of the tunnel is what most seem to remember about that day but the first thing that registered with me, and it is still a great memory, was Fin Calder taking a free-kick near the halfway line and driving straight into the English; classic position, what I called number-one position – ball gripped under the arm, legs strong, staying upright, holding off the English. The whole Scottish pack came in behind him and they drove England back 15 to 20 metres. And whoof! The crowd noise just lifted into the sky, the hair went up on the back of my neck and Scotland were on the move.

It was nip and tuck in that game and we were never really on top. Guscott scored a beautiful try and we only led 9–4 at half-time through three penalties from Craig Chalmers. We lost Derek White to injury, brought Derek Turnbull on and moved Jeffrey to number 8. J.J. played there for his club Kelso, so it wasn't new to him and, as it turned out, he sparked the crucial try.

Just after half-time, he picked up at the base of the scrum, made ground and passed the ball to Gary, who fed Gavin. He chipped and Tony Stanger won the race to touch it down, despite having suffered with badly bruised ribs all week after playing for Hawick. If that try was scored today, I think it would go to the video referee because from certain angles it doesn't look like Tony actually gets the ball down. But who knows? Thankfully, we didn't have video refs then and that magical moment in our history cannot be undone.

It was an incredible feeling when the final whistle blew and the boys realised what they had achieved. Of course, as in 1984, the day we won the Grand Slam was also my birthday, which was a strange twist of fate. I was 44 the first time but I turned 50 on 17 March 1990. Because it's St Patrick's Day, the fans remembered it – I got lots of birthday cakes again!

It was a great night for the Scottish players and their families – the wives and girlfriends all lined the staircase of the Carlton

Highland Hotel to welcome the team back – and it was marvellous for Scottish rugby and Scottish sport. But I don't think the English players involved that day ever got over it. The way they have talked about the game and Scotland since then always seems to have a hint of bitterness, and sometimes more than a hint.

I knew we were in the presence of some great Scottish players – not just the obvious stars but also men like Chris Gray, who was the engine of the team, a real unsung hero like Bill Cuthbertson or Jim Calder in the 1984 team – extraordinary blokes. In some ways, these boys were full of themselves but, in others, very humble. They were mentally tough. In the history of Scottish rugby, they were exceptionally good players but it had nonetheless taken most of them a lot of work over several years to achieve that success.

We did not have time to rest on our laurels because we were then looking ahead to a World Cup year, only the second in the game's history and the first in which the competition would be held in the northern hemisphere – in the UK, Ireland and France. We had a tour to New Zealand after the Championship, which I couldn't go on because I had to be in school, so Derrick Grant assisted Ian. In fact, by that time, we had a great four-man coaching team, with Ian, Dougie Morgan, Derrick and me all working together. Scotland did very well on that tour and nearly beat the All Blacks; the 21–18 defeat, two Scotland tries to one All Blacks try, was the closest those players ever came to achieving that rare feat for a Scottish team.

The beauty of having four coaches involved was the amount of ideas you got from each other on different aspects of play, which undoubtedly helped improve the team. Perhaps because we'd all been Lions, and Derrick had coached the national team as well, there was great respect and no one-upmanship. Derrick never said that much but he thought a lot about the game. If any of us had a point to make, the others would listen. I remember Derrick occasionally interrupting team meetings to say, 'I think that's a lot of rubbish you're talking,' and invariably he was right.

The players seemed to be more mature in those days and knew fine the coaches had arguments with each other; but they also knew the message that was coming across was consistent. They wouldn't moan to the media about coaches arguing and cause rifts by blowing things out of proportion.

The big surprise when the team came back from New Zealand was that Finlay had by then decided to retire. Things seem to have a finite lifespan for Finlay. He is a very straight, honest but almost naive person. He would say some things which made you wonder what he was thinking. In 1998, he said on TV that we should come out of the Five Nations Championship because we weren't good enough to compete any more and should play teams like Spain in a second division. The next season we beat France and won the Championship!

Fin and I have been through a lot and have had differing, strong opinions on a variety of things but we have remained close. At that point, Fin felt he'd had enough and couldn't play to his best at international level any more. Retiring is a very personal decision and I would not argue with someone over it, but the players did speak to Finlay and they managed to persuade him to change his mind the next year and come back for the World Cup.

That was to have been my final term as a coach, as well. I had agreed that I would help only to the conclusion of the 1991 World Cup, so I was keen to make the most of what I thought then would be my last year as a coach with Scotland.

In the autumn of 1990, we beat Argentina 49–3 – nine tries to nil – which remains, at the time of writing, our only official Test victory over them, as 1969 was not classed as a Test. In the 1991 Championship, we lost away to France and England but beat Ireland, narrowly, and had a comfortable victory over the Welsh. An 18–12 defeat out in Romania – a repeat of the embarrassment heaped upon the 1984 team who lost there after winning the Grand Slam – was not the best preparation for the World Cup but, with many players missing for that match, it was not a major worry.

The World Cup then loomed large on the horizon. All our games were to take place at our home, Murrayfield, which is probably the first and last time a team will have that luxury in the tournament, but the manager, Dunc Paterson, and Ian decided we would stay and prepare at St Andrews, training at Madras College, to try and keep the players away from the hype and excitement in Edinburgh. The players loved it: they were able to train quite happily, without distraction, and enjoyed going into the town at night and having a quiet, relaxed drink with the students!

We opened the tournament with a good performance against Ireland. That was the game in which Jim Staples suffered a bad facial injury after Finlay caught him with a short-arm and, typically of the competitive Craig Chalmers, we then put high balls up on him while he was groggy. With good but expected wins over Japan and Zimbabwe, we were ensured a quarter-final place, and we met the surprise package, Samoa. Everyone expected us to play Wales but Samoa beat them. In fact, Samoa were known as Western Samoa then and I laughed at the comment from some Welshman, who said, 'If that's what Western Samoa are capable of, thank God we weren't playing the whole of Samoa.'

Craig and Sean were injured after the pool games and we got them into one of these hyperbaric chambers, which was quite revolutionary at the time. Our medical team, Dave McLean and Donald McLeod, were well ahead of the game and Craig was soon passed fit, while Sean only missed the quarter-final and came back to face England in the semi-final.

On the day we played Western Samoa, it was very windy and I suggested to Ian that we use a tactic against the wind that I had employed successfully at club level, namely, putting the full-back – Craig Redpath in Melrose's case, but Gavin Hastings for Scotland – in a short stand-off position and using him against the opposition as a battering-ram.

The tactic worked very well and did what I'd hoped it would, leaving the back row and virtually the whole back line available to take advantage. That was just a small part of the game but Scotland played well overall, too. The Samoans were cocky going into the game but we took them on physically and never gave them a chance to get going. We won 28–6.

It was a shame that we then had a poor, dour game in the semi-final, where we met England. Because the Grand Slam memory was still quite fresh, the whole of Scotland expected us to repeat the result of the year before, but it's difficult to record back-to-back wins over England. England were very physical and took us apart up front. It's well documented that Gavin missed a kick in front of the posts when it was 6–6 but there was always time for them to come back and drop a goal, which Rob Andrew duly did.

We then had to go to Wales to face New Zealand in the third-place play-off match and I recall that, when we arrived in Cardiff, Dunc Paterson refused to allow us to stay at the Angel Hotel, saying it wasn't good enough for our players, and we found better accommodation in Bristol.

But it was tough going into a play-off match in Cardiff when for most of the team it seemed like the World Cup had finished for us. And then we had probably our toughest game, against the All Blacks. I remember saying I didn't want the boys to drink the night before that game, which didn't please some but, to give them their due, they agreed and stuck to it.

Gavin left his mark on that play-off match in Cardiff when he rampaged over the famous All Blacks prop Richard Loe right in front of the main stand and sent him tumbling head over heels. It was beautiful to watch, at least for us Scots! We lost 13–6, with a late try from Walter Little sealing it for them, which was another chance to end the hoodoo gone.

We then travelled to Twickenham for the final and that was where I was quite embarrassed by the behaviour of some of our players. As we got off the bus, a crowd of them bought Australian scarves. I don't think there was any malice in it but it was at best naive to think that English supporters would see the gesture as anything other than a very public snub to the English team. I certainly didn't agree with what they did.

I thought it was in bad taste and blamed that for the abuse we later received from English fans. In 1995 when we played at Twickenham, Gavin and the team were booed onto the field to practise. It might not seem much but that was the first time I'd ever come across that in decades of rugby and I think it emanated from the 1990 Grand Slam game and the antics at the 1991 World Cup.

The mood of players was also changing at that time. There was quite a degree of agitation from some wanting more from the game, to be treated more like professionals and to be given some kind of financial recompense for their efforts. I'm not talking only about Scots and I wouldn't say our players led it at all; it was more that they became aware that money was being paid to players in other nations. South Africa were coming back into the fold and they always 'recompensated' players in various ways, and it was happening closer to home as well. The tours opened the Scots' eyes to that.

But the SRU were working hard to do as much for the players as they could. Dunc really did everything possible to make sure arrangements were the best for the team. Some of the players have since criticised the Union, but they omit to mention what was done for them. During the World Cup, for example, Dunc arranged for a room to be set aside at the team hotel on Sundays for all the players' families so they could relax, bring in their children and have a day together. We also used to stop off at a pub in Sighthill in Edinburgh on the way back after a game. We'd all troop in and there would be all these locals, many of whom would ordinarily have had no interest in rugby, but because we were doing so well, they'd be excited to see us. Everyone entered into the spirit and it was great PR.

The squad started to break up after the tournament. J.J. and Fin retired straight away; Chris Gray didn't play for Scotland again; Derek White went after the Five Nations in 1992; and David and Sean followed after the summer tour to Australia. Ian McGeechan was also having great difficulty getting away from work in Leeds, where he was trying to juggle his day job as a faculty head in a school with coaching the Scotland team.

Once again, I found myself folding up the tracksuit and returning to teaching full-time, where I had the altogether different, but nonetheless exciting, challenge of overseeing the refurbishment of Hawick High School. I was delighted to be back but only two years were to pass before Scottish rugby called again and this time I decided it had to be all or nothing – it was either teaching or rugby, and no trying to do the best for both any more.

15

The Final Bell Sounds for Teaching

Roy Laidlaw
Scotland (47 caps)
British and Irish Lions (1983)
Former Borders, Scotland Under-21s and sevens coach, and
SRU national squad coordinator
Now a self-employed electrician

The early 1990s were an interesting period for Scottish rugby, but they were years fraught with frustration. It was clear that Scottish rugby was falling far behind the rest of the world. Jim Telfer walked right into this difficult situation when he left teaching to become the SRU's first director of rugby. There was some irony in the fact that he had lost out in the Union committee elections voted for by the clubs on no fewer than four occasions only for the Union to realise independently that we actually needed someone like him on board – someone with a deep knowledge of world rugby. Sadly, many others did not have the same depth of knowledge and lacked understanding.

To me, it was clear. During the Rugby World Cup in 1987, I remember watching John Kirwan, the All Blacks winger, on television in New Zealand explaining how his daily routine involved training for a couple of hours each morning, resting, having a good healthy lunch, popping into an office for an hour or so of PR work and then returning for afternoon training, rest and recovery. This was still eight years before the game went professional.

We knew that similar approaches were being taken in France

and even Wales, while in Scotland our international players were still in real jobs and working full days, training at night with their clubs twice or thrice a week.

In 1995, as the SRU's national squad coordinator, I spent time at the World Cup in South Africa. There, directors of Western Province told me they were battling to avoid a players' strike over 'wages' or 'expenses'. This was still before the IRB had sanctioned the payment of players to play rugby; it was an example of 'shamateurism' at its most blatant.

I travelled all over the world in my role with the SRU, so when the game finally did go open in 1995, I knew that Scottish rugby had a lot of catching up to do. Time spent in professional sport, including with the Bradford Bulls rugby league team and in New Zealand with the sevens set-up, showed us that it would take Scottish rugby three years of fully professional training and much-improved skills work to realise the benefits of professonalism. Instead, the SRU gave us six months before the four district teams were cut to two.

Jim had witnessed the growing difference in standards for more years than I and was much more aware of the speed of development elsewhere. He was regularly in contact with leading coaches and administrators from throughout the UK, France and the southern hemisphere, read loads of magazines and watched tapes all the time. His research convinced us that we had to push a new professional tier between club and international rugby. It is interesting to watch the Welsh now go down that route and win silverware in the Celtic League and Six Nations Championship.

It was bizarre that many people in the northern hemisphere, particularly in Scotland, did not see professional rugby coming, though I accept that not everybody was fortunate enough to travel as extensively as others and see first-hand what was going on. To my mind, however, there are no excuses for the way in which Scottish rugby has failed, quite astonishingly, to grasp the fact professionalism is here and to move forward.

As director of rugby, Jim bore the brunt of the political infighting in Scottish rugby and I believe we would not have a professional game today had we not had such a strong character leading us through the changes. Others would have been broken by what he went through and Scottish rugby would have become an amateur backwater.

The World Cup was always supposed to mark the end of my return to coaching for Scotland, as I was still very much the head teacher at Hawick High School and committed to my work in education.

However, there was something in me at that time which made me want to be part of the Scottish Rugby Union's amateur committee. I cannot put my finger on a specific motivaton, but clearly I wanted to be at the coalface of rugby administration and, despite the odd battle with committee members, I had always believed in the committee system. I had stood for election on three occasions since 1977 and failed each time. Though still coaching Melrose, I stood for a fourth time for election to the SRU committee as a representative of the Borders district at the AGM of 1992. Unfortunately, I didn't get on. I couldn't really understand what I was doing wrong.

Near the election, some club officials at Melrose asked if I wanted them to canvass support round the clubs for me and I said I didn't think it was necessary, that surely my record in club, district and international rugby was creditable enough. Years later, it was suggested to me that the clubs had actually been wary of me. Apparently, they preferred the 'safety' of having someone who had come up through the administrative side, possibly secretary then president of their own club and then member of the district committee.

Ironically, I was asked to join the SRU committee only a few months later by Bob Munro, convener of the SRU coaching and youth development committee. He asked me if I would take over from him, commenting that he knew little about coaching. So I arrived on the SRU as a co-opted member through the back door, but sometimes I wonder what my future may have yielded had I been voted onto the committee and ended up trying to influence Scottish rugby from that perspective.

Being a convener did give me a unique insight into the workings of the SRU committee. At that time, the SRU was run like a large rugby club, with lots of sub-committees which reported to the main committee once a month. Even before I joined, the SRU was very proactive in looking at appointing more professional staff, and I remember being part of a group which looked into the introduction of a new post of 'director of rugby' to build on the work done in the technical department which was headed by John Roxburgh and his assistant Douglas Arneil.

They had virtually rescued Scottish rugby after the teachers' strike in 1985. With thousands of teachers suddenly withdrawing their expertise from extra-curricular sessions, the spine of teaching and coaching of many young players across Scotland crumbled. The school population of 20,000 rugby players was reduced to 6,000 in just 2 years and a wealth of underrated teaching expertise was lost to the sport. The SRU initiated the setting up of a whole network of development officers throughout the country. These development officers stepped in to fill the sudden void and worked closely with clubs and schools to promote the game. Even 20 years on, while the numbers involved in schools rugby have significantly improved, with great work at the SRU to develop schools competitions, they are still not back at the pre-strike levels. There is a different ethos in teaching now towards extra-curricular work, which has forced sports like rugby, football and many others to come up with new, cohesive programmes for young players away from schools. Rugby has not been alone in finding that extremely difficult.

It is a sad indictment of some elements in Scottish rugby that the part played by schoolteachers in developing the game has often been decried and devalued. There has been an assumption in some quarters that schoolteachers teach 'soft' rugby and that players do not properly develop until they are coached by men with 'real' jobs or with senior rugby experience. That is simply not the case and it mystifies me that, while other parts of the world set great store by the expertise of teachers and also embrace the different skills and experience brought to shaping young players by people of various backgrounds, many in Scottish rugby prefer to create artificial divisions. It is noticeable in the lack of some of the fundamental skills in young players that we are now missing the professional expertise and attention to detail of trained teachers in the formative years.

Ian McGeechan and I were both involved in drafting a job

description for the new director of rugby. I didn't consider applying initially because I was very happy with my job at Hawick High School and was looking forward to reaping the benefits which the refurbishments would bring to the staff and pupils. Frances encouraged me to apply for the new post and there was an obvious attraction. For the first time, I could be working in rugby not just at nights and weekends but full time, with no worries over how I would support my family and with a team of dedicated staff alongside me. Ultimately, that proved too good an opportunity to ignore.

The director's main job was to oversee the development of all aspects of rugby, from the grass-roots right up to international level, and to look in particular at the creation of a national playing strategy for all levels. He was also to evolve strategies for developing young players of outstanding ability and to keep pace with coaching trends in Scotland, the UK and the rest of the world.

I don't know who else applied for the job but I was appointed to the new post in late August 1993 – one condition of my appointment being that I would be allowed to continue to coach Melrose for a final season in 1993–94, including the planned tour to South Africa in August 1994. I took up the post on Monday, 29 November 1993 and knew instantly that keeping Scotland competitive on the world stage would be an enormous challenge.

Just two days earlier, I had been at Twickenham where I saw England beat the All Blacks 15–9, having watched the Scotland national team lose 51–15 to the same New Zealanders at Murrayfield the previous week. I was also mindful of the debacle at Netherdale earlier in the tour, when the All Blacks second team had beaten the South of Scotland 84–5. The South had been chosen to play the tourists because they were the Inter-district champions; the team included eight of the Melrose team which had won the Scottish Championship, so this was close to the best available talent in Scotland.

In one of my first interviews after taking over, in the *Sunday Times*, I said:

> As far as top quality players are concerned, I would like to
> see the structure organised so that these players could

188

acquire a competitive edge before they came to Scottish squads, so that the international coaches didn't have to extract a lot more out of them than is necessary. I see the main role of the Scottish coach as gelling the players together.

Even in late 1993, I was advocating a truncated league programme for the top players and more district matches. In the same article, the writer finished by stating that, if the recent heavy defeat to the All Blacks was any indication, Scotland was well on the way to the second division of international rugby. When you consider that only two years previously Scotland had been placed fourth in the World Cup, it was an amazing fall from grace.

The structure of competition in New Zealand was such that the best young players regularly took part in high-quality provincial matches. In the early to mid-'90s, this structure had been improved by the introduction of the Super 10 competition, which included the top provinces from New Zealand, Australia and South Africa, as well as, initially, sides from Samoa and Tonga. That competition became the Super 12 in 1996 and will, in 2006, be enlarged to the Super 14, though it remains a matter of some disappointment that since 1995 the 'big three' nations have not included any other southern-hemisphere nations in what is a fine competition.

I said in an SRU report at the time that Scotland had to be able to compete in that kind of provincial environment both at home and abroad, and we should adopt the slogan 'Small is beautiful, small is quality'. I pointed out that for young Scottish players to compete successfully, the SRU would have to improve in two crucial areas. These were: the nurturing of talent from senior school age upwards; and the development of a competitive structure which would adequately equip young players to compete at the highest level.

The defeats of the South and Scotland by the All Blacks should have acted as a wake-up call to Scottish rugby but, not for the first or last time – remember 1983, when the All Blacks beat the South by over 30 points – the warning fell on deaf ears. As far back as the World Cup in 1987, it was clear to me that our main competitors, especially in the southern hemisphere, were gearing up for the game going professional and it became even more obvious when South Africa were allowed back into the international fold in 1992.

In the summer of 1994, I embarked on three fact-finding missions: to Australia on my own; to Argentina with the Scotland team; and to South Africa with Melrose. The reason I went to Australia rather than New Zealand was that they were world champions at that time. Also, in Australia rugby union was competing with two major professional sports – Aussie rules and rugby league. Besides which, I wanted to look at the world-renowned Institute of Sport in Canberra.

As in other countries in the southern hemisphere, I found the hospitality first class and there was a great willingness to share ideas. When I arrived in Sydney, a local development officer by the name of Matt Williams met me and, of course, I got to know him quite well in later years, when he became the Waratahs coach, then moved to Leinster and more recently to Scotland as our national coach.

He was a great host and only too happy to show me what New South Wales rugby was doing. The set-up at one of the top schools in Sydney, St Joseph's College, where Matt helped out with the coaching of the boys, was very impressive. The school had the biggest weights room I have ever seen and state-of-the-art video analysis facilities. The boys had four or five practical sessions a week, on top of pre-school weights sessions, and I was as impressed by the quality of passing as I had been on my last visit to Australia in 1982. Of course, all the outdoor sessions were taken in perfect weather – but don't start me on my campaign for better-weather rugby in this country!

Watching them playing on the Saturday morning, I was struck by the high levels of individual and collective skills, and also by the speed and intensity. The physical development of the boys was very marked, which gave me the impression that I was watching an adult game, and one specific aspect of play which was exciting was the ability of the three-quarters to create opportunities out wide and, with flat, accurate passes, convert them into tries.

In a couple of days with John 'Box' O'Shea, a senior coach with the Australian Institute of Sport, I discovered how he spent his time working with video analysis, assessing individual players and devising tailored programmes to develop them. There were two major rugby-playing states at that time, Queensland and New South Wales. Each had their own institute and the best young rugby players were developed locally. I remember Box telling me that the holistic approach was central to the development of each player, usually starting immediately after he had left school.

We adopted similar guiding principles in Scotland when Bob Easson was appointed performance coach at the Scottish Institute of Sport in 2000. You may notice that there was quite a gap between my coming across the ideas in 1994 and their implementation in 2000, but that is indicative of how long it takes for anything to happen in rugby in Scotland.

Box was also responsible for monitoring new technical developments around the world. Monitoring trends on video was not new to me, as I had always been a video freak and most of my practices were based on finding out how the best players did things under pressure, then trying to replicate this with the players I coached.

A club match in Sydney produced rugby of a reasonably high standard even though the best players were away playing for New South Wales; but watching New South Wales v. Queensland a few days later was like watching an international. In Australia at that time, the clubs played for part of the season without their top players and then, after the provincial and Test matches were over and all the top players came back to their clubs, the club season was rounded off with a premiership. This was another idea I could see working in Scotland and which I proposed some time later, but our clubs knocked it on the head.

I also visited the Australian Institute of Sport headquarters in Canberra and, although I didn't see rugby there, I watched the top swimmers, under their Russian coach, and netball players going through their paces. Particularly interesting were the netball players, who showed tremendous strength in their wrists when they pinged the ball to each other – it was like a ball being shot from a cannon.

Everyone I met was very positive about developing their sport to new levels and relishing the challenges of competition, not only against international opposition but also between sports. Conferences were held where Aussie rules, rugby union and rugby league shared ideas. I left Australia feeling that the way in which a country with such a relatively small population was able to create top-level success in a wide variety of individual and team sports was quite remarkable.

Of course, money and resources are made available by central and state government, which encourages the whole population to take up a sport. Rugby union had been given a tremendous boost by Australia's win in the World Cup in 1991 and thousands of youngsters had flocked to try it. It was clear even during the World Cup in 2003 that rugby union was still not the major sport in the country, yet the rugby authorities worked tremendously hard to use the tournament to attract more people to the game and were very successful, with large crowds at every match, even in Tasmania, where Romania played against Namibia.

Argentina was the touring destination for Scotland in 1994. I travelled there after the early matches but in time to go to Rosario and Buenos Aires. This time there were no strikes or buses on fire, thankfully, and it was less painful than my tour of the 1960s. The Pumas have a reputation for being limited and capable only of a ten-man game, and in Mendoza and Córdoba the Scottish squad came across that kind of approach.

Rosario, however, were quite different and played a lovely brand of rugby which took the Scottish team by surprise. Interestingly, the exciting players at the heart of their adventurous play were pulled into a far more controlled kicking game by the Pumas in the Tests.

Scotland played two Tests and were desperately unlucky to lose 16–15 in the first and 19–17 in the second a week later. Considering that quite a number of established players were unavailable, including captain Gavin Hastings, Scott Hastings, Tony Stanger, Kenny Milne and Damian Cronin, the tour was regarded as quite successful.

People often wonder why Argentina has such a good record in international rugby, given that to this day it doesn't have any professional rugby. I discovered that rugby is very much a middle-class sport there and the system produces players who develop physically very quickly, so that, at Under-19 and Under-21 levels in particular, Argentinian players are often amongst the strongest in the world. When you ally that to a very good system at school, club and provincial levels, you clearly have a recipe for success.

The final visit of 1994 was to South Africa with Melrose in August. We left as Scottish club champions and most of our internationals, including Craig Chalmers, Bryan Redpath, Graham Shiel, Doddie Weir and Craig Joiner, were there.

We played four matches against club sides: Glenwood and Durban High School Old Boys in Durban, and Cape Town University and Villagers in Cape Town. Although we won the four matches, we struggled for long periods in some of them and the opposition were not even the best in Natal and Western Province respectively.

After the game at Glenwood, I spoke with Rodney Gould, the Springbok full-back who I had played against in 1968, and he told me that their club game was only 'average', as all the best players were playing for Natal in the Currie Cup. With my SRU director of rugby hat on, this worried me because, in many ways, the Melrose team at that time was not far short of a district side and here they were struggling against club teams.

The Melrose v. Villagers game was played at Newlands as a warm-up before their Western Province Currie Cup match, and the standard was markedly higher than it had been against the depleted Glenwood side. And yet South Africa was soon to introduce a new, higher level above the Currie Cup with the advent of the Super 10 and then Super 12 competitions.

Of all the experiences which I stored in my mind for future debate that summer, that club tour to South Africa was probably the most disturbing. Whilst in South Africa, I drove from Durban to Pretoria with Dunc Paterson, the Scottish manager, along with a mutual friend, Jim Chisholm. The purpose of the visit to Pretoria was to inspect the playing, training and hotel facilities for Scotland's World Cup campaign in 1995.

The car journey itself was a great learning experience, as we went up through the Drakensberg Mountains, passing through towns like Ladysmith and Harrismith with great Boer War significance, and I enjoyed the feeling of great space and the variety of the landscape. We passed a little school, a small one-room building in the middle of nowhere, and watching the young black children playing outside, all immaculate in their school uniforms, brought a tear to an old headmaster's eye.

We drove on to Rustenburg, where we were to play against the Ivory Coast in a World Cup pool match. Driving through the city, we eventually found this rather dilapidated ground with a small stand. Seeing the groundsman near the stand, we asked if we could have a look around. Having spent some time with us, showing us the dressing-rooms and other facilities, the groundsman eventually worked out why we were there.

'Oh, this isn't the World Cup ground,' he said. 'That's out the city a little bit.' He gave us directions and, on reaching it, we were amazed at what we saw. The city of Rustenburg was building a completely new ground for our game against the Ivory Coast and, although it was not yet finished, it was to be ready for the World Cup. A city official took us up to the top of the partly completed stand to show us that the rugby ground, complete with a superb irrigation system, was only part of a huge sports complex with a golf course and expansive car parks.

When I arrived home after three very enlightening tours, I was brimful of ideas and looking forward to the new season, to culminate in a World Cup in South Africa in 1995. The competitive structures and the development of elite players in Australia and South Africa were incredibly impressive. Of course, these countries were, as far as resources were concerned, way ahead of us but it was clear that Scottish rugby was being left behind and I knew we had to move to maximise the resources we had. If we could replicate some of their practices, that would represent a positive start.

Another of the things I did early on in my job was to meet with the head teachers of the independent schools in Scotland. The schools had always made a significant contribution to the game and had produced many quality players, so I wanted to see how the SRU and the schools could forge closer links for Scottish rugby's benefit. Although I felt that I had a fair hearing, the headmasters made it quite clear that the SRU would not be allowed to influence their collective thinking. They said that rugby was just one of many sports they played at their schools and they would continue playing it only if they believed it to be beneficial to their pupils and their schools.

Although I didn't mention the possibility of a more competitive structure within schools rugby, they wrong-footed me by saying that before the fixture lists could be changed, every single one of their schools would have to agree. If one objected, that amounted to a veto and there would be no change. I left the meeting quite downbeat, realising that this was another significant area of Scottish rugby which had to be won over.

Happily, the two organisations did begin to work together and within a few years most of the independent schools entered the Scottish Schools Cup competition. With the help of sponsors Bell Lawrie White, it has gone from strength to strength and evolved into several levels of Under-15 and Under-18 competitions.

But prior to 2000, Scotland fielded separate Under-18 Youth and Schools teams, and both suffered countless disappointing defeats, with only isolated victories. Clearly, something had to be done. It was agreed that the two sections should have one team at Under-18 international level and one at Under-18 A level, and that a national pathway for elite player development would be put into place from Under-15 level upwards. This development stemmed from what I and other people involved in Scottish rugby had witnessed around the world. Colin Thomson in particular, as national age-grade manager, had worked extremely hard and with great vision to create a structure that fitted the Scottish game, and it was good to see that beginning to pay dividends before I retired. But it took a lot of time and work to make people accept the problems we had.

Of course, my focus still had to be on the top level, where creating a competitive Test side remained a consuming challenge. Scotland had a fairly successful season leading up to the World Cup in 1995. South Africa were the guests in a game to mark the opening of the new stand at Murrayfield in November 1994. We were beaten 34–10 but the Scotland A team had beaten a strong Springboks side, which included Joel Stransky, who went on to kick the winning drop-goal in the World Cup final. The Scots won 19–17 at Melrose, thanks to a drop-goal by a young Duncan Hodge.

Scotland defeated Canada, Ireland and Wales at home, and then came the famous victory in Paris, when Gavin Hastings scored under the posts as a result of a sublime underarm reverse pass, the celebrated 'Toony flip', from Gregor Townsend. We went to Twickenham full of hope, another Grand Slam in the air, but after a poor game strewn with mistakes and penalties, we lost 24–12.

Our preparation for the World Cup in South Africa was very thorough. I had no direct responsibility for the team but I was included in the management during the build-up and the tournament. At the start of the season, I had set up a group called the World Cup countdown committee, which met regularly to monitor the progress being made towards the event. This group – including the chief executive, team manager, coach, captain, fitness adviser, medic and a representative from the media – looked at all aspects of preparation and was an excellent vehicle for keeping all interested parties informed.

Because we were due to play all our pool games at high altitude, in Pretoria and Rustenburg, it was important that the players were properly conditioned. We had asked the IRB if it was possible to do our acclimatisation in Zimbabwe, but the rules insisted that each country had to start their journey to the World Cup after a certain date from their place of origin. This was designed to ensure that the rich countries did not have great advantages over the poorer ones, which could not afford preparation camps. Because of the ruling, we would have had to return home from Zimbabwe and go back out to South Africa, so we abandoned that project.

Instead, after a warm-up match with Romania at Murrayfield, the tour squad spent a week at Navacerrada in Spain, which is at a similar altitude to Pretoria, and we played Spain in a final warm-up game. Unfortunately, Gregor Townsend injured ligaments playing in Gala's last league match of the season and he was added to a list of leading players unavailable, including Gary Armstrong, Andy Nicol and Andy Reed.

The World Cup squad enjoyed staying and playing in Pretoria – it is the most rugby-mad city in South Africa – and the locals appreciated Scotland's style of playing. For the second time in three tournaments, Scotland were beaten into second place in the pool stage by France under controversial circumstances. We were ahead going beyond full-time, having led France for the whole game, but after endless injury-time, Emile N'Tamack scored in the last seconds and France snatched victory from us, 22–19.

That defeat meant we were again paired with New Zealand in the quarter-final. The phenomenon Jonah Lomu had taken over the event and Scotland were very much a sideshow. Although the All Blacks won by a convincing 48–30, Scotland put in a gritty performance and actually played quite well. Doddie Weir went into the record books as the first Scot to score two tries against New Zealand in a Test match and Gavin Hastings set a new record with 44 points against the Ivory Coast in our first pool match as we won 89–0 at Rustenburg. He retired after the tournament and was chaired off the pitch after the All Blacks game by the players.

In the final analysis, the World Cup had been a success for Scotland; we'd reached the quarter-final for the second time, thus qualifying for the next tournament, to be hosted by Great Britain, Ireland and France in 1999.

Off the field, too, the tour was a success. Pretoria is a very historic city, so many of us walked to the impressive government buildings just up the road from the hotel or visited the Voortrekker Monument, on the outskirts of the city, which commemorates the famous Boer victory over the Zulus which led to the creation of the South African Republic. What many of the players were perhaps more excited about was the three-day trip to the exclusive game reserve Mala Mala after the French defeat, organised by team sponsors The Famous Grouse. The SRU also paid for a trip to Sun City and some posh golf on Gary Player's course there.

There was more evidence of the SRU being anything but mean: all the wives and girlfriends of the players and management were flown out to South Africa for three weeks and given spending money – one of Dunc's initiatives as manager.

It certainly helped make that World Cup a terrific experience for all involved, and though there was to be no repeat of the semi-finals of 1991 for us, I look back on that tournament with fond memories.

16

At Last – We Turn Professional

Gary Armstrong
Scotland (51 caps)
British and Irish Lions (1989)

It was never going to be easy in Scotland. But I don't think the players expected it to be quite as hard as it proved over the last decade.

Basically, when the game went professional, Scotland panicked. They put everything on hold for a year and as clubs started jumping on the bandwagon, thinking they could turn pro themselves, the SRU put around 100 players on three-year district contracts, and for a lot of money, including some who were never going to make the grade. Professionalism was moving much quicker elsewhere and Doddie [Weir] and I saw the chance of a fresh start when Newcastle coach Rob Andrew made us an offer to head south. It was the right decision for us.

But in pushing professional districts, Jim Telfer was right all along and if Scottish clubs had realised that at the start, we could have had a very different picture in Scottish rugby. There was no way clubs like Melrose, Stirling County, Heriot's or Watsonians, the top clubs at the time, could have turned pro. They would never have survived in the European competitions; the Scotland A team would struggle in the Heineken Cup. How it has taken them 10 years to accept that, I don't know. In fact, some still believe they could compete with the likes of Leicester, Toulouse and Munster. What a joke!

When Jim approached me, as well as Doddie and George [Graham], to return in 2002 and help him start up a new Borders team, it was a hard decision. I was offered a three-year deal to stay at Newcastle and play in the Zurich Premiership, go for more titles, with a youngster called Jonny Wilkinson to help through. But Jim knew I wanted to finish my career in the Borders – although if it hadn't been Jim asking, I don't know if I'd have come back.

It is a scandal that people have tried to lay the blame for what we've gone through since 1995 at the door of people like Jim and Ian McGeechan when the clubs, who have been very naive, and the bufties on committees who would get on the team bus with their golf clubs should take a long hard look at themselves. Jim committed everything to improving Scottish rugby and if he made mistakes, his intentions were good. Players like myself, J.J., Fin Calder, Derek White and Gregor Townsend will always have tremendous respect for him.

He took stick from some players over things like drink bans when he was simply trying to do things differently because he knew that for Scotland to win, especially against southern-hemisphere nations, things had to be done differently. Similarly, Jim realised that if Scottish professional rugby was to be a success, a fresh approach was needed. It's a pity more players and clubs did not understand that.

Some things in life are inevitable and rugby union turning professional was a certainty.

The 1987 inaugural Rugby World Cup was the catalyst for the move and as soon as South Africa were reinstated into world rugby, it was not a question of 'if', but 'when'. Although the SRU has often been accused of dragging its feet on instigating change, there is no doubt that in the last 25 years the committee could not have been more proactive in trying to maintain Scotland as a top rugby nation.

As most people in rugby know, the birth of the open game was very messy. For years, there were rumours that players in the southern hemisphere were being paid in some form or another and that rugby in France and Italy was semi-professional as well.

Despite all those underhand dealings, the SRU through its clubs was still staunchly in favour of keeping the game amateur. At the 1994 annual general meeting, one year before the changeover to professionalism was announced, two clubs, Heriot's FP and Aberdeen GSFP, put forward a motion that the SRU representatives on the IRB should resist any change to the status quo. Clubs were clearly not in favour of the game going professional.

Around the same time, the IRB set up a four-man working party, which included Fred McLeod, who was then the senior vice-president of the SRU and, along with Allan Hosie, our representative on the IRB. The purpose was to assess whether the regulations on amateurism were being breached. Its report was completed in early 1995 and presented to the IRB that March; it indicated that there were widespread breaches and concluded that the status quo was not viable. The IRB then told its members to take the report back to their unions; they would meet again after the World Cup to assess the future.

The media magnates Rupert Murdoch and his arch-rival Kerry Packer had become involved in proceedings, however, bidding to sign players up to televised professional circuses, ultimately forcing the hand of the IRB. If they were to enable clubs and unions to keep their best players – if, in effect, they were to keep the world game together – they would have to act quickly. After a momentous meeting in Paris from 26 to 28 August 1995, the IRB declared that the game was now open at all levels, almost exactly 100 years after the game had split in England into union and league after a similar dispute over whether players should be paid. The press statement said: 'Subsequent to the repeal of the amateur regulations, rugby will become an open game and there will be no prohibition on payment or the provision of other material benefit to any person involved in the game.' 'What a relief!' I thought. As a student of the game, I welcomed the change and although I knew that it would be very tough to compete with countries of greater resources at international level, I realised that professionalism would bring the potential for development.

For years, rugby union had been looked on as a Cinderella sport compared with football and rugby league, a game that its players and officials nurtured only in their spare time. This decision presented those involved with rugby union with opportunities for full-time careers in the sport. It was a chance, I felt, for the game finally to be taken seriously around the sporting world. I only wished that the change had come 30 years earlier, when I was a player – I would have grabbed the opportunity with both hands.

With my experience of Scotland's struggles to stay near the top of international rugby, I viewed the advent of professionalism as a chance to create once and for all a proper playing structure in our domestic game. I spoke earlier in the book of my feelings of despair on the Lions tour in 1983 when I saw first-hand the gulf between our structures and those of New Zealand. The preparation their players had for international rugby was so far superior to what our Lions came through; this was a chance to make a significant improvement.

With the thumping of the South and Scotland by the All Blacks and the recent Melrose tour to South Africa fresh in my mind, I knew that we had to put in place a new, fully professional competitive tier above club rugby as a preparation for consistently good results at international level. Naively, I believed that everyone in Scottish rugby would think the same and I put forward the idea that professional district rugby should be the new tier. After having studied the structures in so many other countries, I never countenanced the idea that Scottish clubs could turn professional.

Because of the constitution, the clubs *are* the SRU and so have always had the major say in how Scottish rugby is run. As a result, the resistance of a few to the professional districts has been able to significantly hold back development of that tier. Critics of mine said that districts had no identity, but that is bunkum. In the past, when touring teams came to Scotland, it was always district teams that played them, not clubs, simply because clubs were not strong enough. The Edinburgh v. Glasgow game was the oldest district fixture in the world and the Inter-district Championship had been going since 1953.

When districts played against touring teams, they always attracted huge crowds. There is a black-and-white picture of the South v. New South Wales in 1927 just inside the clubhouse door at Melrose Rugby Club and the crowd is huge and I have a video of the South v. All Blacks game at Hawick in 1963 when the crowd must have been in the region of 10,000.

Ireland is very similar to Scotland in rugby population and culture. They have four provinces, just like us, and those provinces played visiting touring teams and in inter-provincial championships. They had an advantage in having their own grounds, and a well-established administration in place; but then a key reason why our districts didn't have their own grounds was that the clubs didn't want them to become too powerful and made sure they remained peripatetic.

This brings me to perhaps the fundamental difference between Ireland and Scotland, which explains why they were able to move forward at a speed we could only dream of. Their union, the Irish Rugby Football Union (IRFU), is actually a union of the provinces, whereas the Scottish Rugby Union is a union of the clubs. Some clubs in Ireland were concerned about losing their star players as well but, after consultation, the IRFU decided which route they were taking. And the Irish provinces have been very successful.

The main reason why I favoured districts was because every club in Scotland could have an investment in the professional game: all young, quality players would have an avenue for promotion within their own area and all supporters would have a local professional team to get behind. Had we chosen clubs, then only a handful could be supported financially and I believed that that would alienate a lot of players and supporters. Players would inevitably be less inclined to move from, say, Hawick to Melrose, than they would from Hawick to Borders, which would be a natural progression and allow them to remain loyal to the club which brought them up and that club to be proud of them. In terms of supporters, could Melrose, Watsonians, Ayr or Kirkcaldy have attracted support across their whole district in the same way the Borders, Edinburgh, Glasgow and Caledonia might? In other words, if we went with districts, everyone in Scottish rugby could be part of this new revolution. The opportunities for people to get involved would be more evenly spread than if professionalism was limited to certain clubs.

Unfortunately, that was not the view taken by everybody and I had some very prominent opponents. At that time, the European

Cup was in the early stages of being developed, and in its first season, 1995–96, the SRU, as well as the RFU, decided not to enter any teams. However, for season 1996–97, Scotland was offered three places in the new cup competition. The SRU had by then decided that districts would be the way forward.

At an extraordinary general meeting on 8 February 1996, there was a challenge from eight clubs who wanted to put forward the case for clubs to represent Scotland instead. The Union's committee had listened closely to the views of the players and the consensus was that they preferred the district route.

At the debate, the senior vice-president Fred McLeod and myself put the Union's case for districts and two former Scotland players, Gavin Hastings of Watsonians and Melrose's Keith Robertson, put the case for clubs. The main thrust of the SRU's case was that we wanted a system where we had strong clubs and strong districts, leading to strong international teams; and that our resources, particularly in terms of player numbers, would be maximised if we went for district rugby, putting us in a position to compete on the European stage.

Fred pointed out that a French 'club' like Toulouse had 1,500 players to choose from, that Bègles-Bordeaux represented a great city and all the surrounding area, and he asked that we compare like with like. Scottish clubs, he stated, could not compete on an equal footing with those kinds of clubs. He also made the point that the clubs wanted district rugby up to Under-21 level and for the players then to play only club rugby, and added that following a clubs-into-Europe route would create super-clubs in perpetuity, leaving the rest of club rugby to wither.

I argued that in Edinburgh, for example, there would be the opportunity for all young players, from clubs like Heriot's, Boroughmuir, Currie, Watsonians, Stewart's Melville, Edinburgh Accies and others, to graduate to one professional club, Edinburgh. The top club in the Borders at that time was Melrose and it seemed very unfair to me that, to become professional, all young players from the surrounding clubs would have to go there.

There was also the fact that the presentation by Gavin and Keith worried smaller clubs, who could envisage the scenario of super-clubs taking all the money from the SRU to turn professional and threatening the existence of the rest by moving too far ahead. Over the next few seasons, when Melrose (1996–97) and Watsonians (1997–98) won the Division One championship, there was a feeling that they were almost state-sponsored, because they both had a lot of SRU-contracted professional players involved, and we were accused of having given them an unfair advantage.

Another thing which I don't think many realised at that time was that turning professional would change the whole ethos of a club. No longer would it be simply about serving the community and bringing on youngsters, attracting people into the clubrooms socially; instead it would become a business. Look at Wasps, the most successful English club of the moment, and how they relocated from Sudbury, their traditional home for a century, first to Queens Park Rangers' Loftus Road and then out of London altogether to High Wycombe, where they currently share with Wycombe Wanderers. Saracens are at Vicarage Road and Sale left their age-old home for Stockport County's ground.

These moves are made to improve the business and Melrose, who struggled with the council just to get floodlights, would have had to look at a similar move, to a town with more than 2,500 inhabitants and a stadium with more space for development. How would that have gone down at the Greenyards? Each club would also need 34 professional players to be registered to take part in the European Cup. Today, we only have three professional teams and, even scouring Scotland, it can be a struggle to fill those squads with experienced players.

At that 1996 meeting, there was animosity towards the club proposals from the floor. Leading that was Brian Simmers, then of Glasgow Accies and more recently chairman of Glasgow Hawks. He said that he had thought and read more about Scottish rugby in the months preceding that meeting than he had in 30 years of club involvement. And then, to audible intakes of breath in the room, he challenged the motives of the two great former internationalists for putting forward the club view.

Brian said he did not believe Gavin and Keith had the best interests of Scottish rugby at heart and that they were motivated purely by what was in the best interests of their respective clubs, Watsonians and Melrose. In a measured, well-delivered oratory, he insisted that money was the motivating factor in all power struggles between clubs and unions, and went further, stating that selfish ambition was driving Scotland's top clubs in their quest to play in Europe.

Interestingly, he spelled out how Scottish rugby's playing numbers were a fraction of the leading nations' and followed Fred in highlighting that the populations of areas around Bath, Toulouse, Leicester and Cardiff were so great that they should be compared with Scottish districts and not clubs. He added that Scotland should be looking to southern-hemisphere rugby, to their provincial structure, and setting our standards at their level.

The conclusion to a trenchant speech was quite clear – district rugby was the logical progression for Scotland's leading players, and districts, not clubs, should compete in Europe. He concluded by stating he was '100 per cent' in favour of districts in Europe.

Brian, a former Scotland internationalist and one-time Glasgow district coach, said a lot of what I was thinking and I was pleased with the audience's reaction – they voted 178 to 24 in favour of district teams leading Scotland into Europe. Only 12 clubs, with 2 votes each, voted for clubs in Europe at that time. I left that meeting honestly believing that that was the end of the arguments and we could move forward apace.

Ironically, a year or so later, Simmers became chairman of the new, ambitious club Glasgow Hawks – I helped advise them on their inception – and when they moved up the leagues, he changed his tune, arguing just as vigorously for districts to be scrapped and clubs to go into Europe. What about self-interest, then? He has since been quoted at length, many times, attacking me as some kind of devil figure for the direction in which I tried to take Scottish rugby.

That underlines just how Scottish rugby was riven by vested interests and such an about-face was a depressing example of how difficult it was to take a consistent, dynamic route when clubs were the major influence on any change. With that kind of thinking, I found it impossible to move forward with purpose and speed.

We decided to go down the district route, forming four professional district teams. Our approach was well researched and studied. For example, we looked at the Boston Report, an investigation into professional sport around the world, from

American football to basketball and many others, which had come out in New Zealand in the early 1990s. It stated that a population base of around 500,000 was necessary to sustain a professional sports team. I was well aware that the Borders had a population of only 100,000 but felt that, because of its traditions and the fact that it is the only region of Scotland where rugby is considered the number-one sport, it could be made viable.

But that statistic was the reason why the North and Midlands region (rebranded as 'Caledonia' after professionalism), which encompassed Dundee, Stirling, Aberdeen, Perth and Inverness, was an obvious choice to host another pro team, as were the cities of Glasgow and Edinburgh – all districts with a rugby tradition and a relatively large population.

The players were to be centrally contracted, as was the case in almost every other major rugby nation. England were different, as powerful clubs had stolen a march through their wealthy owners. The 12 Premiership clubs have also relied on RFU grants of close to £2 million each per season and have said quite openly that without that they would go under. And that is with crowds of around 10,000. Interestingly, this past season was the first in which even highly successful clubs like Newcastle and Sale actually made a profit, so there has been a lot of investment there over the past decade for little return, even at that level.

We began that 1996–97 season with three of the four districts entering Europe for the first time. We had full-time players, but part-time district coaches because the players still spent most of their time at their clubs.

The results showed a disappointing start, with the Borders Reivers launching their European Cup campaign in Pau, in France, and conceding 85 points, which was a humbling experience considering they had some of the leading Scotland players at the time on their team. Tony Stanger, Bryan Redpath, Craig Chalmers, Graham Shiel, Peter Wright, Steve Brotherstone, Adam Roxburgh, Jim Hay, Carl Hogg and Iain Fairley were among them. But back in the Borders, in front of a terrific 6,000-strong crowd at Mansfield Park, Gary Parker kicked them to victory over a Llanelli team which included Frano Botica. There were more great crowds for Glasgow, Edinburgh, the Borders and Caledonia in those early seasons, so there was a base to build on.

However, some clubs never accepted the district scenario and, before a year was up, there were renewed calls for a review of how Scottish rugby was being run. I agreed that the issue of governance was very important, but I was concerned at the proposals from the clubs for lumping together the professional game with the club game again, especially when the previous season had seen an overwhelming majority in favour of districts in Europe.

Four of my former international captains – Jim Aitken, Gavin Hastings, Fin Calder and David Sole – then joined forces in a bid to reverse that direction and put clubs into Europe as the professional standard-bearers of Scottish rugby.

Earlier in the '90s, through the initiative of Dunc Paterson, the convener of rugby, we had tried to involve well-known former players in administration, and we asked Finlay and David to become managers of the Scotland Under-18 and Under-19 teams. They accepted and proved very successful but they stepped down after one season due to pressure of work.

But I feared that there were underlying tensions simmering among the 'Gang of Four' which lay behind their desire to attack the SRU. David had had a run-in with the Union when he was suspended as a coach for criticising a referee after a club game and Jim Aitken had also had a tiff with the authorities when involved with Penicuik Rugby Club.

Gavin was a surprise to me because, although he was now strongly in support of clubs, he had advocated just as strongly in his 1994 book *High Balls and Happy Hours* that if Scottish rugby was to improve, it had to have more district games in order to allow players to compete regularly at a higher level. To quote him:

> It is my belief that . . . we should be playing more games at a district level, which would be a sort of equivalent of the provincial level in New Zealand, Australia and South Africa. Our district teams, the South, Edinburgh, Glasgow and the North and Midlands, are only barely comparable with club sides such as Leicester, Bath, Gloucester, Swansea or Cardiff.
>
> At the moment there are eight clubs in the first division of the Scottish league from Edinburgh. If these clubs act as

feeder teams then automatically the standard of rugby being played by the Edinburgh district team will be far higher.

He went on to criticise the SRU of that time for attempting to improve the quality of the club game and not taking the district route. I thought he spoke a lot of sense in that book. It mirrored what I believed, having, like him, spent a lot of time in the southern hemisphere. So, what changed, Gavin?

Finlay had always been a close friend and I retain a lot of respect for him but I couldn't understand why he was taking a strong stance for clubs then either.

The Gang of Four travelled the country putting on roadshows at clubs in which they would shoot down the SRU's policies and maintain that clubs were the way ahead. When you remember that Keith Robertson was with that group, you can see that it was quite a powerful lobby. Of all of them, Keith had the best ideas and had put the most thought into them. He advocated an eight-team semi-professional set-up, with two teams in each of the districts. But I could not envisage that really working in Scotland.

The criticism was not unexpected, because we knew it was never going to be an easy transition, but the manner of the attacks and the way respected men like those in the Gang of Four were changing their minds and swaying public opinion with what I felt was a surprising lack of knowledge of what was going on I found baffling and incredibly frustrating. We were doing our very best to make it work and never stopped working with people from other countries and sports to try and uncover the best route forward for our players and teams.

We had sent Roy Laidlaw and Douglas Arneil from the Union's Rugby Division down to Bradford Bulls in the summer of 1996 and they were advised by the fitness coaches there that players who went full time would become much stronger and quicker than part-timers, so that a gulf would swiftly appear. They told us that our players would need three years to reap the benefits of a professional regime. As a result of this advice, Roy and Douglas recommended in their report to the Union that Scottish rugby be split into two distinct games – professional and amateur. In the event, we were not given three years to develop four professional

Top: This Scotland squad – visiting a coal mine at Mount Isa – were the first, and last to date, to beat Australia on their own soil.

Above left: Colin Telfer, one of Scotland's best stand-offs, was my right-hand man as we headed towards a Grand Slam.

Above right: Mark Ella, the Australian master, shaped my back play.
(© Fotosport)

Top left and right: Willie John McBride and myself worked
hard to try and uncover Lions success in 1983.
(both © Popperfoto/Bob Thomas Sports Photography)

Above: The Scottish Lions were: back row (l–r): Dr Donald McLeod,
Jim Calder, Iain Paxton, John Beattie and me;
front row (l–r): John Rutherford, Roy Laidlaw, Colin Deans and Roger
Baird. Iain Milne was possibly investigating lunch!

Top: Ya beauty! The Triple Crown is ours for the first time in 46 years after a 32–9 victory at Lansdowne Road.

Above left and right: Winning the Grand Slam at Murrayfield was quite unbelievable and even outshone my 44th birthday! (left © Eric McCowat; right © The Scotsman Publications Ltd)

Try-scorer Tony Stanger, a former pupil of mine, delights in the 1990 Grand Slam (left) and the players celebrate (below), while the 'Brainstormers' (above) – Ian McGeechan, myself, Douglas Morgan and Derrick Grant – play it cool after beating England. (top and bottom © The Scotsman Publications Ltd)

Top: The British and Irish Lions victory over South Africa in 1997 was my career highlight, and even won Ian and me a 'golden boot'!

Below: These Lions heroes earned their place in history. (© Fotosport)

Celebrating the last Five Nations Championship victory in 1999, and consoling my greatest Scot, Gary Armstrong, after our defeat, and his last game, against the All Blacks in the 1999 World Cup.
(above courtesy of Ian Stewart; below © The Scotsman Publications Ltd/Ian Rutherford)

Top left: Receiving my MBE at Buckingham Palace in 1984
with Mark, Frances and Louise.

Top right: 'Meeting' Dr Danie Craven at Stellenbosch University in 1999.

Above left: A commemorative gift from The Famous Grouse,
very good sponsors, after the World Cup in 1999.
(© The Scotsman Publications Ltd)

Above right: Becoming 'Dr James Telfer' at Napier University in 2001.

The life of an international coach – you see it all!
(© The Scotsman Publications Limited)

districts. After only six months the SRU decided to cut two teams – 60 players – before our first season was even finished.

Roy also went to Hearts for some advice and asked if he could see around their fitness facilities, look at the gym and see how they did professional weight-training. What he found was a room with some rusty old weights lying in a corner and a table-tennis table in the middle of the room. He asked why the table-tennis table was up and was told that the players weren't really into weights and preferred playing table-tennis! There were no great lessons to be learned from Scottish football about creating athletes and it was somewhat disappointing to think about the way Australian sports work together to improve each other, while we in Scotland often work away in isolation.

There was no doubt that the SRU was struggling to cope with the demands of professionalism. Some committeemen – unpaid amateurs, of course – were at Murrayfield almost every day trying to cope with it all. So the Union set up an executive board, appointed Bill Watson as chief executive and moved Bill Hogg back to secretary to make the most of his expertise on club and international rugby. Three subordinate boards were established: the international game board; the domestic game board; and the business and development board. Andy Irvine, John Jeffrey and Iain Paxton joined the international board, and two prominent businessmen – Sir William Purves and Sir George Mathewson, both from the financial world – joined the committee.

The big dilemma the SRU had then, and wrestled with until this year, was that the organisation had a board which was trying to run a business and had to deliver winning teams and profits, but it was also a governing body with a responsibility to develop and run the sport. That was not an easy fit.

In season 1997–98, we took the decision to go full-time with four districts, each with a full-time coaching staff of two. We advertised for head coaches in the newspapers and had a tremendous response. Short leets were drawn up, interviews took place and Rob Moffat was appointed to the Borders, Ian Rankin to Caledonia Reds, Bob Easson to Edinburgh, and New Zealander Keith Robertson to Glasgow.

Keith had been an assistant coach with Otago Highlanders; Bob had coached Edinburgh Accies, and North and Midlands; Ian was coach at North and Midlands; and Rob was the coach of the Scottish club champions, Melrose. I remember going down to Heathrow Airport with Roy Laidlaw to interview Keith, as Otago were touring here at the time.

They were given the chance to choose their assistant coaches. Frank Hadden (Caledonia), Peter Gallagher (Borders), Henry Edwards (Edinburgh) and Gordon Macpherson (Glasgow) joined up. This was a difficult time for them because they all had to give up good jobs to come into Scottish professional rugby; none were close to retirement age, so it was a major statement of commitment.

The teams may not have been hugely successful but, just like the year before, there were some great games with very good crowds. Glasgow beat Ulster home and away, and beat Swansea at home to reach the quarter-final play-offs. Unfortunately, they came up against Leicester and suffered a humiliating 90–19 defeat at Welford Road. The Borders played in front of big crowds at Hawick, Kelso and Gala, and though they failed to win a game, they came very close to beating Bath away.

We had at last started a real professional tier and I was confident that it would become a competitive one, given time. And then we got the shock of our lives. Early in 1998, I had heard rumours that the committee was discussing cutting the number of professional teams to two. I was asked to put forward a case for the teams and the Rugby Division produced a paper outlining the advantages of the four-team system. I met with Bill Watson and other committee members to discuss it and I stressed to them that to go to two teams would be to narrow the base far too much and it would stunt the development of the age groups we had put in place.

I thought we'd won the argument, so when a meeting was called, I went along fully confident that the teams would remain. I had been told there would only be a discussion, so I was absolutely amazed when a vote was taken – I did not have a vote – and only a few people supported me. The committe voted to get rid of two teams by merging the four into two, which would be based in Edinburgh and Glasgow. The Caledonia representatives and the late Ken Crichton from Stirling County, who was a Glasgow rep, felt we should stick with four districts but their support was not enough to stop the mergers. They perhaps had an interest in keeping the Caledonia team; even the Borders representatives, however, voted to cut the teams to two.

The reason was mainly finance, I was told, but it was later said that the committee believed they were making a rugby decision. I know that some senior clubs were 'nipping the ears' of the committee about the number of players who were being taken away from them, and that probably swayed them.

It was obvious that the first batch of players to be lifted into professional rugby would leave a big hole in club rugby; but they would be replaced by younger players coming through. What the complainers seemed to be ignoring was the fact that the game elsewhere was now professional: Doddie Weir and Gary Armstong had already left Melrose and Jed-Forest respectively to go to Newcastle. Gregor Townsend had moved to Northampton, followed by Michael Dods, and the best players were always going to leave amateur clubs to join professional ones.

That vote shattered me and I seriously contemplated resigning at that point. I thought long and hard about what the future held, and then decided that it would be better to fight from within rather than watch it unravel from the outside. I didn't fall out with either Bill Watson or Dunc Paterson over the decision – I respected their expertise in both rugby and business. No matter how incredulous I felt at the decision, I resolved to try and make the new arrangement work; I felt I had to try and make a go of it for the benefit of all the players and officials who had committed themselves to us.

I have received criticism for not producing a stream of quality young players, but that decision to reduce the number of teams was a key factor in disrupting the development of many of our best young players. Caledonia and the Borders lost their star players, so the younger players had no local heroes to look up to – a valuable part of motivating young talent.

I was particularly disappointed that administrators, coaches and players who had placed their trust in the new system had been let down. What also angered me was the sudden loss of some of the network of development, academy systems and the growing number of young supporters who had been carefully nurtured in that first year. The Caledonia team in particular had made huge strides and had found a real identity at all levels of the game, with its shortened moniker 'Caley Reds'. There were great swathes of enthusiastic 'Young Reds' growing up all of a sudden and we received very positive reports from clubs, schools and development officers.

As director of rugby, it was my responsibility to contact the coaches of the four teams, including some who were in New Zealand with Super 12 teams as part of a fact-finding exercise, and break the news to them. I had received an agreement from Bill that each coaching team would be increased to three. So Keith Robertson remained the head coach at Glasgow, supported by Gordon Macpherson with Rob Moffat moved west, from the Borders, and Ian Rankin transferred to Edinburgh with Bob Easson and Henry Edwards as his assistants.

Frank Hadden went back to his job at Merchiston Castle School, from which he had been given a sabbatical year anyway, and I brought Peter Gallagher in to Murrayfield to work with underage teams. He is now Scotland Sevens manager. Although shell shocked by the decisions taken, they all acted very professionally and got on with the jobs given to them.

Although I had no direct dealings with the players who were made redundant, I felt sorry for them as well. Many had given up good jobs to try professional rugby and now were left to pick up the pieces. As I forecast at the time, many of them didn't return to their clubs but looked for new challenges in professional rugby outside Scotland. I thought that even the players who remained in the new teams must have felt very uncomfortable having just been herded together, but when I raised the issue, I was told by the SRU that they were the lucky ones and they just had to get on with it.

The new merged teams were termed 'super-districts', an unfortunate name which came back to haunt us. They were given the names Edinburgh Reivers and Glasgow Caledonians to try and maintain aspects of the four identities, and the SRU was ambitious, putting them into football grounds. Easter Road was to be Edinburgh Reivers' home and Firhill became Glasgow Caledonians' home, and, while the idea was ridiculed at the time, recent developments in other countries have shown that it was very innovative. As it turned out, most of the players liked playing at soccer grounds because of the even surface and short grass.

It was ambitious, to seek to build crowds over 10,000; but there was great resistance. Borders supporters wouldn't go to Edinburgh to watch a game and rugby supporters in general just wouldn't go to football grounds (mainly because of snobbery), except perhaps at McDiarmid Park in Perth, where the Caley Reds had built up a good following. Yet Wasps, Saracens, Sale and London Irish all play at soccer grounds in England, Toulouse go to 'Le Stadium', a soccer ground, for big games, and Munster and Biarritz played a cracking Heineken Cup quarter-final in 2005 at San Sebastián in Spain.

The lack of identity was a problem, despite some great games – Toulouse and Edinburgh at Easter Road on a sunny day in season 1998–9, which finished with the French nicking a 29–25 win stands out. But a major problem was that we did not have enough fixtures, so we had to create competitions for the teams. They went into the Scottish-Welsh League, which, mainly thanks to the efforts of Bill Watson, was eventually enlarged to the Celtic League.

It was a very difficult time at the top end of Scottish rugby, with so much hostility directed towards the professional set-ups, and I felt for the players, who were just pawns in the middle of a cultural and political maelstrom.

Administration was also taking up a lot of my time by this stage and there was also the small matter of coaching the Scotland team again, which kind of sneaked up on me. It was clear that being director of rugby was becoming more than a full-time job, however, and I laughed recently when people wondered what Ian McGeechan, my successor, actually did, the underlying suggestion being that it wasn't very much. The ex-players, including Jim Aitken and Ian McLauchlan, who voiced their opinions at the time were just plain ignorant!

The director of rugby was actively involved in recruiting players and, while I would leave interviewing them to the professional-team chief executives and coaches, I had to sign off on every one. I also attended practical sessions because I was the coaches' line manager on the playing side and was responsible for their appraisals. Responsibility for strategy on young players coming through in the districts fell to me and I also worked closely with Bob Easson, who had left his position at Edinburgh and joined the

Scottish Institute of Sport. I helped to appoint the fitness coaches, physiotherapists and medical staff for the professional teams, and I appointed and appraised the managements of all the Scotland national squads.

One of my responsibilities was obviously to attend board meetings and there was a lot of work on the club front, including going to club and district meetings, focus group meetings and attending games every weekend. Anti-doping procedures and child protection legislation had recently become huge issues and they were both part of the Rugby Division's responsibility, as were player registration and eligibility, women's rugby, referees, development officers, coach education and coaching Scottish Vocational Qualifications, domestic league and cup competitions, schools and youth rugby, the lot. I also attended meetings with government agencies and the local authorities, and I frequently met my opposite numbers in other unions. Oh, and of course overseeing the budgets for these areas was not an easy task in the cash-strapped SRU. I was fortunate to have a very committed and competent staff, to whom I delegated a lot of responsibility and major decision-making.

By the time Ian took over, the job had grown enormously from what it had been when I'd first started, and I wasn't surprised when the Genesis Review of 2005 suggested two directors of rugby, one responsible for the professional game and one for the amateur. It is worth pointing out that the Lord Mackay Report in 2000 had made the same suggestion but it was not implemented. It wasn't the only aspect of that wide-ranging independent report to be ignored.

17

Time to Make Changes

Richie Dixon
Scotland B captain
Scotland coach (1995–98)
SRU interim director of rugby (2005)
SRU head of coach development

Coaching Scotland was a great honour and I felt confident I was doing a good job, so it was a big shock when my assistant coach David Johnston and I were sacked.

As I have said, Jim and I have always had a great friendship founded on a deep mutual respect. But there is no doubt that that was tested to the full in 1998 when he and the SRU decided David and I should no longer coach the national side. I was bloody annoyed, I can tell you. We had only been denied a Grand Slam by an 18-9 defeat at Twickenham in 1996, and had beaten Ireland at Murrayfield by a record 38–10 scoreline in 1997. We lost the other three games and conceded 47 points in France, which was our worst up to then, but the 90 points we scored set a new Scottish record for a Championship.

We were developing a new style of play, moving away from the rucking which opposition teams were reading much better and instead working on moving the ball out of contact. The forwards were playing better rugby than they had in some time and we were scoring more tries. David was a very good backs coach. As a player and coach, he was very much a free spirit and, having played football and rugby to high levels, was comfortable with how he played and coached.

215

David and Jim did not always see eye to eye but they were professional and did not let that get in the way of their work. As a manager, Jim was very good in his role and I don't agree with players who said he overstepped the mark. That was not true. There are different reasons why players are critical and often it's a knee-jerk reaction and should not be taken too seriously.

David and Jim were both very good at what they did, but they came from different directions. Jim had been there, seen it and done it all, like I had, whereas David was a youngster and full of ambition. But they were both committed and, for that matter, so was I. I felt I was a good national coach.

The sack came after a last-minute try cost us victory to Italy at the start of 1998. It was a much better Italian team than the one that came into the Six Nations Championship two years later, and other coaches have lost to worse teams. So I think the decision was as much to do with the mood around Scottish rugby at the time, with the media calling for the heads of everyone – Dunc Paterson, Charlie Bisset, Jim, the coaches. We were all apparently to blame for the fact Scottish rugby was struggling to cope with the demands of professionalism. David and I were the wrong people in the wrong place at the wrong time.

I thought it was a mistake to sack us but I got on with it. I was head of coach development at Murrayfield at the same time, so I turned up for work on the Monday, didn't let anyone see how upset I was and just got on with it; it was about being professional. The sacking didn't alter the respect I have for Jim, to be honest, because we went through a lot before and after then, but I do wish it could have been different.

No matter how much I believed coaching to be something in my past, the role of guiding the Scotland team just kept on coming back.

I have to admit that getting away from the administration and office work was not something that displeased me, but the manner in which I returned to the post of head coach with Scotland was not a happy experience. It involved me removing coaches Richie Dixon and David Johnston, perhaps the toughest decision I ever took in my career.

After the 1995 World Cup, Dunc Paterson, the manager, and coach Dougie Morgan stood down, and I recommended Richie and David to take over. Richie, who had been assistant coach, was appointed head coach and David, who had been the A team coach, was promoted to assistant coach. They had worked together on quite a number of occasions in the late 1980s and early 1990s, including a South Seas tour in 1993, and though they were different, they seemed to work well as a pair.

At the same time, Dunc in his capacity as convener of rugby asked if I would replace him as manager. The committee felt my experience would help the squad at that time, especially with a tour to New Zealand coming up at the end of Richie and David's first season.

We changed the name from manager to 'national coaching director' to reflect the changing role which I took on. Up until then, the manager had been a member of the committee and did all the administrative duties – usually to a very high standard, I might add.

As I did not come from that background, I took a different approach. I was to be the chairman of selectors, as the manager had been in the past, but I was also in overall charge of the general playing strategy. I had no practical coaching responsibility, however, and was very conscious of not interfering in the coaching sessions and team meetings, which were the domain of the two coaches.

Early in September 1995, Richie, David and I had a meeting to discuss our roles, and later that month these were explained to the players. I have since discovered that David was resentful of my appointment, probably because he felt that I would have too much say in how the games were to be played. Richie was happy; he knew me well and we had like minds.

Richie was very keen to get the forwards in particular to play the ball out of contact, which was a reflection of the way the game was going and something the players had been encouraged to do in the World Cup in South Africa the previous year.

Their first game in charge was a 15–15 draw with Western Samoa at Murrayfield in the autumn of 1995 in which we were outscored two tries to nil and were a bit lucky. They then led the team to good wins against Ireland, France and Wales. The team played very well but I was a bit frustrated that we nearly let the Welsh and French back in to steal those games. We were capable of quite comprehensive wins but we beat France just 19–14 and Wales just 16–14 a fortnight later.

We approached the Grand Slam game with England with a fair amount of confidence, only to fail to see the ball for most of the 80 minutes because it was wrapped in the big hands or up the jumper of Dean Richards. We cited Jason Leonard for a straight-arm hit on Rob Wainwright which left our captain groggy for part of the game. Richie and I went down to London to put our case to the hearing. We put forward a strong case but were outflanked by Jason's City lawyer from Harlequins, who insisted his client would never attempt such a thing, and the video evidence was not as helpful as we had hoped.

I went on the Lions tour with Jason the following year and we got on very well, so he obviously did not bear a grudge.

I was beginning to find David a bit different. I was chairman of selectors and we had a meeting in late March 1996 to discuss the tour squad for New Zealand. David sent me a pretty ridiculous letter beforehand, outlining how the meeting should be organised. It detailed how much time we should spend on discussion of games played and of players, namely ten minutes for this and twenty minutes for something else. Having run a school for ten years with around 1,200 pupils and 80 staff, I had developed a fair idea of how to run a meeting efficiently and thought it was a bit of a cheek. It reminded me of the time when a friend of mine went in to see his accountant and the accountant sat a big clock in front of him and switched it on, indicating that time was money.

Ironically, a year later when Arthur Hastie was manager and chairman, some of the selection meetings went on far longer than mine, mainly because the coaches couldn't make their minds up. I sometimes wondered if Arthur got the same memo as I did!

When it came to the New Zealand tour, I seemed to cause a bit of a furore at the press announcement of the squad when I was asked why Michael Dods was left out and said quite honestly that it was because he wasn't good enough. I always try to be honest with the media and, though it had been a collective decision, I felt it was important that I took responsibility.

218

Michael had started four internationals and kicked points in all of them; he had scored the two tries and kicked the other points in the 19–14 win over France, which was a great achievement for him. But I explained that the selectors had decided they did not consider him good enough to go as a wing, possibly facing Jonah Lomu, and that the fact was that his goal-kicking success rate was only 47 per cent, which wasn't good enough for that role. I felt I was being open and fair, but the media criticised me for that.

The wingers we opted for were Kenny Logan, Tony Stanger, Craig Joiner and Derek Stark, with Rowen Shepherd and Stuart Lang going as full-backs. They all had a physical presence, which we felt was vital for a tour to New Zealand. We had already lost Bryan Redpath before the tour because of a stress fracture in his lower back.

I became the target of a bit of criticism from within the tour party as well. Scott Hastings was very unfavourable in his autobiography because we had tried to advise the players against taking drink during the week. It was the first chapter of his book and I think there was probably a need to make an early impact, but it disappointed me because I have always had a good relationship with Scott. He accused me of being an interfering schoolmaster, out-of-touch with the players' needs in the professional era. According to David Johnston in a report made after the tour, there was nearly a mutiny against me. I've since wondered if he was part of the alleged conspiracy!

I have no qualms about criticism when it is fair but this upset and baffled me. The feedback I had was that a few of the players did not like the idea of being told they should not drink, which was not my own decision but a collective management one. Certainly, no player or coach ever came to me and said there was a problem, and there were players there who would have no hesitation in telling me straight – Craig Chalmers, Gary Armstrong, the captain Rob Wainwright, Damian Cronin and Peter Wright, for example – and Richie Dixon was never scared to tell me what he thought. Yet no one said anything.

To me, it was a normal, happy tour, but there was a major difference to tours before: this was the first professional tour for a Scotland squad and I felt strongly about making it one to remember for everybody – the players, the management and the nation. We actually decided to call our opposition not the All Blacks but just plain New Zealand in an effort to take away some of the aura around them.

I used my speech at the start of the tour to say to them, 'Look, lads, we have never beaten New Zealand before. If we do the same things as we have done in the past, we will just go home as the happy losers. Why don't we try something different for the next five weeks – shut up shop, have no drinking during the week and put all our efforts into beating New Zealand?'

There was no stopping social events, the players played golf and they could have a drink at weekends, but I tried to emphasise how we might feel psychologically and physically better in the games if we had 'dry' weeks. Scott said I ruined the camaraderie of the tour but I don't think he understood what we were trying to do. I had discussed the issue with David McLean, our fitness coach, who was trying to educate the players on diet and alcohol consumption. He was keen to have alcohol removed from the weekday routine and, having studied the latest research on how alcohol affects sports performance, I fully supported him.

The 1971 Lions, who won the series in New Zealand, had the very same rule: players were advised and agreed right at the start of that tour that they would not drink during the week. There was a clear focus among them, a desire to achieve something the Lions hadn't done before, and that was over 20 years before professionalism. To me, what was good enough for the Lions was good enough for Scotland.

In fact, after the First Test in 1996, one seasoned New Zealand reporter commented on how fresh the All Blacks were on the Sunday morning after the game, having not taken any drink the night before. They had been up at 7.30 a.m., watched the video of the game, and were ready to move on at 8.30 a.m. That was how they approached professional rugby.

It wasn't only the alcohol that concerned me, to be honest, because by that stage the media in general were taking a greater interest in the game, the tours and the players, and tabloids were beginning to turn up looking to see what the players were doing at nights. It's a different kind of interest, not straightforward rugby reporting, and it was clear to me that a lot of our players weren't at all aware of that. I'm not into spilling beans about things that go on on tours and that's not what this book is about; but some things have traditionally been hushed up, even by journalists.

That changed when the game became professional. I was warned about it and saw it myself: players could no longer expect their occasional excesses to be ignored. But I'm talking about players in general because, in fairness, there were not many on that 1996 tour I would worry about. These were a good bunch of Scottish players but, collectively, rugby players can get a bit boisterous. Things get misinterpreted and when it's in print, you can't retract it. As manager on Scotland's first professional tour, I was keen to avoid those kinds of off-the-field pitfalls.

The suggestion from Scott that his upset at not being allowed to drink meant that I was the wrong choice to be the manager is one I would strongly refute. Richie even praised me in his tour report. He said, 'Jim Telfer's previous knowledge of New Zealand was of great value to me. His organisation and administration of the tour were, in my opinion, exemplary.'

I did wear a tracksuit because it seemed natural and, yes, I led team talks before we played, perhaps because of the experience I had of playing in New Zealand with Scotland and Lions teams over the years. Bear in mind this was the first tour to New Zealand for either coach. The manager on the Lions tour the next year, Fran Cotton, had the same approach and would speak to the players before games. With him, the job was much more than just being an administrator.

There are clear parallels with the modern style of Sir Clive Woodward. According to players and coaches who have worked with him, he is a great organiser, manages players on and off the field, is involved in tactics, but does not actually coach or work on player technique. That was the kind of role I envisaged for myself as a manager at that time.

When I read Scott's book and articles by David Johnston on the tour, I was at a loss as to what they were getting at. I have had a fair bit of criticism in my time, particularly from past players, but some things become exaggerated and twisted over time, often because of personal feelings about other matters. I do take criticism harder than perhaps I have shown outwardly and it was difficult reading people, many of whom have never worked with me, spread the myth that I was poor at 'man-management' or treated all my players like schoolchildren. That hurt me more than the criticism of alcohol bans ever did, to be honest.

Having worked as a headmaster for nearly ten years, I felt that man-management was one of my strengths. My feeling is that these perceived problems on my part were just excuses used by some of the older players who wanted 'a good time', whatever that was. It was a lack of maturity over what professionalism was about. Surely, for just five weeks they could have given that up for the cause of trying to win for Scotland; that's what annoys me. I know in my heart that some Scotland teams have been capable of laying that ghost of beating New Zealand in the same way the other home nations have and have not taken the opportunity.

I would never say that any Scotland player did not care about winning for his country, but some are prepared to go further than others to do it. Many of these players had been to New Zealand with the Lions in 1993 – Scott got his face badly smashed on that tour – and I felt that they, in particular, would want revenge, the chance to take on and beat the All Blacks. Yet Richie's report of the matches showed that our game was riddled with inconsistency right through the tour: playing well, playing poorly, scoring some lovely tries, losing silly tries.

We had a good squad with us and we knew the quality we would face from the start. David and I had gone up to Auckland to watch the Super 12 final between the Blues and the Sharks before our first game against Wanganui. That merely underlined the high standard of provincial rugby in New Zealand. We beat Wanganui comfortably and then played very poorly against Northland on a wet and windy Friday night, with some senior players in particular unable to lift their game.

We played well against a quality Waikato side full of Super 12 players and were leading 22–12 at half-time. We lost the lead late on and missed several scoring chances so the win slipped through our fingers, but it had been an improvement. Yet we then let our standards drop against Southland. Having again built up an early lead, we, the Scotland national team, really struggled to win in the end against a second-division NPC side.

I had a blast at the team after that game. Scotland always seem to have a period of playing bloody awful, and the purpose of that

222

blast was to try and get rid of that – to impress upon the players the need to get consistency and concentration for 80 minutes. But that was where David reckoned I had gone too far and almost provoked a mutiny.

The team reacted by beating a third-division team by 60 points in Blenheim, despite not actually playing that well. Unfortunately, we lost both centres, Graham Shiel and Scott Hastings, with knee injuries in that game. Graham, sadly, didn't win another cap until 2000, but Scott returned before the end of the tour.

We went down to Dunedin and played some nice rugby against the All Blacks in the First Test, and won as much possession as them. But they had Christian Cullen, Jonah Lomu and Jeff Wilson – not a bad back three. Craig Joiner was introduced to the star that was Lomu, and Ronnie Eriksson won his first Test cap, against the renowned Frank Bunce. We worked hard and were termed 'defiant' by our media, but we lost 62–31, a record number of points conceded at that time, and the players had seen first-hand how much they had to step up to take on a New Zealand side.

Cullen had made his Test debut in their warm-up match against Western Samoa, in which he'd scored three tries, and the 'Paekakariki Express' followed up with four against us. The New Zealand media dismissed our performance as merely another indication of 'the widening gulf between the hemispheres'.

We had more worries off the field to contend with before the Second Test when we were training for the Bay of Plenty game in Rotorua. Volcanic ash from Mount Ruapehu, 50 miles away, created a pall of thick smoke across the training pitch at the Rotorua Boys High School and Richie had to curtail the session. Craig Chalmers, for one, couldn't see; he was rubbing his eyes and looked like he was wearing mascara. We had already had to deal with a fire alarm going off in our hotel in Wanganui and an earthquake on tour – were they trying to tell us something?

The Bay of Plenty game was in doubt as there was ash on the pitch and there was a fear it might burn the players. We met the town officials at 7 a.m. on the morning of the match in a bunker with all the seismic apparatus around us, but the ash was swept up by a mower and the game went ahead. It was a beautiful day, the ground was perfect and we won 35–31 after a bit of a struggle.

223

Chalmers' kicking wasn't great and Stuart Lang, the former Kelso and Heriot's full-back, took over. After Andy Nicol scored a second try, Lang converted superbly from the touch-line, and then sealed the win with two late penalties.

We played very well in the Second Test, when the Eden Park pitch in Auckland was almost unplayable because of torrential rain. We were only behind 21–7 at half-time, despite playing into the driving rain and swirling wind, and Richie told the team they were just '40 minutes from glory'. However, this was an occasion very similar to that of my Lions experience in the Second Test at Wellington in 1983, when the All Blacks, especially Dave Loveridge, came out and showed how to play the conditions.

Outstanding displays, this time by Michael Jones and Justin Marshall, who was playing in only his fourth Test, turned the match and they eventually won 36–12. Four of the five All Blacks tries stemmed from scrum dominance, which suited them in the conditions, while we were giving young prop Barry Stewart his first cap against Craig Dowd, one of the best scrummagers in the world.

Unfortunately, two players were cited in that game by an independent match commissioner, Australian Terry Willis, and the hearing took place just before the after-match function. The two players, Frank Bunce and Kevin McKenzie, were accused of foul play – they were fighting with each other. In view of my experience in London earlier in the year after the citing of Jason Leonard, I took David Johnston, a lawyer, into the hearing with me. John Hart, the New Zealand coach, represented Bunce.

Both John and David disappointed me in their attitude towards the commissioner, John remonstrating that the whole hearing was a waste of time, especially when there was a dinner being held, and David trying to baffle him with legal jargon and references to past case histories. The commissioner, having heard both submissions, was quite laid back and said something to the effect of, 'Do you think I came up the river in a banana boat?'

A qualified QC, he knew exactly what had gone on, that it had not been too serious, and he was almost laughing to himself at the way the two coaches were trying to pull the wool over his eyes. He duly wrapped it up quickly, saying they could actually have got 30-day suspensions each for striking each other but that he felt that there was no need in this instance. It was quite obvious to me that he was planning that line of action all along, and that John and David nearly cost us something worse.

Unbeknown to me, David, Richie and Rob, the tour captain, were working on a paper in New Zealand called 'The Future of Scottish Rugby', which they produced at the end of the tour. To me it merely underlined why we should continue down the district route, for which I have been heavily criticised by some Scottish clubs since. They had spoken to players, management and media, and in the paper they pointed to the gulf between northern- and southern-hemisphere rugby in advocating a route for Scotland of strong districts and strong clubs. They suggested that we should have a draft system, which meant moving players around the country to make up squads as they do in American football, and also proposed district leagues to replace the existing top-level domestic set-up.

The report's introduction read:

> The call for provincial/district rugby is again sounding from the rooftops, with the rider that whereas previous calls have gone unheeded, action must now be taken immediately if we are not to be consigned to the second division of world rugby or even slipping into the third. Parochialism and self-interest cannot, however, stand in the way of the future of our game. This paper is an attempt by the coaches and captain of the New Zealand tour to accelerate the process . . . by putting some meat on the bones of the proposal for more district rugby.

The report's conclusions did not surprise me because tours to New Zealand invariably illustrated the difference between a leading nation and ours, yet also highlighted the similarities between us. And yet I spent the next eight years fighting, year after year, to drive district rugby forward. Agreement in Scottish rugby? If it hadn't been such a painful time, I would laugh at how ridiculous that hope turned out to be.

One other innovation which struck me during that tour to New Zealand was the launching of a new rugby academy, run by Brendan Radcliffe, who later became Wayne Smith's assistant at

Northampton. Some of the first-year inductees, taken from provinces all over the country, were: Doug Howlett, Christian Cullen, Pita Alatini, Norm Maxwell and Quentin Sanft, who Kirkcaldy and Biggar supporters will know very well.

Two years later, I watched the NZ Academy side on TV taking on England in that 1998 'Tour from Hell', which Jonny Wilkinson still talks about as being a massive learning curve, and they wiped the floor with the tourists.

Our tour was memorable for Scott Hastings in more positive ways, I'm sure, as, having missed the First Test through injury, he won his 62nd cap in the Second Test to overtake his brother and become Scotland's most-capped player. It was a great honour for Scott, who has at times lived in the shadow of Gavin, but who has undoubtedly been as good a servant to Scottish rugby.

The following season, 1996–97, was quite a difficult one. It was our first full season of professionalism with the players contracted centrally to the Scottish Rugby Union. The district coaches were still only part-time. The players spent most of the season with their clubs but came together in the district teams for the European Cup and Inter-district Championship.

The contracted players would come to Murrayfield during the day and be coached by Richie Dixon mainly and myself occasionally. I remember that Ian Barnes was one of the Edinburgh coaches at that time, with Graham Hogg. He has become an outspoken critic of district rugby since then, but he was certainly in favour of districts when he was coaching in the set-up. I have been left wondering whether the vitriolic, personal attacks on me were the result of him being passed over for one of the full-time coaching jobs in 1997.

But my relationship with David Johnston was again becoming strained. He was still an assistant to Richie, but I was concerned that he was spending a lot of his energies on Union politics to the possible detriment of the time spent with Richie and the national squad.

He was working full time as a lawyer and was contracted to come to Murrayfield for two sessions a week and two-thirds of his working time in the lead-up to the games. In a memo to me, he wrote that he couldn't divorce the roles of coach and lawyer, and that, as well as coaching, he wanted to represent management –

and probably the players as well – in salary negotiations, suggesting, for example, that everyone – the coaches, manager and selectors – should be paid the same as Scotland's top players. He insisted the players would not respect the management if they weren't on the same salaries, but I would have thought that confidentiality would have ensured they didn't know what salaries were being paid. It seemed to be a big issue with him – he insisted that he was acting on behalf of future managements – despite the fact that, unbeknown to me, he had negotiated his own fee with the top officials at the SRU. I usually negotiated all the fees of the national management team with Bill Hogg, the chief executive. I discovered later that, pro rata, he was the highest-paid individual in our entire Rugby Division, including myself.

I believe that coaches deserve to be properly recompensed, but the amount paid has to be relative to the wealth of the employer. By the time I left Murrayfield in 2003, the Union was so cash-strapped that the managements working with age-grade teams were doing it for practically nothing, surely an indication of how dedicated they were.

The next period was marked by negotiations, as players, the exiles in particular, began to test the will of the SRU over professional payments. It sometimes led to fall-outs and refusals to train. I had some sympathy with the players because the SRU moved so slowly then and it was frustrating. The whole issue of paying players and assessing their real value in the marketplace was a major headache. What were players worth? What should Scots in Scotland and Scots earning much more out of Scotland be paid to represent their country? It was very new to us, but it was clearly an issue which had to be sorted out quite quickly to allow us all to concentrate on improving performances on the field.

Season 1996–97 was not nearly as successful as the one before, when we'd come close to the Grand Slam. The inconsistencies of the tour continued, and frustrated Richie and David quite a bit. We lost to Australia in November, 29–19, and then lost to Wales and England by big margins before beating Ireland 38–10 to lift our spirits a bit.

That was the first time Alan Tait returned to the Scotland team after a period in rugby league. David, as backs coach, had resisted Alan's selection, despite him showing up well for the A team against Wales, and insisted he should stay in the A team for a bit longer. But by this stage, the British and Irish Lions had announced Alan in their big squad of 62.

I was not involved in Scottish selection but I was one of the Lions selectors. I remember Bill Lothian of the *Edinburgh Evening News* reporting that the Scottish selectors had delivered 'a massive snub to Murrayfield reject Tait' by only picking him in the Scotland A team and not the full Scotland side for the next game.

Alan actually withdrew from the next game, against England A, with a groin injury, and the selectors then persuaded David that he had to be in when he recovered. There was a month between the England and Ireland games, so he was fit and duly scored a try on his return. But the team were heavily beaten by France in the final game – the 47–20 defeat was our worst in the Championship at that point.

Ian McGeechan and I enjoyed the Lions adventure in South Africa in the summer of 1997 – more of that in the next chapter – and came back keen to encourage the Scotland management and players to learn from some of the discoveries we had made about leading players on that tour. There was no quick fix. That autumn, the team lost to Australia 37–8 and then suffered a humiliating defeat – a record which still stands – going down 68–10 to South Africa, in a game in which Percy Montgomery really came into his own as a world-class full-back.

The next year merely saw the gloom deepen. We headed to Italy in January 1998 before the Five Nations got underway for a match which two years later would become part of the new Six Nations Championship but which at that stage was still a friendly. We lost the game 25–21, despite feeling we had a very good team. Players like Tony Stanger, Alan Tait, Craig Chalmers, Gregor Townsend, Gary Armstrong, Dave Hilton, Doddie Weir, Scott Murray and Rob Wainwright were all involved, yet it was another embarrassment for Scottish rugby.

As was the custom at that time, the coaches met the players the morning after the match before departing for home. I remember quite clearly the meeting after the Italy game. There was a real sense of doom and gloom. I knew at that point that something had to be done to change that mood before the next game, against Ireland in a fortnight. I wasn't sure what, however.

The selectors met on the Monday night following the game and picked a squad to face Ireland, but Bill Watson, Dunc Paterson and I met later to discuss concerns about the direction the team was going in. At the meeting, I recommended that the coaches be replaced, indicating that I felt that there was a staleness about the relationship between the players and the coaches, and that it might even deteriorate further. I thought they had lost faith in each other and that the best solution was to bring in fresh faces.

It was an incredibly tough decision and I felt extremely sorry for both coaches, because they had undoubtedly done a lot for Scottish rugby, both as players and as coaches. What I have to make clear, as it has been questioned since, is that this was purely a rugby decision, based on the coaches' abilities to lead the Scotland team forward and upwards. The sometimes rocky relationship I had with David had nothing to do with my decision, and I say that with a clear conscience.

The next question was who would take over. Bill and Dunc asked if I would take the reins in the short term, but no specific tenure was agreed as they considered their next move. I said I would, although I still had my director of rugby role so, at that stage, I didn't envisage the coaching role lasting very long.

It was a pity that David walked away from coaching altogether. He had been coaching for less than a decade and I was disappointed that he blamed me for ending his coaching career. I had hoped that he would continue, learn from the experience and come back stronger. It had been very hard for me to take such a serious decision and, as a coach, I sympathised with him, but I still feel it was the right thing to do at that time. I admired Richie for the way he accepted the decision. Although he was bitterly disappointed, he remained committed to his coach-development role at Murrayfield and continues to do a very professional job.

18

The Lions Roar – At Last!

Ian McGeechan
Scotland (32 caps)
British and Irish Lions (1974, 1977)
Scotland coach (1988–94, 2000–03)
British and Irish Lions coach (1989, 1993, 1997, 2005)

A long-haired skinny lad from Leeds and a gruff back-row forward from the Border hills – the perfect combination for British and Irish Lions success?

I only really got to know Jim when I stopped playing as, thankfully, I had never been dropped when I played for Scotland, so I didn't play in the B team when he coached them in the 1970s. Having moved into coaching myself, I stepped up and took the B team when he went on the Lions tour in 1983, and when he returned, we started to discover we had similar outlooks on the game.

We had a long night in Benevento in Italy with the B team, and we just sat and talked rugby through the night and into the morning. My first impression of him was that he was a very gentle man; he is actually a very good listener. Jim has always had the bigger picture in his mind, not just Melrose or the Borders, but what he can do for Scottish rugby.

When we coached together with Scotland in the 1980s and early '90s, we would disagree, sometimes in front of the players, and it wasn't ever us having great fall-outs. We just had this absolutely open relationship where we were both trying to drive things forward.

When I was asked to be Scotland coach in 1988, I wanted him to be my assistant and I used players to help persuade him to join us – he was head of Hawick High School then. Fin Calder was one who went to see him about it and he still jokes, 'We knew what we were letting ourselves in for, but we knew we needed him for the forwards.' There are some past players who are now highly critical of Jim, yet some of them would never even have played international rugby had it not been for him. He was a master at lifting players up to a level they didn't know they could achieve.

Jim and I just grew from there. Our wives became very good friends and we've discussed, very personally, things we've done, or would do, which I certainly wouldn't discuss with others. So when it came to 1996 and I was asked to coach the 1997 Lions, I asked if I could pick my own assistant. Fran Cotton, the manager, said yes, and I told him I wanted Jim with me.

We thought the same way; we each had absolute confidence in what the other was doing at either end of the field. It sounds stupid because our backgrounds are so different but it was a very easy working relationship. I did the tactics, Jim worked with the forwards and I oversaw the team. It worked very well and, with Jim with me on the Lions tour, I had somebody I could trust and rely on, and that was vital for what I had planned.

He knew I wanted to do things differently in 1997. I sent him a report I had done on the kind of player we were looking for and the kind of game I felt we had to play. But he was a bit worried because he hadn't coached internationally since the 1991 World Cup and had been a director of rugby in Murrayfield, a position which hadn't involved him in coaching at the top level.

I had no doubts. There wasn't anyone else I would have wanted in that environment and I was so glad he took up the challenge. I have never seen Jim smile and enjoy himself as much as he did in 1997. I think it was because he was with good players, the environment we had was good and he was relaxed. I genuinely believe it helped his view of coaching in the game. He changed in 1997 and I think he did the best coaching of his career in 1999, when Scotland won the Five Nations Championship.

We took a lot of strides forward on that tour and did things that British players had never experienced before in terms of the analysis of contact and what it led to, splitting forwards to attack in layers and grouping players in a new way. The players were excited about it; we all were.

He had changed the personality of Scottish players in making them work as a group; he created Scottish packs that were formidable although they had no right to be; and in 1997, he worked his magic with some of the best players in the British Isles. We achieved something that year, as coaches and players, that will never fade from the memory.

Being involved with the Lions is like no other rugby experience. Each tour is unique, a ten-week phenomenon where players and management come together to prepare and to play against one of the strongest nations in the world, the results of which stand forever as a testament to their efforts. And the group's place in history is determined by the results of the Test matches.

This was my fourth Lions tour, as I had been twice as a player and once as a coach. Each one had been memorable but all had ended in failure as regards Test results.

Fran Cotton was chosen as manager in June 1996 and he had asked Ian McGeechan to be his head coach. Ian asked if I would be his assistant not long after I'd returned from Scotland's New Zealand tour and I was delighted to accept. There was some criticism of my appointment, mainly in the Scottish press, because I was a full-time official with the Scottish Rugby Union and not an active coach.

We had a twelve-strong management, which included five coaches – Ian and me; Andy Keast, technical coach; Dave Alred, kicking coach; and Dave McLean, fitness coach – and one of the strengths of that team was that we all had a specific remit, with very few overlaps. That was a big change from my previous Lions tour, when I was the only coach.

This was the first professional Lions tour, against South Africa, who were the reigning world champions, and it was the first Lions tour to that country since 1980. There has been a great love affair between South Africa and the Lions, particularly since 1974, when the Lions won three Test matches and drew the other.

Once I'd accepted the job, I was actually quite worried about returning to coaching at that level. I had not coached with Scotland for six years and had even stepped down with Melrose in 1994. I had been in South Africa in 1995 with the Scottish World Cup team and in New Zealand in 1996 as national coaching director, but it wasn't the same, and I had failed the last time I worked with the Lions.

I drew confidence from Ian, however, and, as you would expect with people like Fran and him, the preparation was meticulous and very professional. Ian had gone to South Africa in 1996 and stayed with the All Blacks for two or three weeks, and he wrote a report about what he'd found out there. The trip allowed him both to witness at first-hand how New Zealand dealt with touring South Africa and to closely study the Springboks. He found that the All Blacks had been self-contained in that all the training equipment was their own and was carted around the country from place to place. He suggested that we do the same and also, on the advice of the All Blacks, that we take five extra players to alleviate the pressure on key positions like hooker and scrum-half, so they did not have to be on the bench when not playing but instead could have a rest and, after the problems of 1983, I wholeheartedly agreed.

The most important aspect of that tour was Ian's playing philosophy. He believed he had found a way to beat the Springboks which involved introducing layers of attacking players and a generally quicker, more expansive style of attack. We then went looking for the kind of players we needed to carry that out and four sub-selectors were chosen: Derek Quinnell from Wales, a Lion in 1971, 1974 and 1977; Peter Rossborough, a former England full-back; Donal Lenihan, an Irish Lion in 1983 and 1989, and manager in 2001; and Ian Lawrie, a former district prop and experienced Scotland selector.

The seven of us had specific duties: Ian Lawrie and Fran looked at the front row; Donal looked at the second row; Derek and I were in charge of back-row players; Ian McGeechan looked at half-backs and midfield; and Peter at the back three. We scoured the countries and had regular selection meetings at the Metropole Hotel at Birmingham Airport, as it was easy for everyone to get to.

I went with Richie Dixon and Ian to London when the New Zealand Barbarians were over in the autumn of 1996 to discuss the latest about South Africa with John Hart, the All Blacks coach. I also went down to deepest Wiltshire to see a scrummaging machine built by Nigel Horton, the former England and Lions second row. It was called 'the Predator' and we took it with us on tour.

Selection is the key for any team but especially with the Lions, with whom I had learned in 1983 the folly of compromise. Making the right decisions is not always easy with Scotland teams but with the Lions it is possible because there are so many good players to choose from. When it comes to selection, your head must rule your heart. We chose a group of 62 in February, 1997. Quite a number of players didn't make the first meeting, I recall, because there was a bomb scare on the M40 and traffic was brought to a standstill.

Fran, Ian and I reduced the number to the final 35 in April, and, inevitably, there was disappointment for some. The final group included some who had recently been playing rugby league – Scott Quinnell, David Young, Alan Tait, John Bentley, Allan Bateman and Scott Gibbs – which surprised some people, but it was appreciated that we needed their experience, strength and professional approach. Alan Tait was listed as a utility player, but actually every one of the 35 was a specialist in our mind.

There was one player not in the original 62 who made it: Neil Back. Ian and I were determined to get him in the squad. We both felt he should have gone to New Zealand in 1993. Ian was the coach and he wanted him, but he couldn't get the selectors to agree, mainly because the English coaches at that time felt Neil was too small. Neither Ian nor myself agreed with that.

In the 35, there were 5 Scottish players, and the criteria for them was the same as the rest: they had to be capable of playing in Test matches – and they were. It was a fairly young squad and in some ways inexperienced. Only a handful had gone on previous Lions tours – Martin Johnson, Ieuan Evans, Jeremy Guscott, Jason Leonard, David Young and Scott Gibbs.

Martin was chosen as captain by Ian mainly because he was certain of his place and was a couple of inches taller than the Springbok captain Gary Teichmann. I liked that. Size is very

234

important in South African rugby, so we were making sure we had a psychological advantage from the start.

We planned to have a practical session at Murrayfield but it was cancelled because we felt some of the players were being overplayed through the season. Some of them were playing in the English Cup final on 10 May, two days before we were due to meet, and Martin Johnson, our captain, had played in 52 games and had to be rested for the first couple of matches on tour.

We met at Weybridge, Surrey, on 12 May and we had a week in Britain and a week in South Africa before the first game. In that first week, a specialist team-building company from the Lake District, called Impact, organised us into groups and set up games; I'll not forget being suspended about 30 feet up in the branches of a tree with my safety in the hands of players. This was to get everyone working with each other to engender team spirit. In the afternoons, we would do rugby sessions and it was a good balance.

We were also given a small laminated card which identified 20 different characteristics of the Lions. We were to carry that in our wallets, and pull it out and look at it when we thought it was appropriate. We also had mock press conferences and interviews, and discussed how we would handle difficult times – when selections were made, for example, or the period five or six weeks into the tour, a critical point beyond the honeymoon phase and into the real work.

There were a lot of little issues to get right – some wives and partners coming out, for instance, some not. 'Duty boys' responsible for tasks such as collecting kit were traditional on tours but we dispensed with that and did not use tour numbers either. Right from the start, I was very impressed with the maturity and enthusiasm of the players.

I also took senior forwards – people like Martin, Lawrence Dallaglio, Tim Rodber and Jason Leonard – into my confidence and asked them questions about how they felt we should practise. They didn't know me and I didn't know them, we only knew each other by reputation. I was keen to seek their views and advice, and I was aiming for player empowerment, making sure they believed in what we were trying to do. Only then do you get true commitment. All of them demanded high standards of themselves and were prepared to work hard, which was great news for me.

My approach to begin with was to get back to basic, very simple drills, so that everyone knew what I was after. I have kept notes of the drills we did each day, and also charted how often we did each one and how long we took to do them. My four essential principles – body position, tightness, leg drive and support from depth – were coached and if I had not ticked one off for a day or two, I made sure that it was covered soon after. I liked to have a balance and also a picture of what I was doing with technique.

It was clear the players had enjoyed themselves after that first week in London. They had got to know each other, begun to like and trust each other but, most importantly, they liked the rugby product – it was the way they wanted to play. That meant that from the moment we boarded the plane, they wanted to be salesmen for it, to sell their game as best they could.

At the first press conference in Johannesburg after we arrived, we were greeted by Dr Louis Luyt, chairman of the South African Rugby Football Union. I remember that Ian and Fran were looked on as idols because they had been part of the 1974 tour; there was a tremendous reverence shown towards them and that boosted us all.

Our first few games were at sea level, so we trained at Durban, in perfect weather in the shadow of King's Park, the home ground of Natal Sharks. I'd been there with Melrose three years before, so I was quite familiar with the place, but we stayed out of town at Umhlanga Rocks and travelled in each day. Everything was geared towards the Test matches in our intensity and training levels, and before we knew it, the first game, against an Eastern Province invitational XV at Port Elizabeth, was upon us. We played quite well and scored five tries there, winning 39–11 with Jason Leonard captaining the side.

We then moved to East London and faced Border, which became a real struggle and a game we were lucky to win. It was a wet and windy day, and we scraped home 18–14 with a Rob Wainwright try. Rob also captained the side. The next game was against Western Province in Cape Town and we decided to introduce Martin, hopefully fully rested, for his first game. We lost Paul Grayson to injury, however – he had been struggling with a hamstring injury – and Mike Catt came out to join us. There was also some doubt over Tom Smith, whom we feared had a back injury which could have forced him to go home. But it proved to be an old injury, from which he quickly recovered, and he was allowed to stay.

Rob Howley was outstanding in that game. He made a beautiful cut and break to put Ieuan Evans in for a try in the corner and we won 38–21 against a side which was one of the best in South Africa.

I remember a comment from Martin afterwards, when he was asked at the press conference why the Lions hadn't closed the game up after going ahead and he said, 'The modern game we play doesn't allow us to stop playing rugby. We won because we kept playing.'

There were a number of principles that were important to us on that tour and we saw them working early on. The body language of the player in front of the man with the ball and the quality of control in contact were vital new things for the players. Ian had devised scales of different types of contact, graded according to how good they were for us.

The best level was simple hand to hand; the second was the man turning in the tackle and the supporting man ripping the ball from him; the third was going to ground and putting the ball back quickly for the first supporting player to pick up; and the fourth was the man on the ground with bodies forming a bridge ruck over him. We worked hard on these in training so the players knew what they were aiming for in terms of specificity and accuracy in contact.

We also worked on how and where we ran – running at spaces, running late, but always being dynamic. We knew that the South African team were physically bigger than most of our players, so we coached them to target spaces and shoulders, and urged support runners to come from deep with the ball-carrier at the apex of the diamond to ensure that support was available right and left but, most importantly, always behind.

Second waves of support were introduced and we stressed that players taken out of the game had to get back to their feet quickly to become a second wave of attack. It was all part of our approach to developing the shape we wanted. There were key things that had to happen throughout the provincial games in order for us to create that team shape which we felt would beat the Springboks: the angles of running of the midfield and the back three, the support lines of the back row and the second-support-line awareness of the front five. 'Teams within teams,' Ian called it. The players had to understand that and buy into it for it to mean anything, and we saw that happening in those first few games, which gave us real hope. But it was not plain sailing.

Although we won the game, we were badly beaten in the scrums by Western Province and I was worried. We knew we had to sort that quickly, because the pride of South African rugby then and even now rests on dominating the scrum area. We moved up to the high veld for the next three games and chose the team to play against Mpumalanga at Witbank.

I had a tough heart-to-heart talk with the forwards when we arrived in Pretoria, our base for the next three games, and I spelt out what we had to do to improve. The basic principle of what I was saying was that the players had to be honest with themselves; they had to look themselves in the mirror and understand what was required. From now on, we would be taking no prisoners and we would not field anyone not prepared to do the work. We had to adapt to the conditions, no whinging, all positivity.

It was agreed that there would be an extra forwards session immediately after the next game, against Mpumalanga. We chose for the first time a smaller scrum – Tom Smith, Keith Wood and Paul Wallace – in the front row and we destroyed the Mpumalanga scrum, which was supposed to be the strongest in South Africa.

Unfortunately, we lost Doddie Weir in that game when he received a nasty kick on the knee from Marius Bosman. It was a horrendous ligament injury which threatened his whole future in the game. I spoke to him after the game and he was trying to put a brave face on it but I knew he was hurting deeply inside. Doddie had to leave the tour soon after, as there was no chance of him being fit for the remaining matches. He was one of the great characters of the group, always positive and keeping the spirits up, and he was a great loss.

We played very well against Mpumalanga and beat them 64–14, Rob Wainwright scoring three tries, I remember. That provided me with some confidence, but after the talk on the

Monday morning, we still had a scrummaging session with the substitutes and forwards who did not play.

I remember that being the most concentrated session I've ever done on a scrummaging machine. We probably did about 60 scrums in 30 minutes but not one player complained, not one player bitched. We actually had pressmen watching – they'd heard about this mammoth session and had come back after the game specially to see it.

That took a lot out of the players and it maybe showed in the next game. It was designed to be as much a mental exercise as a physical one because I knew that we were moving into the toughest part of the provincial tour. We were due to play against three of the most famous provinces in South Africa – Northern Transvaal (Blue Bulls), Gauteng (Golden Lions) and the then top province, Natal (Sharks) – in eight days. Fran Cotton called it 'the Bermuda Triangle', possibly because any players who didn't stand up here would disappear.

We made sure at this point that the senior players were alert to the fact that we were in the fifth week of the tour and some players would be finding it difficult, so they took on the responsibility of going around speaking with the younger ones and encouraging them. By this time, we had gained some respect in South Africa – four wins in four games – but we were now to face our first Super 12 opposition, the Blue Bulls.

We were beaten 35–30 and although we had opportunities to win, we didn't deserve to. We made so many basic mistakes in the first half that we didn't give ourselves a chance. We were perhaps complacent. Pretoria is a real rugby city, so the locals were cock-a-hoop. Scott Gibbs was cited for a short-arm tackle and that added to our woes. But to be quite honest, it was a wake-up call for our players.

Some of them had been getting just a little bit cocky but we knew, after that defeat, that our backs were against the wall. We lost two players in that week: first Doddie, who was replaced by Nigel Redman, who had been touring with England in Argentina; and then Scott Quinnell was forced to go home with a recurring groin strain. Tony Diprose, who had also been on the England tour, came in for him.

The next game was against the Gauteng Lions at Ellis Park, a fabulous stadium and arguably the most intimidating rugby park in the world when full of partisan Boks fans. This was a make-or-break game and the team chosen simply had to lift their spirits.

One thing I realised for the first time was that the pitch at Ellis Park is actually below ground level, so that when you come in off the street the changing-rooms are at ground level but then you walk down a very long tunnel to reach the pitch.

The game, billed as the 'Battle of the Big Cats', was to be played at a ground where few visiting international teams won. We didn't start very well and were down 9–3 at half-time, but I remember an incident early in the second half which I believe was the turning point of the game and perhaps the whole tour.

There was a cross-field kick by a Gauteng Lions player and the ball trundled towards the Lions line. It was fielded by Tony Underwood all on his own. Two home Lions got to him but he held his ground superbly until Tim Rodber got there and helped him. We cleared the ball away and the recovery started. Austin Healey scored a superb try to bring us back into the game and then John Bentley scored what some would say was the try of the tour when he ran 70 metres, beating players sometimes twice, before going in under the posts.

It was a great victory – winning at the home of South African rugby – and the atmosphere was just as great after the game. The players who had not played applauded the team up the tunnel and into the dressing-room. The tour was rescued by that game, largely because of the players who played but also because of the reaction of the players who didn't.

Dr Luyt, our host, was not too pleased, because he had a grand dinner organised to celebrate his team's victory but the occasion was a bit muted as we were the only ones celebrating.

That game showed us that we had cracked it at provincial level and, when we played well, we could handle any team at that level. A lot of younger players came through – Tom Smith, Paul Wallace, Jeremy Davidson, Neil Back, Barry Williams. Tim Rodber was again captain and did an excellent job.

The home Lions had one or two players of note as well. Kobus Wiese, the huge international lock, was back to get fit for the Test matches, and Roberto Grau, the famed Argentinian loose-head, who had played the previous weekend when Argentina had beaten

England, was there. Andre Vos, the captain of Harlequins in recent years, was also playing for Gauteng.

We then moved to Durban for the last Saturday game before the First Test and we were spoiled for choice in selection, with so many players putting their hands up to play. A lot of them were peaking at the right time and it was tremendous.

Natal were the provincial champions and had been beaten in the Super 12 final in Auckland in 1996. I remember at the team talk before the game when Fran spoke to the players he said that although we were acquiring quite a large support in South Africa, we also had loads of support back at home. He had received a lot of faxes from home saying how well people felt the boys were playing and he told them that everyone was behind them.

There was one from Marjorie Reynolds, whose husband Jeff had been a Lion in 1935 and owned the hotel which was wrecked by the 1968 Lions. She had taken the trouble to send a fax saying how much people were enjoying the Lions displays and to keep it up.

We played well against Natal and won 42–12. The most important thing to us was the style of our win. One benefit of having Andy Keast with us was that he had been an assistant coach at Natal for two years. He had put together videos of key players whom he felt were vital to how South Africa played and that shaped how we approached games. Andy knew how Henry Honiball, the stand-off, in particular would play, and though he didn't play against us for Natal, he was a vital cog for South Africa in the Test matches.

We also received crucial help from Keith Lyons of the Centre for Notational Analysis in Cardiff. The relationship Ian built up with Keith was another significant factor in the quality of information we had to work with. Keith supplied us with videos of the Super 12 games and statistical information on South Africa. Even when we were in South Africa, he supplied analysis of game-time and other important data.

The Natal game was also notable because playing his last game for them was the former Scotland hooker John Allan, who had played for Edinburgh Accies in the early '90s. He was well known in South Africa as a player, coach and commentator. Another former Accies player at Natal was Jeremy Thompson.

Having beaten Natal convincingly, we set off in good heart for the Western Cape. Unfortunately, we lost another great player, Rob Howley, who suffered a bad shoulder injury which put him out of the tour. He had been playing very well and was an excellent tourist. I was pleased to see him play in a Lions Test match four years later on the 2001 Lions tour of Australia.

We then moved to Cape Town for the build-up to the Test and had one game against the Emerging Springboks, under Nick Mallet, who later coached the Springboks on a fantastic 17-game unbeaten run. The match was at Wellington, out in a good wine-growing area.

The game was viewed as the final opportunity for some players to shine before the Test team was picked. We played some lovely 15-man rugby that day and thoroughly deserved our 51–22 victory. We didn't announce the Test team selection to the press until a few hours before the Test, which was a new thing. We wanted to keep them guessing. However, we did announce the team to the players on the Wednesday morning after the Emerging Springboks game.

Selecting a Test team is never easy, but no sentiment can be involved. With some players injured, notably Doddie Weir, Scott Quinnell and Rob Howley, the choice had narrowed somewhat. I was concerned with the pack, obviously, and looked closely at the front five.

One of the aims we had was to withstand the pressure in the scrums from the start, and during the last few games before the Test match, it was fairly obvious that the lower the props could get the better it would be. So we picked Tom Smith and Paul Wallace as the props, both technically good and able to get lower than their Springbok opponents Os du Randt and Adrian Garvey, who were both well over 6 ft. Keith Wood was the outstanding hooker, so he was picked.

The in-form second row was Jeremy Davidson, so he had to go in alongside Martin Johnson. There was some debate about the back row. Tim Rodber and Lawrence Dallaglio were certainties at that stage. It was between Richard Hill and Neil Back for the number 7 shirt. It was a tough one, but we decided to go with Richard, mainly because he was such a hard, intelligent player with a high work rate. But I still felt I wanted to have Neil in at some point.

When the squad had been announced back in April, there was a feeling that most of the Test team would be Englishmen because they made up the bulk of the squad, but actually, for the First Test only six Englishmen were chosen and, had Howley been on tour still, there would only have been five. There were three Welsh, three Scots, three Irish and six English players, which shows how players can come through with the right conditions and incentives.

One thing that still sticks in my mind is the attitude of the players not chosen. Jason Leonard had been on two tours before and he could play either side of the scrum, but his attitude when he was not chosen was so positive – he helped Paul Wallace through that week enormously – and that, I have no doubt, played a significant part in ensuring the Test players had the confidence to go into that First Test believing they could win.

In that team, everyone was a skilful and athletic rugby player, comfortable on the ball; I was very happy with the pack chosen. We trained at Stellenbosch during the week and there was a scare when Paul Wallace limped off during training. But with expert advice and treatment from our medical team, Dr James Robson and physiotherapist Mark Davies, he was fit for the Test.

I was convinced that the key to success was the front row and I told the players that there was no way we would annihilate the Springbok pack – very few teams have ever done that in South Africa – but if we got parity, we had a chance.

We picked from strength in the backs as well, with three former Lions in Evans, Guscott and Gibbs. Gregor Townsend was the form player at stand-off, Alan Tait was given the job of playing on the wing and Neil Jenkins was at full-back, in large part because of his excellent goal-kicking.

People who have seen the *Living with Lions* documentary will no doubt remember my team talk before the First Test. It was my custom to give the forwards a pep talk just before their pre-match meal. I remember setting out the room in the hotel near the Newlands ground, putting the chairs in a circle and draping a net over other chairs to remind them of the height they had to be in all the forward exchanges. It was a psychological thing: I wanted them to be lower in the scrums, lower in the driving, lower in the tackle, and the only way for us to succeed was to be lower than that net.

A few expletives obviously came out in my talk, but I spoke about them reaching their Everest, a summit very few ever get the chance to reach. I emphasised that being picked was one thing but winning for the Lions was something different altogether.

The game was at 5.30 p.m., which suited us because it was cooler then, but nobody outside the squad of 47 expected us to win even though we'd been playing very well in the provincial games. Ian, however, had always insisted to the team that if we were in the game with 20 minutes to go, our superior rugby would come through. And in that First Test, that's exactly what happened.

We kept in the game with Neil Jenkins kicking goals and in the last 10 minutes we scored two memorable tries. The first was by Matt Dawson, who broke down the blind side and fooled the South African back row with a dummy pass. Gary Teichmann must have nightmares about that try. And of course, in the 80th minute, Alan Tait streaked away down the left-hand touch-line to take us beyond the seven-point margin, which might still have allowed them victory, to give us a 25–16 win.

Such was the spirit that the next morning all the players, even the ones who had played the day before, were down to train at the Villagers ground before we got ready to move off.

We left Cape Town for Durban to prepare for the Second Test. The home media was full of criticism of the Boks, taunting them for their poor display. We weren't fooled; we knew the press were trying to provoke the team to stronger performances.

We were due to play Free State on the Tuesday and what had been agreed was that those playing there would fly up to Bloemfontein, play the match and come back the same night, while the rest remained in Durban and watched the game on TV.

Ian was indisposed with the flu and James Robson said he shouldn't go, so I was in charge of the team. Nigel Redman was the captain. This was our second team, but it absolutely mesmerised Free State in probably the best display of all the provincial games – and this was against a Super 12 team.

But we have to put 'second team' into context. We had Tim Stimpson at full-back, John Bentley and Tony Underwood on the wings, Allan Bateman and Will Greenwood in the centre, and Mike Catt and Austin Healey at half-back. So you could see the quality of the players competing for Test places who had not got their chance so far.

Unfortunately, Will Greenwood suffered a very nasty and worrying injury, swallowing his tongue after banging his head on the ground. He lay motionless for a while but eventually revived. James Robson reacted quickly to ensure his air passages were clear but there remained a fear that he had been seriously concussed. Fortunately, he recovered within a few days and joined the party in Durban, although he did not play again on tour.

The Lions were beating Free State 31–6 at half-time and eventually won 52–30. Team talks at half-time were never my strength, but that one was perhaps the easiest I ever had to make. I said to forget about the scoreboard and start the second half believing the score was 0–0. I was pleased that we started well and scored again on the restart, and though we lost 24 points, we still scored another 21 to win handsomely in what was the last tough provincial test.

I remember we had to change our hotel from Umhlanga Rocks and move into Durban because the Springboks had been allocated 'our' hotel. It wasn't any great hardship, although we were now a lot nearer to the noise of the city. It actually worked to our advantage because the players were able to mingle a bit more with fans and then switch back into game mode when they had to.

Injuries, however, were now becoming a real problem. In the lead-up to the Second Test, Ieuan Evans broke down in training at King's Park and the team from the First Test started to change. On the positive side, it gave opportunities to players who had been doing well in provincial games. John Bentley was brought in for Ieuan and that was a great boost to him, because he'd had some very good games and some not so good.

Interestingly, I was also in contact with the Scotland squad who were out in South Africa at the same time and spoke often on the phone with Hugh Campbell, the assistant coach. Scotland were mirroring some parts of our tour and played Mpmalanga, Eastern Province, Gauteng Lions and Northern Transvaal. I sent reports to Hugh on how these teams had played against us. Before the Second Test, on the Friday night, Scotland played Northern Transvaal and it was on the TV. They had been the only team to beat the Lions up to that point. Scotland won – I was shouting and jumping about, punching the air in my room. I phoned Dougie Morgan, the Scotland manager, because I had to speak to somebody.

I went down to the dining room in the hotel but couldn't tell anybody Scotland had won, because nobody was interested really and the Lions had their own focus. But I mouthed to Ian across the room, 'We won,' and he knew what I meant. That was a great victory for Scotland.

Prior to the Test match, our hotel was besieged by Lions supporters. By the time we were ready to leave for the match, we had to use a secret door to get out to the bus because the throng in the main foyer was so great it would have taken us ages to get through.

When I spoke to the forwards before we left, I warned them that the Springboks would be like a wounded animal and that their forwards would want to play very well to restore the reputation of South African rugby. They had taken a lot of flak during the week.

In fact, I felt some of the Lions forwards froze in the Second Test, possibly due to the sense of history around the occasion and the fact they knew we were on the verge of something memorable. We took a bit of a pounding for most of the game and the Springboks scored three tries to none. But as we all know, after Neil Jenkins had scored five penalties Jerry Guscott put over a memorable drop-goal to win the game 18–15. But there was a cameo piece of play before that which proved crucial to the win.

A Springbok was tackled on the halfway line near the touch-line and Neil Back, who had just replaced Richard Hill, came across and won a vital ball at the breakdown; Keith Wood took the ball and chipped it along the touch-line and South Africa were forced to take the ball into touch. We won the lineout and Gregor Townsend drove into a ruck. The ball came back, Matt Dawson fed Jerry and he kicked the drop-goal. But it would not have happened had Neil not reached that breakdown as quickly as he did and stolen possession.

Living with Lions picked up my irritation about where Ian and I were forced to sit during these Test matches. For some unknown reason, we were placed right in the middle of the crowd rather than in a special coaches' area. It was not an ideal place to be and we had to rely on James Robson getting messages to players on the pitch. But we came through it and when the final whistle went there was a tremendous, overwhelming feeling of achievement. It is still, even now, difficult for me to describe the incredible emotions that were flowing through me, after three Lions Test series and three defeats, to finally know what it was like to win with the Lions.

We were too drained to celebrate much that night but the players mingled with supporters on the back pitches after the game and had a great time with barbecues and so on. The next day, when we were leaving to go to Cape Town, there was a huge throng of people in reception and everyone got loud cheers as they got onto the bus. We also had a court session where Keith Wood, as the judge, cropped Ian's hair because he had said if we won the series he would get his hair cut. Keith left him looking like a convict!

We were due to play our last provincial game at Welkom before the final Test at Ellis Park and Fran Cotton admitted that he had chosen a secure, quiet place for us to stay (Vanderbijlpark, about an hour south of Johannesburg) because he thought the series would be 1–1 at that stage and we'd need space away from everyone.

Because of injuries, we called up Tony Stanger from the Scotland squad and he actually played at Welkom. It took him a little time to adjust to what we were doing, such was the level of expertise in the Lions backs. I was delighted that he became a Lion because he had been one of the most consistent Scottish players for years and was a former pupil of mine! After the game, he returned to the Scotland party – for him, it was a question of being in the right place at the right time.

We played on a bone-hard pitch at Welkom and Fran complained about it, though he apologised a couple of days later for doing so. There was really nothing to complain about and it was the only pitch on the tour which was not of a good quality.

We were struggling to get a team together for the Third Test because Tait, Townsend, Wood, Leonard, Rodber and Eric Miller were all injured. Only three players who were fit from the original 35 did not feature in a Test squad – Nick Beal, Graham Rowntree and Simon Shaw. We brought in Underwood, Catt, Wainwright and Back. South Africa introduced Jannie de Beer for Honiball and he played a more open game.

We were more relaxed, but we weren't really in the game and were quite well beaten. In many ways, the match was a damp squib because we had already won the series.

Even at the age of 57, I learned a lot on that tour. With top-quality players available, you can choose the style in which you want to play and then pick the players to suit that style. I had tried to operate that system in 1983 but it failed and I was castigated for it. But in 1997, that tour underlined for me the fact that you have to be bold and follow your own judgement in selection.

In the forwards, I always prefer to choose skilful rugby players ahead of those with limited ball skills. Ball players always have more game awareness and can adapt more readily under pressure. As I said earlier, it is vital that you develop leaders on and off the field early in the tour and empower them in all your playing strategies and work ethic. Experience will tell you when to draw the line, because, ultimately, players like to have a boss.

I now judge all rugby players, especially at international level, against the benchmark set by those Lions. When I was involved with Scotland in the World Cup in 2003 and things were not going well, I would discuss things with the forwards and I'd often stop and think, 'What would Jason Leonard, Martin Johnson or Lawrence Dallaglio have done here?' I have to say that in some cases they would have taken a different route to the one which the Scotland players decided on.

Those Lions set a standard of mental toughness, which really boiled down to honesty and hard work, leading to consistency of performance for 80 minutes in every match.

They were such a good bunch of players it would be very hard to pick out individuals. The real heroes for me were the ones not considered the big stars, especially those who did not get into the Test team. They played so much good rugby in what you would call the second team and supported wholeheartedly the players who'd got the nod ahead of them. They were all a tremendous credit to themselves, their families, and the British and Irish Lions.

Fran Cotton was an excellent manager, a big man in every sense, and assembled a great team around him. They all deserve credit for contributing to a memorable ten weeks.

I enjoyed working with Ian again. Our coaching relationship seems very natural; we are so alike in rugby philosophy and so different in delivery. The challenge of working with top players brought out the best in of both of us.

One aspect that was new to me was the production of a documentary about the tour, *Living with Lions*, which was shot in and around the camp. In some people's eyes, it was a bit crude. I happened to be in a lot of the shots and I seem to get recognised a lot more now as a result of that film. Even at the Heineken Cup final at Murrayfield this year, a young Irishman who played Gaelic football came over and said he had watched the video several times and that my speeches still inspired him. And in Wales in particular, people often shout across the street, 'Great video, Jim.'

But just as the video brought me some fame, if you like, it also brought me notoriety. I received a lot of nasty letters and emails telling me my language in the film was a disgrace, especially as I was an ex-headmaster. I received one from a doctor who said that if I had spoken to him and his mates the way I had spoken to the Lions players, he would have walked out of the room. That is not how I spoke in normal life either and I was actually quite shocked when it was pointed out to me how many times I swore on that video. But then, it was more than two months squeezed into less than two hours. I was perhaps a bit naive, but I had not expected the final film to include quite so much detail. We never got the chance to see the film and give our opinions on it before it was released.

But what the doctor did not appreciate was the unique environment in which the best rugby players in the world prepare themselves to suffer some physical and mental pain in order to become winners, to go into battle and put their bodies on the line – because essentially that is how it feels. I did not bother replying to him, but if he had been in that situation and had walked out of the room, I would have told him to continue walking and never to come back.

The only person I apologised to was my mother, who had to watch it, only once, I believe, She said, 'Jim, that's terrible language.'

19

Back on Top

Gregor Townsend
Scotland (82 caps)
British and Irish Lions (1997)

The period between 1995 and 1999 saw tremendous changes in rugby union as the game finally rid itself of its amateur status. This was a turbulent time for almost every rugby nation, especially the northern-hemisphere countries, which struggled to adapt to the new professional game.

Scotland was certainly not immune, and squabbles and disagreements raged over the structural changes being introduced. However, this discord did not seem to affect the performance of the national side, which came up one game short of a Grand Slam in three of the five seasons leading up to the 1999 World Cup.

At the onset of professionalism, the best players in Scotland were contracted to four districts, which participated in two European competitions, initially known as the European Cup and the European Shield. The players favoured that district route – almost identical to the set-up in Ireland. However, the SRU cut short any further development of the domestic game and created mistrust and resentment when it merged the four professional sides into two 'super-teams' to help ease the financial burden.

It was a disastrous decision and I was surprised that Jim allowed such a scenario to occur. But he found much more success when he returned to us as the national coach in 1998, culminating in Scotland being crowned the last-ever Five Nations champions in 1999.

Before that historic season, Jim was the manager, and a selector, of the 1996 Scotland side that lost out on a Grand Slam in the final game of the season against England. That season was to be one of my happiest times in a Scotland jersey, as I was chosen at stand-off and as vice-captain. Jim was the most hands-on manager I have ever had and, although he didn't coach us, his pre-match speeches were inspiring and sometimes physically demanding. On one occasion, we had to do press-ups while still in our number-ones [shirts and ties]!

The following season, I had the honour of representing the Lions in South Africa, and Jim and Geech's coaching combination played a major part in our success. They worked well together and won the respect and admiration of all the players on the tour. The *Living with Lions* documentary about the tour demonstrated to a wider audience that Jim had become one of the leading coaches of all time.

Jim was head coach of Scotland in 1999 and his positive approach helped produce some of the best rugby the Championship had ever seen, ending with a magnificent 36–22 Scottish win over the French in Paris. A key factor was the quick ball we received from our forward pack, as Jim demanded aggressive, low-to-the-ground rucking, which made my job at stand-off much easier.

There was no little experience in the team and Jim urged the players to have a significant say in how we trained and played. We formed a trust, which produced some outstanding training sessions. From 1995 to 1999, I had Jim as a manager, assistant coach and head coach. I also had to negotiate with him in his capacity as director of rugby a remuneration package for exiled Scottish players. He was as passionate there as on the field, but always showed me respect.

There were times later in my career when we disagreed with each other, which infuriated both of us, but my lasting memories are of Jim driving us forward in his own inimitable way. He is the best coach I have ever worked with.

John Leslie
Scotland (23 caps, 1998–2002)

Playing for Scotland remains the biggest highlight of my rugby career, and had it all been like it was in my first season, I would probably have been floating on some cloud somewhere now. It all just seemed to click in 1999 and the bounce of the ball went with us; but when you look at successful teams, there is a common denominator – a happy, ambitious environment.

Jim Telfer encouraged us to enjoy the game, to go out and be brave and try things. There was sometimes a madness about things he did but when you got to the Friday or Saturday, the reasons, usually, became clear. It was always well structured, of course, and I enjoyed the tactical side, but that 1999 triumph owed a lot to the good atmosphere. Jim was a fantastic coach, one of the best I've ever come across, and I played under several leading coaches in both hemispheres. It was an honour to represent Scotland and a privilege to be coached by Jim Telfer.

The 1997 Lions tour was tremendous but it was intended to mark the end of my coaching career. Everyone has to accept when their time at the helm comes to an end, and I had done so on more than one occasion before then. To finish by assisting Ian and a wonderful squad of players in achieving a real highlight for northern-hemisphere rugby was the perfect way to bow out.

And then season 1997–98 happened. By the end of January, I found myself in charge of a Scottish national squad again, having recommended that the SRU change the coaching structure. As I have said, it was not through any deep-seated desire to be Scotland coach again that I took the reins; I felt I could not leave the team without an experienced coach at what was a difficult time for the players. So here I was, coaching again!

I asked David Leslie and Roy Laidlaw to become my assistant coaches. I remember our first game, in Dublin. To freshen up the team, we picked George Graham for his starting debut at loose-head prop. George had been a good loose-head when he was young but the pundits said he was too small and he went to rugby league before Newcastle brought him back to union.

Gary Armstrong took over from Rob Wainwright as captain and we won 17–16. The game will be remembered for the tactical change when Dave Hilton was brought on for George late in the game and subdued Paul Wallace, the 1997 Lions tight-head, to enable us to secure the win. George, however, learned from that encounter and continued to be an integral part of the Scottish front row for the next few years. We then suffered a heavy defeat, 51–16, to France when Philippe Bernat-Salles, Jean-Luc Sadourny and the Lievremont brothers, Marc and Thomas, ran riot.

We lost narrowly to Wales, 19–13 at Wembley, despite playing very well; the highlight was a try from their kick-off by Gregor Townsend, and they scored a debatable try, as well. We finished the season losing 34–20 to England at Murrayfield.

This was a crucial period for Scottish rugby, however. The selectors had witnessed how difficult it was becoming for Scottish teams to compete at world level, so we turned our attention to Scottish-qualified players outside Scotland, men whose parents or grandparents were born here. It was not new, but a route taken for over a century in Scottish rugby; and in the late 1980s, with a shortage of big, strong forwards in our game, we went to England to uncover new talent.

Since then, players like Damian Cronin, Andy Reed, Ian Smith, Paul Burnell, Alan Sharp, Neil Edwards, Peter Walton, David Hilton, Eric Peters, Mattie Stewart and Budge Pountney, of various backgrounds, made huge contributions to the Scotland international team and helped us to remain competitive.

Of course, we later discovered that David Hilton's connection wasn't as he and his parents had believed and so he wasn't eligible to play for Scotland. It emerged that David's parents' belief that his grandfather had been born in Scotland was not factually supported. His grandfather appears to have believed it to be the case himself before he died but his birth was in fact registered in England. Yet David had been one of the most committed of the exiles and had even brought his family to Scotland and joined the Glasgow Caledonians to show his desire. There was no one more surprised or upset than David to discover that his grandfather had not been born in Scotland. He remained here despite taking an incredible amount of flak, as did we, for the error. I admired the way he dealt with that, returning to the Scotland team after qualifying through the three-year residency rule.

But, in 1997–98, it wasn't a simple matter of scouring England to fill holes any more. We were now being supplied with players' names by agents, as well as videos of them in action. So we became aware of a sizeable number of Scots-qualified players around the world, especially in New Zealand.

I have to say that I can see no difference between a player born in New Zealand and one born and bred in England, if both qualify to play for our country through a grandparent. Certainly I have seen more pipe bands in New Zealand, Australia and South Africa than I've ever seen in England. Other countries with far greater resources than us have used the eligibility rules to their own advantage. France have had a few South Africans as well as New Zealander Tony Marsh; England have used the system to cap Mike Catt, Henry Paul and new prop Matt Stevens among others; and New Zealand draw on talent from Fiji, Samoa and Tonga. Particularly hurtful were accusations that I had devalued the Scottish jersey by bringing Kiwi players into our game. There was an incredible frenzy about the whole issue in the media and among the public in 2001 when Brendan Laney arrived from Otago. While I was not coach then, I do regret Brendan's situation.

The players I brought here in the late 1990s did play a significant role in helping Scotland's performance on the international stage and I thank them as I do everybody who played for me. It goes back to my belief that a person's background should not affect his opportunities – all Scottish-qualified players were equal in my eyes, judged only on ability.

However, while Brendan undoubtedly desrved to play for Scotland, his introduction to the international squad, just days after he had arrived in the country for the first time, was, in hindsight, premature. The reason was that we were short of confident, imposing full-backs – none of those Brendan displaced ever made the jersey theirs despite numerous chances – and the coaches felt Laney might give us that something extra which could help us beat New Zealand for the first time. I did advise Ian McGeechan that Brendan should first play for the A team, and he did, which eased some senior player concerns, and the general committee supported our decision.

It was a shame because Brendan, a great character, became one of the best players in the Scottish game in Edinburgh colours and he did not deserve the hurtful criticism – the selectors and I did. It was a mistake, but one born of wanting to see Scotland win, nothing else.

The Scots rugby psyche has disappointed me over the years – it has sometimes bordered on the xenophobic. Club members, the press and the public at large don't have the responsibility of trying to put out a competitive Scottish team upon which a lot of money, prestige and global respect in our game depends. There are very few clubs in Scotland now or in the past who have not fielded, and in recent years often paid, players from the southern hemisphere. If people from those clubs criticise me, they are guilty of double standards. There is nothing wrong with foreign players and coaches working at all levels in Scottish rugby, because they can help to drive up the standard of our game. But the professional tier and Test sides are reliant on what comes from club level and the strength of Scots therein reflects the quality being produced at the grassroots.

As a past Scotland player, and privileged to have been so, I would love to see Scotland field 22 players born and bred in this country. But working at the level we were, it was as plain as the noses on our faces that the rest of the top-tier nations were moving ahead of us and we had to find something extra.

Two players who became available for us were Glenn Metcalfe and Shaun Longstaff, Kiwis who had come to play in Scotland. They had come to play club rugby but were good enough to make a difference at Test level. We have always been lacking in depth in big, strong tight-head props in Scotland, which was why we recruited Matt Proudfoot, who had been playing Super 12 rugby for South African side the Bulls. Matt had been on the bench for Northern Transvaal against the Lions in 1997, so he had a reasonable pedigree. Gordon Simpson was a Super 12 player recommended to me by Peter Thorburn, one of the New Zealand selectors at the time, who had been Gordon's coach at North Harbour. Matt played for Melrose and Edinburgh Reivers, Gordon joined Kirkcaldy and Glasgow Caledonian, and both played in the Tests against the Wallabies on the 1998 tour.

At the end of the Five Nations Championship, David and Roy had stood down as my assistant coaches and gone back to their work with the Under-21s. I had given them the opportunity to taste international coaching and hoped they would come through as the next generation of Scotland coache. However, neither chose to be a front-line coaches, David largely due to business commitments and Roy because he preferred to work in the background, but they remained committed to the game with age-grade sides and I respected their decisions.

I then approached Hugh Campbell and John Rutherford, another two Scots whom I felt had widespread respect and were ambitious in coaching. They came with me to Australia, along with Frank Hadden, the former Caley Reds assistant, as our technical coach.

Gary Armstrong and Alan Tait couldn't go on tour because they were needed at Newcastle. There was some controversy over whether we should have played Fiji first up. In retrospect, it was a mistake to go there first, but the idea was that we would be fresh and free of injuries to face them on their own ground. It was a very hot day; we played reasonably well in the first half but then ran out of steam. Fiji won quite comfortably, 51–26.

It was only the Test team who went to Fiji and it was a hell of a journey. The result capped a miserable few days. One thing I remember is that it was a holiday when we went there and it seemed as if every bit of spare ground was taken up with youngsters and men playing sevens in bare feet.

In Australia, the players preferred to stay in cities, so we did that and travelled out from Sydney to small towns like Bathurst and Penrith to play matches. Our best match on that tour was against New South Wales, coached by Matt Williams. Hugh, John and I got to know him quite well, as he took us for a sightseeing tour around Sydney. We were beaten in both Tests, 45–3 in Sydney and 33–11 in Brisbane, which was disappointing, but we blooded a number of new players and overall it was a worthwhile tour.

The two Leslie brothers, John and Martin, were next on the horizon in season 1998–99. They had Scottish grandparents, both had proved themselves in the Super 12 and we had been told they were keen to come to Scotland. I knew their dad, Andy, a former All Blacks captain, having met him on a number of occasions in New

Zealand and when he toured Britain with supporters' groups.

They proved to be excellent acquisitions and played some terrific rugby for Scotland. John's baptism was for Glasgow Caledonians against the touring Springboks in the autumn of 1998 at Firhill, where he seemed to be the only home player on the field who took them on, with great straight running. Unfortunately, he had already agreed a deal with Japanese club Sanix before we got him, and he then played for Newcastle and Northampton. But his allegiance to Scotland was shown when he drove his wife, Carmel, north from Newcastle so that she could deliver their first child in Scotland, at Borders General Hospital near Melrose.

Both Martin and John made their debuts in November 1998 against South Africa, as did Budge Pountney and Jamie Mayer, and though we lost 35–10, it was nowhere near as bad as the visit by the Springboks the year before. John Leslie's impact was certainly greater in his first Five Nations Championship match, when he scored within nine seconds of the kick-off – still a world record – against Wales at Murrayfield.

Unfortunately, Duncan Hodge and Doddie Weir broke bones – two more suffered similarly in the Championship – and our captain Bryan Redpath had been ruled out before the competition started. Gregor Townsend came into the side at stand-off and Alan Tait took over at outside-centre. The rest is well known, as Scotland went on to win the last Five Nations Championship.

The Grand Slam was taken from us when England emerged victorious at Twickenham, 24–21. We both scored three converted tries and they kicked a penalty. Our tries were superb, Tait scoring at both ends and Townsend grabbing an interception and racing clear from halfway. But we just couldn't turn pressure into points, missed some penalties at goal and were made to pay.

However, the influence of the Leslie brothers came home to me in that game. I remember at half-time, after I'd spoken about a few things, Martin took the forwards into one area and John took the backs into another and they spoke to each group about what was not being done very well, what had to change and how we could get the better of England in the second half. And the players listened and understood.

John was very good at that – weighing up what was right and

wrong during a game. It was not passion but purely technical. He had captained Otago many times and had taken them to the NPC title the year before. I could understand why Ian McGeechan later made him captain, because, while he was quite a shy character in everyday life, in an international squad his leadership qualities were clear.

By that time, I had worked hard to make the team feel empowered to take their own decisions and play the kind of game they wanted to play. This particular group of Scots had some very good on-the-field leaders – Gregor Townsend, Gary Armstrong, John and Martin Leslie, Eric Peters, Alan Tait and Tom Smith – players with great maturity and a desire to take responsibility.

We beat Italy easily, 30–12, and then Ireland by 30 points to 13, so we headed to Paris believing that, although the Grand Slam was gone, we could give a good account of ourselves at the Stade de France. We had lost Tom Smith and Eric Peters to injury by then, Eric breaking his kneecap in a club match with Bath, while Tom broke his leg. Dave Hilton and Stuart Reid came in for them respectively.

We also selected two open-side flankers for the first time – Budge and Martin. That was because the match was in April and the weather in Paris was sunny; we knew it was going to be a fast-paced, top-of-the-ground game. We didn't go there thinking the Championship was up for grabs, because England had beaten everyone and only had to overcome Wales at Wembley, which they, as always, seemed confident of doing.

But what a weekend that turned out to be. It started with Thomas Castaignède being injured after just two minutes, in the act of creating the game's opening try for Emile N'Tamack. It was a bad start for us but it proved fortuitous and the Scottish players responded with good running rugby to take France on at their own game. Gregor, John and Alan, a key midfield axis, were really on the same wavelength and they created so much in that first half. The forwards played well to provide the ball and Glenn Metcalfe made several great intrusions from full-back to slice open the French defence. A very open half ensued, with tries coming thick and fast.

The half-time whistle brought a resounding sigh of relief after an incredible 40 minutes which left Scotland 33–22 in front –

Martin Leslie and Alan Tait scoring twice and Townsend writing his own chapter in Scottish rugby history by scoring in every game of the Championship. France had responded with one each by Christophe Juillet and Christophe Dominici to add to N'Tamack's early score.

The second half was a completely different affair. Both teams played very conservatively – we scored one penalty and they scored none – but a good defensive effort carried us to a great win.

The next day was a normal trip home and I was back in time to watch England's game with Wales on the television. When Scott Gibbs destroyed English hopes with a late try which Neil Jenkins converted to win the game, I realised that we were Five Nations Champions, and it was an incredible feeling. The telephone rang non-stop for the next couple of hours and the SRU hurriedly made plans for a trophy presentation at Murrayfield the next night.

Over 10,000 tremendous supporters from all over Scotland turned up at Murrayfield on a lovely night, which just shows how people respond to success.

We opted for a low-key tour to South Africa before the World Cup, for which we would leave a number of players at home to rest and recover from injuries, giving us a chance to build up our reserve squad. We took some young, uncapped players, including Chris Paterson, Jason White, James McLaren and Iain Fullarton, but still had nine of the team which had beaten France. We defeated Border and Northern Free State Griffons but were completely outmuscled by Mpumalanga and then lost narrowly to the Golden Lions in the final game in Johannesburg.

After a short break with my wife Frances in South Africa to recharge the batteries, it was straight into preparations for the World Cup. We went around the country in training for it, to Perth Academy, Kingussie Academy, spent three days at Alvie House, near Aviemore, at the expense of The Famous Grouse, where we did some falconry, and we also stayed at Troon and Peebles.

In two warm-up games, we lost to Argentina in August and then put 60 points past Romania at Hampden Park. But the crowd of just 5,000 was a taste of what was going to happen in the World Cup with regard to crowds at grounds away from Murrayfield.

We opened our World Cup campaign against South Africa, which was a daunting task, as we had lost over 100 points to them in our previous two meetings. We actually played well and were ahead by 16 points to 13 at half-time, but they came back and led 18–16 when we lost John Leslie, who caught a high ball from Gregor under their posts and injured his ankle. That was a major loss because he was one of the most influential players in the team, at the heart of the back line. We lost the game 46–29 in the end.

We beat Uruguay and Spain easily and then got Samoa in the quarter-final play-offs. We disempowered them in every way possible and won comfortably, 35–20. It was Pat Lam's last game for Samoa, but it wasn't the last time he would be at Murrayfield, as he came back as our forwards coach for the 2003 World Cup.

I remember the quarter-final game against New Zealand vividly because it was the last time I was in charge of a Scotland team. It was a Sunday night and pouring with rain. Despite that, there was a capacity crowd and the atmosphere was the best I'd felt at Murrayfield for years – it was electric. The All Blacks were favourites for the tournament and we were seen as just another casualty on the way.

To be honest, we showed them too much respect in the first half. They scored twice early on and controlled the ball superbly in the wet, so they were comfortably ahead at half-time. As usual with Scotland, when the game was lost we played well, and we 'won' the second half, with glorious tries by Martin Leslie, scoring against his home country, and Cammie Murray, who dummied the great man himself, Lomu, to score. But we still lost 30–18.

It was an emotional night because it was the final game for several players: Alan Tait, Gary Armstrong and Paul Burnell. It was tremendous for them to get a great reception from the crowd. Paul had been an excellent servant of Scotland over 11 years; Alan had lit up our game when he returned from league and he played well both for Scotland and the Lions; and Gary was just Gary!

He epitomises everything that is good in a Scotsman; he is honest, loyal and extremely courageous. I was delighted that professional rugby came along in time for him to benefit. Some players use their rugby fame to get on in business but Gary wasn't like that and it was no surprise to me when he went back to driving lorries when he eventually retired from rugby. He had some great years at Newcastle, first with Rob Andrew as his partner and then with Jonny Wilkinson, and finished off with Gregor Townsend at the Borders.

Although I retired after that match, the assistant coach s Hugh Campbell and John Rutherford continued, and they deserve praise for what they did for Scotland. Ian McGeechan came back before the tournament and we formed a four-man coaching team so he got a feel for the coaching systems before taking over from me.

It cannot be ignored that the Lord Mackay Report was soon to be published and the Five Nations and the World Cup were played against a backdrop of tremendous unrest in the domestic game in Scotland that year. This was shown in the very poor attendances at games, especially at Netherdale, where Uruguay played Spain, and in Glasgow where only a few thousand watched the world champions South Africa play Uruguay – a stark contrast to Australia's crowd-pulling endeavours in 2003.

20

Plotting New Paths,
Finding New Obstacles

Tony Gilbert
New Zealand coach (2000–2001)
Borders coach (2002–2004)

When I finished coaching the All Blacks, I still wanted to coach but I didn't want to do the same thing again. When Jim Telfer contacted me, the lure of starting a new team in the Scottish Borders, a place with a great history of rugby, was very strong, but what swayed it for me was Jim – he was the talisman, really.

I had first seen him in 1966 when he played against Otago with the Lions and that was the first time that the Borders reared its head with me. People talked of Jim's style of rugby as being the 'Borderers' style'; I watched him throwing himself about at number 8 and he was into everything. So when he came calling, there was an instant appeal for me.

We had also met as coaches, when Scotland came to New Zealand on tour, and when I initially came across to look at the Borders, it became clear that we had the same mindset about rugby, as well as about life. If I was going to leave New Zealand, it would have to be to go where my heart was, and after that visit, it was in the Borders.

I did not come with any expectations other than that my wife and I were coming to a proud rugby area where there was a great rugby ethos and a commitment by people to their clubs. The negative was that we were constantly under pressure financially from the SRU and it was difficult to make the side

262

work under such constraints. I have to admit that I looked a little bit askance at some of the inward-looking approaches to the game, which we had had a long time ago in New Zealand but had moved on from.

But there were far more positives than negatives. I just loved the players, the team and people who worked hard for the team, and the support we got from the Johnny Grays of this world. Johnny's a former player and coach, Gala through and through but very progressive, with a great outlook on life and sport. The Borders has some tremendous characters and great rugby people.

I will never forget some wonderful times in Jim's lounge or mine, with a cushion, discussing the finer aspects of contact or collisions, and one or other of us would be on our feet and the other on the floor. It was just wonderful at my age to meet someone who was as enthusiastic about rugby as I was and be taken into his home and heart and his circle of friends. I will forever treasure my two years in the Borders.

With all the emotion and the terrific send-off of the Rugby World Cup behind me, rugby politics was to pull me back down to earth with an almighty bump on my return back inside Murrayfield.

Coaching has always sustained me but I also loved the challenge of trying to map out a clearer, more successful picture for the whole of Scottish rugby. There were few challenges which would have taken me away from my job as a headmaster, but being able to help direct Scottish rugby was one.

If only I had known how far that job remit was to reach. When I returned to my desk, now retired as national coach, my attention quickly returned to the Lord Mackay Report – a wide-ranging, independent review of Scottish rugby which had been published in July 1999. I had been involved in the report to the extent that I gave my views at the Greenyards on 12 May in one of the many public hearings the panel staged around the country.

My presentation stuck to the structure of the game and left alone issues like governance, constitution and finance, which were not my areas of expertise. The SRU committee was struggling with professionalism and a review was inevitable; we were still working from a 130-year-old constitution which said that the clubs were the SRU. That was all right for a sport's governing body but we now had a business to run as well and combining the two was a major problem. The constitution had been a central part of the problem in Scottish rugby's struggles to move with the times.

The publication of the Lord Mackay Report was pleasing and I agreed with what it said: a successful national team was important for the health of the game in Scotland; a strong base of professionals playing in Scotland should form the core of the national team; the 'super-teams' should continue to make up the European Cup representation.

The report also stated that we should work towards having three professional teams when the finances and playing strengths warranted it and return eventually to the four-team scenario, and I was pleased with that.

Leading clubs had submitted that we should instead move to a semi-professional eight-to-ten-team league but the panel rejected that for the same reasons we had debated many times before. The report also recommended that there should be 12-team amateur leagues, running right from September to March, and that was something I did not agree with. I believe that 10-team leagues suit Scottish rugby when you take into account our weather. Games are often postponed because of poor conditions and we haven't finished a season in the allocated time since 12-team leagues were introduced.

Interestingly, the panel also said we should have more rugby-skills training in schools, and that mini and midi rugby should be coached in the summer months. Apart from the 12-team leagues, I agreed with everything it said and believed that, within the five years I had remaining at the Union, we'd get back to four district teams.

The report was agreed to in principle but that did not stop some clubs trying to alter sections they felt did not suit them. A big issue was the panel's advice that committeemen should be appointed only for two years, with the option of another two. It also recommended that special representative status – whereby committeemen who had been elected several times consecutively were no longer subject to elections – should be done away with, which I also agreed with.

But the clubs allowed themselves to be talked out of that new way of electing members by the general committee. Five years later, it became a massive issue again and this time the clubs agreed to the change. Had they stuck to the report's recommendation in 2000, the committee members' power might not have come back to haunt them in 2005 and taken everyone back to square one.

The fundamental issue at the heart of the last few years' strife has been who actually runs Scottish rugby. Lord Mackay said then that there should be a clear distinction between the roles of the new executive board and the general committee. Defining and adhering to that distinction, which was supposed to ensure the board ran the business end of the game, with the committee effectively acting as a body of checks and balances, has been fought over every year since then and led to the recent civil war in the game's administration. Now, however, we seem to be making that divide much clearer and more workable.

The board included the directors of finance, rugby and marketing, as well as the chief executive and four non-executive directors. The SRU chose the non-executive directors, mainly through Bill Watson, the chief executive, who brought in people with a wide variety of experience in relevant specialist fields.

The first board consisted of chairman Ken Scobie, a well-respected London-based Scottish businessman; Andrew Flanagan, the chief executive of Scottish Media Group, who was on the board at Hearts football club; Fraser Livingston, the chairman of a large firm of quantity surveyors; and the late Bill Wilson, a director of the Royal Bank of Scotland. I felt the qualities of the executive board were excellent, and all of them had some knowledge of and interest in rugby.

But the real weakness of the new system, in my opinion, was that although the panel recommended that the chairman of the board and chief executive should attend committee meetings to discuss common issues, in reality there was not nearly enough collaboration or communication between the two bodies. In hindsight Lord Mackay should have suggested that representatives from the committee sat on the executive board, which, after great unrest in the early part of 2005, has now finally occurred.

There are, however, still potential problems ahead. I actually see the Scottish Rugby Board effectively running professional and international rugby and the new Scottish Rugby Council running the amateur game, hopefully working closely together, but with almost all of the power with the board. Whether everyone agrees to that and allows the new structure to develop, we must wait and see.

Latterly, the committeemen received a lot of criticism, sometimes from clubs but mainly from the press. Some of it was justified but some was well wide of the mark. But, like all authority figures, be it in government or local councils, they were easy targets.

They are very dedicated people who spend hours and hours involved in the game, often with very little thanks for what they do. They are a cross section of the rugby community who spend a lot of their own time supporting all areas of the sport. Even I have been amazed at the number of things they have to do.

But sometimes, if they were there for a long time, power went to their heads. As in any club committee, there were always one or two more powerful than the rest and they became the leaders. If the leaders are the right people, then the club progresses, but if they are not, all kinds of trouble can ensue; and it's the same with the SRU, which is why I was in favour of limiting the terms of committeemen to two or three years.

After the Mackay Report, the committee started to concentrate far more on the rugby side than on finance and marketing, mainly because they knew little about those areas. I found, however, that they wanted the same level of involvement in rugby matters as before the report came out. Obviously, this wasn't part of their remit and I felt that the work of the Rugby Division was being stifled. One of the things which I found most frustrating was the struggle to get academy managers appointed in the three remaining districts, the Borders having appointed one when the new professional team was set up in 2002. I knew that some clubs didn't like the principle of academies because of the fear of losing their players to the professional teams, and that these same clubs were also influencing the committee, but I was determined that each district would have an academy before I retired. Thankfully, after about a year of procrastination by the committee, I managed to get the principle passed before I went to the World Cup in 2003 and I believe the structure, now in place, is working satisfactorily. Actually, I know that privately most committee members were in favour of the structure but were afraid of the backlash from some prominent clubs.

Politics aside, one of the biggest challenges confronting Scottish rugby is putting in place the mechanisms for producing the next crop of quality young players. There are two aspects to this: first, the individual development of each player in physical conditioning and skills; and second, the quality of competition the players are exposed to.

Efforts have been made on all sides to ensure that the second improves. However, as yet, a workable and effective relationship between the leading clubs, professional teams and national age-grade squads has still to be created. In the meantime, some of our best talent has bounced about between the tiers, sitting on benches, playing for clubs' seconds teams and going nowhere fast. If Scottish rugby is to move forward, this has to be sorted out as a matter of priority.

When he coached the Scotland Under-19 team in the late 1990s, Frank Hadden suggested that all the players be taken away from their clubs at Christmas, to give them the best possible preparation for the FIRA World Championships. He recognised a need to help the boys step up to reach the level of the opposition they faced. But that need has since become more acute, because at that time countries like England, New Zealand and Australia were not involved in the competition. I knew that the clubs would never agree to his suggestion, so it went no further then. Eight years on, the top clubs have finally agreed . . . in principle, at least!

From 2000 onwards, age-grade international rugby became even more competitive and spawned annual Under-19 and Under-21 world championships, at which Scottish rugby is scrutinised around the world. But still our Under-19 and Under-21 elite players were playing at a lower standard than most leading nations and then expected to step up into the international arena to play against some fully professional teams in those competitions.

Two initiatives were set up to try and streamline the process: the National Pathway, driven by Colin Thomson, intended to identify and develop talent in youngsters from 15 to 18; and our first national rugby academy, funded by the Scottish Institute of Sport. Bob Easson took over as the institute's rugby coach and he started with about 24 hopefuls. The initatives have been successful to an extent, but our best young players are still going into those world championships underprepared.

The other route which can be taken to produce elite players is, as in England, through a fully professional set-up with a first, a second and an academy team in each club. Although academy and second-team players will often play with local clubs as well, the young players are contracted to the professional clubs and reap the benefits of working with full-time players.

I find it sad that three of Scotland's national Under-21 team, including the captain, opted this year to go to England to pursue their careers. I haven't spoken with them, but I suspect that they all believe they will benefit from the better development programme in England. It is a bit like a young man at 18 choosing which university to attend and making the decision on the basis of which one is likely to give him the best career opportunities when he qualifies.

So Scottish rugby has a simple choice as far as elite development is concerned: either set up the ideal scenario, which is what they have in England; or do as we have done so far, and continue to compromise by using the senior amateur clubs as the mechanism for developing young players, with all its inherent problems. Until the clubs can be persuaded to release some of their best young players into the professional system, we cannot set up a more efficient programme and we will continue to underdevelop Scottish players and underachieve in these world events.

I have been involved in Scottish rugby long enough to realise that people have different ambitions and that mine often vary greatly from those of some club members. The problem is that club members have only to think about what is best for their club, and clearly that differs from the responsibility of a national director of rugby.

One of my jobs in the Rugby Division within Murrayfield was to try and work towards restoring the third and fourth professional teams. Sadly, there was still a great deal of resistance to district rugby from clubs. It is interesting that Wales, who initially opted for a twelve-club professional system, before eventually arriving at a four-club district arrangement in 2004, have seen great success. I know that Graham Henry, the former national coach, and Terry Cobner, the director of rugby when I was at Murrayfield, were very keen to go down the district route. I viewed the change as a vital component in Wales's Grand Slam win in 2005.

The Welsh have always had an abundance of quality players, and a great youth and schools system. But when you analyse that Six Nations success, it is worth acknowledging the following: the players were concentrated in four provincial teams; they were not now losing players to rugby league; and the fitness and conditioning levels of the Welsh players, with a New Zealand fitness coach and an Australian skills coach, had gone up dramatically.

I was delighted when we saw the light at the end of the tunnel in the push for a third professional team. Finance has always been a problem in Scottish rugby. English rugby receives around £8 million in grants and loans from the British government; Welsh around £4 million; and Irish rugby last year received over £2 million as well as around £120 million towards the new Lansdowne Road stadium from their government. Scottish rugby received under £1 million from all government sources last year, meaning that we still rely heavily on finding our own funds. But the Rugby Division pushed for the third team and I, perhaps naively, believed that if the finance was there, everybody would support it, not least because it was a recommendation of the Mackay Report.

Ian McGeechan, who was the national coach at the time, and I spoke to the delegates at the 2001 AGM and I think Ian's speech convinced any doubters. He talked of broadening the base, but he also spoke of his experiences at Northampton and the benefits of having a professional organisation to help the amateur game. Northampton had been a pariah in the early 1990s because they just took the best young players from the clubs in their area and kept them. But in the professional era, the amateur clubs found there were benefits to having a professional club in their midst and developed a closer relationship with Northampton, whereby players moved between the professional and amateur clubs more readily.

Once clubs voted in favour of the third team, there was a debate on whether it went to Caledonia or the Borders. I was in favour of it going to the Borders, mainly because of the area's rugby culture and tradition of having so many people involved in the game; it is the only region in Scotland where rugby is the main sport.

Yet, at the time, most of the top Borders clubs were against it, including my own, Melrose, mainly because they feared they would lose players. Other Borders clubs were in favour – they had already lost their best players to their wealthier neighbours. It was somewhat ironic to read a Melrose spokesman at the time insisting his club was most definitely not in favour of a new Borders team and pointing to the two players he feared losing, Tom Weir and John Dalziel – players whom Melrose had previously enticed away from Gala.

He seemed to have no empathy with some of the obvious benefits which a new professional team could bring, such as local heroes for the young players in the Borders and the chance for them to see stars like Brian O'Driscoll and Gavin Henson close up. The Hawick coach at the time was Ian Barnes, who said that the money being set aside for the new Borders team would be better invested in grassroots rugby. I agreed that we needed to encourage more and more youngsters to play the game at school and clubs, but his argument didn't quite stand up, as his team had just won the Premier 1 Championship with five of his pack coming from the southern hemisphere. So much for developing home-grown talent!

It's a poor reflection on Scottish rugby that an area like that, which produces so many good players, does not enjoy the advantages of having a professional team and I hope that changes soon. I was very disappointed when it went in the first place and I regard not being able to resurrect a fourth team in the North as a failure on my part.

Of all the areas, when the four-team scenario was created, Caledonia was the one which really grasped it with enthusiasm. They played at football grounds and youngsters got right in behind it and there remains, as we have seen with international matches with Japan and the Barbarians at Perth and Aberdeen in the past year, a very positive and passionate approach to the game.

What people at some Borders clubs have not yet grasped is that their enemy is not the professional team. If there is an enemy, it is the city teams because of the natural and increasing drift of young players to cities. That is the real debate at the top end of club rugby now – a city versus small town debate, rather than a professional team versus club debate.

The pendulum of strength in club rugby has swung towards the central Lowlands, especially the cities of Edinburgh and Glasgow. There are many reasons, but chief among them are the increasing opportunities in tertiary education, employment and worldwide travel, and the Borders in particular has struggled to compete.

Even though the sport is uniquely a way of life here, I don't think Borders teams will ever dominate Scottish rugby again – those days are gone – but if they were to use the pro team to their advantage, the area could rediscover success.

But it was an exciting challenge restoring a professional presence to the heart of an area where rugby was taken very seriously. In the setting-up of the new Borders team, we cast our net wide to find a head coach. It's true that I looked to New Zealand; this was because we share similar terrain and weather, and produce a similar type of rugby player, and they had coaches who at worked at a higher level in pro rugby. The outstanding applicants for the post were former All Blacks coaches Wayne Smith and Tony Gilbert.

I interviewed Wayne in London (and discovered he was Scottish qualified!) but it was clear he preferred the idea of an established side; when I interviewed Tony, meanwhile, he was very enthusiastic about the challenge of launching a new team. Tony came over and spent a fortnight in the Borders just before Christmas in 2001, and after taking in some club matches and visiting all the Borders grounds, he accepted the post.

My preference in coaching is for a three-man team, with a head coach and two assistants, but because of the resources available, the new chief executive Alastair Cranston and Tony decided to go for one assistant – Rob Moffat – and instead of a second, they appointed an academy manager, Richie Gray. The decision pleased me because I had been keen for some time to form academies in each of the four districts.

We still had a few hurdles to get over. There was great debate about where the team would play. Most clubs wanted the team to move between all of the Borders venues, as had happened with the district sides in the past, but while that sounds good, all rugby teams will tell you they want their own home.

We settled on having one venue and while my favoured option would have been a completely new stadium, finances did not permit that, and Hawick and Gala emerged as the favourites. Gala was selected, largely because it was more accessible – it is about 18 miles from Peebles, Hawick, Jedburgh and Kelso – and because an independent feasibility study had recommended it.

The next stage was to put together a squad, taking into account the fact that there were a number of talented and popular Borders players scattered around the country. I was never going to bring back all the Borders players who had moved to Edinburgh after the merger four years earlier, but I felt we did need experienced players in the new team, possibly Borderers, as well as some young local talent and other players from inside and outside the country.

I spoke with all the Borders players in the Edinburgh squad and told them it was important we didn't weaken Edinburgh any more than was necessary; but I did target Chris Paterson and Nathan Hines, former Gala players, as key players who could help launch the new team. Both said they didn't want to move, mainly because they enjoyed being part of Edinburgh and felt the team hadn't fully realised its potential yet. I actually offered Chris the opportunity to play stand-off at the Borders.

A group did move – including Cammie Murray, Kevin Utterson, Steve Scott and Iain Fairley – and we went for Gregor Towsend, who was in France, and Gary Armstrong, Doddie Weir and George Graham, who were all at Newcastle. They were the experienced men I felt we needed. We then signed up Aberdonian Chris Cusiter to learn from Gary Armstrong, and Colin Stewart and Jon Stuart joined from Glasgow.

One interesting youngster who came along was Ross Ford, a 17-year-old from Kelso. I met him with his parents and was surprised at what he told me. I had always encouraged youngsters to go to university or college and combine rugby with study, but Ross was the first player who said to me he wanted to play full-time professional rugby, not club rugby, thus giving himself every chance of making it, and that he could study after he'd finished playing. That attitude was quite refreshing to me.

There is no doubt that creating a new team has many trials and tribulations, and I found it disappointing to see a lot of resistance from some Borders clubs. It prompted Tony to ask me, more than once, 'Do the Borders rugby people really want a professional team?' He was used to a place like Otago, where everyone involved in club rugby, from the juniors to the seniors, wanted Otago to be the best in the country and worked to help achieve that aim.

I believe that Alastair, Tony and Rob, and the rest of the management and players, worked tremendously hard in those first two years to give the Borders a foundation. There has been criticism in recent times of foreign coaches coming in, but I know that Tony did a great deal to engender a feeling of belonging and make the team proud of the area it played in, and the area proud of its team. In fact, he knows more about Borders history than I do and used to take the players to a huge sandstone monument to William Wallace – which many local boys did not know existed – to show them a Scottish hero.

The new Borders squad began training in June 2002 and played its first game back in the familiar red and white hoops of the old South against Connacht in August. One job done; now for the rest.

Glasgow was quite a different story. When we reduced the teams from four to two, Keith Robertson became the senior coach, with Rob Moffat and Gordon Macpherson the assistants, but it didn't work out particularly well. In January of 1999, I asked Keith to move and he came in and helped Roy Laidlaw with the Under-21s until the end of the season, when he left. I asked Richie Dixon, whom I trusted and knew well, to help out and take Glasgow.

He still had a full-time job as coaching manager at the SRU, but he had an excellent assistant in Colin Robertson, who took over the reins when he was away. Richie and his team worked hard and Glasgow went reasonably well, but I was conscious that at some point a decision would have to made as to whether he would come back to Murrayfield or stay there. So I asked him at the beginning of his third season whether he wanted to go full-time with Glasgow or return to his coaching manager's post at the end of it.

I wanted to give him plenty of time to think about it and was not expecting a decision until the turn of the year. David Jordan, his chief executive at Glasgow, was keen for him to stay, but he decided to come back. At the end of that season, Rob moved back to the Borders, so there were two vacancies to fill at Glasgow.

Richie was closely involved in our search for a new coach and, after interviews, we went for Kiwi Searancke, an experienced coach who had good references from New Zealand. In an effort to banish the demoralising underachievement, I was keen for our players to experience different styles of coaching, most of them having only had Scottish coaches. We also appointed Steve Anderson from rugby league in an effort to try a different approach. I remember seeing one of the first sessions they took, at Dalziel Country Park after the players came back from holiday. Despite having been given programmes to follow, a few of the players were quite out of condition, including two current Scotland international forwards who were labouring on a 3-km run. Richie and I were very embarrassed. At the time, we had fitness and conditioning records from the Super 12 teams, so we knew exactly what levels we had to be aiming for to compete in professional rugby, and how far behind we were.

Despite that, the season started very well and there were some good results; but as time went on, the consistency dropped off and a rift developed between the players and the coaches. Kiwi became critical of the quality of players he had and I knew that the situation was deteriorating. I went through to Scotstoun in Glasgow and spoke to some senior players – Andy Nicol, Gordon Bulloch and Jason White, in particular – assessed the situation and then had to tell Kiwi and Gordon Macpherson that they would have to go. It was a very difficult decision to make. I had already decided to move Steve Anderson, the third member of the coaching team, to Murrayfield to look at our elite performance plans, as he had particular skills in that field.

At the time, I said that it had been a mistake to appoint Kiwi but, on reflection, I actually regret that I sacked him. I think Kiwi had identified limitations in terms of the players' standards and their ability to push themselves to the levels required to be consistently competitive. I took the players' concerns seriously, as they believed the coaches to have lost the dressing-room and the situation to be irreparable, but, in fact, with the benefit of hindsight, I feel there were more serious questions needing to be asked of some players, including key senior figures.

Hugh Campbell was given the opportunity to move out of the national squad and become head coach at Glasgow. I asked Sean Lineen if he would be one of the assistant coaches; I had asked him twice before if he wanted to be a professional coach but he was not ready to take the plunge. This time he was. Shade Munro, an experienced coach with Glasgow Hawks, was also recruited, to help with the forwards.

Before he left, Kiwi and his coaches had devised plans to try and rectify the situation, and I know that Hugh and his team took most of the advice on board. Sean did remark to me that he was surprised at the limitations of some of the professional players and that it was an uphill struggle to make significant improvements.

Of the three teams – and I still go along to games involving them all – the best atmosphere has been at Glasgow. There is always a buzz there on a Friday night and I really enjoy going to games there. They deserve success.

21

Time to Leave the Stage

Bryan Redpath
Scotland captain (60 caps, 1993–2003)

In his final years in rugby, Jim was questioned by players in a way he wasn't accustomed to and it made for difficult times. Professionalism changed players, not so much those who had come through from the amateur game, more guys who had only known professional rugby.

They had had a different education to those of us who had started as internationals in an era when we all still worked nine to five or, for those of us putting up new houses, eight to six at times. I came from Melrose, where Jim had been a major influence on me on and off the pitch from about the age of 16.

I'll never forget when he used to take us for training at Melrose on Sunday mornings. There would always be someone throwing up, having taken a bit much beer the night before. Jim would lay into him about standards and more than once he was asked to tone down his language as people left the church beside the ground! But I knew that his sole motivation was to make me and my teammates better, to push us to discover new levels and ultimately to win.

It was the same with Scotland. It was quite simple with Jim: playing for Scotland was the ultimate and if you didn't perform well, you trained harder the next week and found the mental toughness to do better the next time.

Latterly, however, as we approached the 2003 World Cup, he found that that approach did not work for every player he had. It didn't faze me but some of the forwards couldn't cope with him being on their backs all the time, pushing and demanding more. They started to tell him that. I remember him standing up during the 2003 tour to South Africa, where we played some good rugby, and he told the whole squad that he wasn't here to upset them, to criticise them for the sake of it, that he simply wanted them to become winners and be a successful team. He said it with real passion and it finally began to sink in with some players. I wish he had said that earlier, to be honest.

If some of those players who challenged him or who were unhappy with him looked at themselves in the mirror, they'd have to admit they were a bit lazy or wanted to find an easier route to success, and that that was what attracted Jim's attention.

The World Cup was difficult because some of the players were upset at being misquoted in the press, and Ian McGeechan, our coach, and the press did not see eye to eye. The feeling in the squad was that it didn't matter what we did on the field, the press had made up their mind that we were failures. We did not play well early on but we overcame Fiji on a sweltering hot afternoon in Sydney. We performed against Australia for a good hour of the game at least and were unlucky to lose crucial tries. So we went out at the quarter-final stage to the eventual finalists, which most supporters expected.

Before the Fiji game, I had torn into the players in the dressing-room. I was angry at the moaning that was going on to the press about kit going missing, training and other little things, as if these were responsible for us not playing well. That was me back to my Border tongue – I did it once also when we barely beat Wales at Murrayfield – and Jim came up to me after that and said that that was the kind of captaincy he admired. He knew something had to be said but by then he had stepped back from doing it himself.

In my eyes, Jim has been the best coach ever in Scottish rugby. He hasn't always been my supporter, but when I deserved to be selected, he backed me.

I remember on the day Scotland was leaving for the World Cup, I first went to a birthday party with my son Cameron. It was for his friend Harvey Ferguson, the son of Jason and grandson of Sir Alex Ferguson. Alex told me he remembered hearing Jim

Telfer had once said to his players, 'You're not just doing this for your teammates, you're doing this for your country.' He said he really liked that quote and I remember thinking, 'You are just like him – two great Scotland coaches.'

There was no doubt that while rugby administration held many challenges, it was never any substitute for working with players and Test-match coaching. I thought that was all behind me as we moved past the millennium but my old friend Ian McGeechan had other ideas. Ian had succeeded me as head coach at the end of 1999. Initially, he invited me down to the back pitches to help out with specific sessions when I could spare the time. But by the autumn of 2002, I was back with the national team again as a specialist coach working on contact, alongside forwards coaches Hugh Campbell and Pat Lam. It was in no way a full-time job, but I enjoyed the opportunity to pass on my experience.

I remember taking the rucking machine up to St Andrews where we were based for the autumn Tests against touring sides Romania, South Africa and Fiji. I put into operation the essential principles I'd worked on with the Lions, namely body positions, leg drive, tightness and coming in from behind. I particularly enjoyed working with the backs; in the modern game it's amazing what backs have to do to keep continuity going. I actually believe the backs enjoyed the experience and perhaps for the first time felt like real rugby players – they were doing the same as the 'men' did!

I also remember our fitness coach Marty Hulme and Ian would come over to see what I was doing under the net or on the rucking machine. I could never work out whether they were there to see what I was doing technically or to check I wasn't working the players too hard! Anyway, I never asked. One of the things I did was to take players for individual sessions. I would teach some of the forwards techniques for spinning in and out of the tackle and for using their legs in the correct way. After a few sessions, however, there seemed to be very little enthusiasm for my help, so I stopped.

We won all three matches, not too convincingly against Romania and Fiji, but we played well against South Africa, considering what they had done to us in 1997, 1998 and at the World Cup in 1999. They didn't know it but we put a spy into the Heriot's clubhouse with a camera at one of their sessions. The South Africans were always very suspicious of being spied on, and it was quite comical because the cameraman had to duck down whenever they came past the window, with the result that parts of the film were missing. But we got the gist of what they were trying to do.

To beat South Africa was to take a great scalp and I remember the two very good tries from Budge Pountney and Nikki Walker on a drizzly day. Gordon Ross kicked well, too, and we won 21–6.

The Fiji game turned out to be Budge's last game and it was very sad when he quit the squad two months later. In the build-up to the first Six Nations match, against Ireland, he took a full part in a morning session and then at lunch-time Ian came in and told me that Budge had decided to pack it in and had left Murrayfield. It was a great shock because he had shown no indication beforehand and had played in all three autumn Tests.

He was a huge loss because he had made himself into a very good international player. He was brave, had a high work rate, with the basic instincts of an open-side flanker, and he was a natural leader on the park.

There were a lot of things stated in the papers about why he resigned. He said there was no water at training, yet we had boxes and boxes of water stacked up at Murrayfield. It was a simple misunderstanding, in that another squad had picked up our water – we sometimes had four squads training at Murrayfield at the same time. There were other things going on in Budge's life, I'm sure, but he never spoke to me about any problems and so I was left at a loss to explain why he felt it necessary to end his international career so suddenly and with a very critical swipe at Scottish rugby.

But you move on; we had to look forward to facing Ireland and we needed a new open-side flanker. In contention were Andrew Mower and Donnie Macfadyen. Donnie had suffered a lot of injuries, so Andrew was the one we called into the side.

Andrew was my type of player. Fearless to the point of being reckless, he could injure as many of his own players in training as he would opponents in games. I used to wonder how Gary

Armstrong and him got through training together at Newcastle without injuring each other. When he came into the side, he gave away a lot of penalties but by the time the World Cup came along, he was beginning to control his game a lot better. It was a great pity that he got injured out in Australia and never played again.

The 2003 Six Nations results were a mixed bag. We lost to Ireland at home and to England and France away, but beat Wales and Italy convincingly at Murrayfield. I had changed my style of coaching by that final year. Because the players were far better conditioned than in previous years, they spent less time practising out on the field and did more talking and watching coaching DVDs, so the amount of coaching I did was limited.

It had been my custom to give the forwards a team talk before games but I stopped doing that after a couple in the autumn because I felt it was right to let them motivate themselves. Around February 2003, one journalist kept going on about some senior players being unhappy with the coaches; I suspected that he was referring to me, and I went into my shell.

I resolved to be as positive as possible and not let players make me the scapegoat if things were to go wrong. I had been used to putting opinions forward at team meetings as honestly as possible, often concerning faults we had, but now I felt that this was being turned against me by players who did not seem to understand that it was done merely to help them improve. So I decided I would speak with Ian before or after meetings and keep quiet during them. The squad seemed to lack the strong mental character of previous sides, despite the fact that there were some very experienced players.

After the Championship, we went to South Africa. It was a happy tour, with a great atmosphere, and I witnessed one of the best performances I've ever seen from a Scotland team in the First Test at Durban. We had built up a lead of 12 points at one stage. We scored three good tries and were leading going into the last ten minutes but we lost 29–25. We were guilty again of not putting the opposition away.

But we were playing a fast, top-of-the-ground game, keeping the ball alive, a game designed to suit the World Cup conditions later that year. Chris Paterson won the Famous Grouse Try of the Year award for finishing a fantastic team try, started by a counter-attack from Kenny Logan, who was in the form of his life. Nathan Hines came within inches of winning the match in the last seconds when he crashed over the try-line, only for the ball to be knocked from his hands inches from the ground.

The Springboks counteracted our style in the Second Test by targeting not the passer but the receiver, and we did not react to the pressure put on the receivers, so we lost the Johannesburg Test 28–19. But it was a good tour, and the players had responded well to the conditions, which would be similar in Sydney and Brisbane.

Ian and Marty spent a lot of time on conditioning work when we came back, the players going to Spala in Poland for cryotherapy-enhanced training, training in the hothouses at the Botanical Garden in Edinburgh and in specially created humid conditions at a resource at Edinburgh University.

The squad also went to the Trossachs for similar team-bonding exercises to those which the Lions did in 1997, using the same people, Jeff Jackson and Paul Broom, who had worked for Impact then and were now running their own company. We all got to know each other better and set out our aims for the World Cup. The players had a big say in how everything was to be done.

We then played three warm-up games, starting with a very good win over Italy. We selected a new team to play against Wales and, despite winning a lot of possession, we scored no tries and were beaten. It was quite a setback. Then we lost to Ireland as well and we realised that some players were a bit weak. Ian had wanted to pick two separate teams for the first two games at the World Cup, but as a result of the warm-up games, we decided we would have to mix and match.

One novelty we brought in towards the end of the preparation was that the home-based players went home every night after training and the exiles were given apartments to stay in rather than hotels; it worked very well.

When we got out to Australia, for the first stage of the tournament we were based in the sleepy Sunshine Coast town of Caloundra, an hour's drive from Brisbane, where Rod Macqueen had taken the Wallabies in previous years. We were keen to give the players independence; they had bikes to cycle to training every day and were allowed to cook their own meals. There was a feeling of togetherness but also a relaxed feel about the stay.

As it happened, the heat and humidity the players had spent so much time preparing for was never a factor because the temperatures were unusually low, and there was a wind in Townsville and Brisbane. Unfortunately, in the second week we lost Andrew Mower when he suffered a serious knee injury in training. That was a huge blow because, having lost Budge Pountney early in the year, we were struggling for open-sides. As it turned out, it was an injury which Andrew, sadly, never recovered from and he retired the following year without playing again.

For the first two games, we picked two teams in advance so that the players knew whether they would be playing against Japan or the USA or both. We flew up to Townsville, about 1,000 miles north of Brisbane, two days before the Japan game. Bryan Redpath was playing his first game in four months, which wasn't ideal but, because he was captain, we wanted him fit for the later matches. We started very well but then lost our shape. The Japanese were quick, good at the breakdown and tackled superbly – targeting the ankles, I remember – and they killed our attacks stone dead. But we came good at the end and scored five tries to get our bonus point.

I had noticed, however, that though the players mixed well, they never criticised or found anything wrong with each other; they were all very 'nice'. I felt this might be our undoing. In any tour, there is always something that does not go particularly well and issues have to be thrashed out, but at the senior players' meetings with management, the players never seemed to have any problems. If pressed, all they would say was they wanted shorter training sessions or better food, the usual things players complain about.

But after games, despite the fact we had not played well, they were not prepared to criticise each other and I think that was a weakness. 'What would a certain M. Johnson have said?' I used to ask myself. We wanted the players to be empowered, to push each other both on the pitch and at training.

The press, meanwhile, were having a field day. A crowd of bikers had rolled into our base at Caloundra and taken over the hotel. They were preparing for a weekend of celebrations and, while the players enjoyed looking at the bikes, we grew concerned when we realised the parties were all-night affairs around the pool. We therefore arranged to move to Brisbane earlier than planned, which would ensure the players could relax prior to the USA game. We were ridiculed in the local press, and by some elements in our own, for supposedly running scared of these bikers, but it didn't adversely affect us.

The atmosphere in Brisbane was tremendous for the USA game, with close to 50,000 people there, most of whom seemed to be Scots. We played well and were up 24–9 at half-time, but then Tom Smith was sin-binned and we lost the place. We ended up winning 39–15. The USA were completely different to Japan. Where the Japanese were very quick across the ground, great tacklers and moved the ball well, the Americans were big and strong, and played a far more structured game.

We had been looking to bring Mike Blair through, knowing that Bryan was retiring at the end of the tournament, but he was very nervy in that game, uncharacteristically so, and we struggled to control it. We had given Chris Paterson ten minutes at stand-off – he'd been practising there at times in training – and we scored late tries through good running and support to finish with five tries again, ensuring maximum points for the first two games, even if that win wasn't too convincing.

It was about that time that the press started to step up the criticism. It was mainly the Scottish press; the foreign press were fine and got on well with Ian and myself. We then moved down to Cronulla, south of Sydney, to prepare for the game with France and were welcomed by a pipe band. We did our rugby training at the Cronulla Sharks' ground, which was in superb condition. Some of the players even met up with Olympic swimmer Ian Thorpe, as we used the same outdoor swimming pool as him for training. Stuart Grimes even measured his feet against Thorpe's to see whose were the longer. Although he's a good swimmer with big feet, Stuart was advised to stick to his day job! A few days before the game, HRH The Princess Royal came and visited us at the training ground and then had lunch with us, which was nice.

Whilst in Cronulla, we learned that Martin Leslie had been cited after the USA game. Martin received a 12-week ban, which was reduced to 8 weeks on appeal. We were very aggrieved at the whole affair, convinced that if the same type of offence – a knee in the back – had been carried out by a player in a top-five-nation team, he would have received a far lighter sentence. I was a bit upset that Rupeni Caucau, the star Fijian winger, was sent off and banned for just three weeks after blatantly punching Olivier Magne in his first match. He was supposed to be one of the stars of the tournament and we believed that his suspension conveniently finished the day before our game.

It was unfortunate that we lost Martin, because he was one of our main back-row players and, having lost Mower, it was the last thing we needed. I enquired about Donnie Macfadyen replacing him but I was told he wasn't match-fit, so Cammy Mather, the Glasgow captain, came out. When Cammy arrived, he injected new life into the forward pack. He came with ideas and took control of certain things. It made me wonder why it took a player like him, with so little experience compared to others, to start bossing the forwards. We put him straight into the team to play France and, despite not being a specialist open-side flanker, he played very well.

We stayed in the game for the first 30 minutes, frustrating them well, and had hoped to go in at half-time only three points down at worst. But we gave away two soft tries and were twelve points down. After half-time, we fell apart and we were completely outplayed, losing 51–9.

Having been beaten by France, we had to beat Fiji to secure a place in the quarter-finals. That was the most tense week that Ian and I had ever experienced. We tried to hide our nerves from the players but they must have felt tremendous pressure as well.

There were a lot of Fijians in Sydney, where we played, and Fiji were also the media favourites because of their easy-going attitude. We also felt that sections of the Scottish press wanted the team to lose because that would mean that we would have to qualify for the next World Cup – bad news sells more papers. Also, the other three home nations, especially Wales, were playing very good rugby and no doubt our pressmen were getting ribbed by their counterparts from those countries. There were also very critical reports coming out saying that old internationalists were very unhappy with the team and were writing us off. It all built up but, to be honest, I was still very confident of winning.

I remember the team talk Bryan Redpath gave before the game.

It was one of the most critical I've ever heard from a player to other players. He really lambasted them and pointed out that they had done nothing but moan about this and that, when in actual fact the preparation had been very good. He was correct in his summation, because it was time they stood up and delivered. I believe they reacted to that tongue-lashing and did stand up and deliver in that game. The match wasn't a classic but we stuck to our game plan of keeping possession and making sure that our defence was secure when they had the ball. We kept playing with discipline and got our reward with a try from Tom Smith, a planned move from a lineout two minutes from the end, to win the match 22–20. Some of the press described us as being 'two minutes from oblivion'.

But when you look at other games in the tournament, like Samoa against England, Wales against England, and Wales against the All Blacks, the underdog was similarly never subdued until the last five or ten minutes but in each case the favourites came through.

I thought we deserved more credit for coming from behind and scoring a very good try to win. Anyway, we had achieved our goal of reaching the quarter-finals. We were to face Australia in Brisbane in the last eight. As had been the case against Fiji, Chris Paterson was picked at stand-off. Unfortunately he was hit by a stray ball in the face in the warm-up and there was a worry he might be concussed and not make it. But, after a very anxious 15 minutes, he recovered and we played very well against Australia. It was the fastest game we'd experienced. The scores were level at half-time, thanks to a great long-range drop-goal from Chris.

Just after half-time, there was a refereeing decision which significantly affected the outcome of the game. Phil Waugh was clearly offside at a ruck, but he was allowed to feed the ball to Stirling Mortlock and the centre raced away for a try. The Wallabies visibly drew great confidence from that and, cheered on by a huge home support, they eventually won 33–16. A French journalist told Ian that he thought we'd played some outstanding rugby in that game, and I believe the performances against Fiji and Australia restored some pride in Scottish rugby.

That final game also marked the end of the international careers of Kenny Logan and Bryan Redpath, which made for another emotional ending to a World Cup. Both of them had been great servants to Scottish rugby, and they got better and better as they got older.

Reflecting on that year, I actually feel the team played its best rugby against South Africa, both at home in the 21–6 victory and in Durban in the summer. I also think that the so-called weaker sides, Japan and the USA, were well prepared and it took us a long time to subdue them. Looking back, the team probably played as well as it was able to, mainly because we had fewer line-breakers, fewer players capable of changing games, than in the past.

At the press conference after that final game, I was quite outspoken, just out of frustration, really. The media began asking me about the reasons why Scotland had struggled and why we had not improved the situation over the past ten years. When you looked back on what we had tried to change and improve, while still trying to get the best out of our leading players, it was frustrating to think that we were still being blamed for everything that was wrong in our game.

Having heard about all the criticism from former players during the tournament, I picked on John Jeffrey because he was the one most fresh in my mind. I now know my reaction was a mistake. I apologised to him as soon as I could. I actually cannot remember saying some of the things I'm reputed to have said. I'm usually very careful about those kinds of remarks but I accept that I must have made them. I've met John a few times since and our friendship is now as it was before the World Cup. I went to see the Scotland Under-21 team training at Peebles last year and John, who is their manager, actually asked me to speak to the team before they played England.

When I started out in coaching in the mid-1970s, working with Scotland B players, the forwards were all heading in different directions across the field, all different heights as they ran, and one of my first tasks was to turn them to face in the same direction in order to present a more competitive, cohesive and challenging face to their opposition. My most used coaching words at that time were 'Go forward!' Some forwards may not have agreed with me at first, as if that approach in some way devalued individuality, but they soon learned that in rugby you need individuals working within a team. That change started a noticeable improvement, for

286

me, and ultimately led to the success we achieved in the next decade, culminating in the 1984 Grand Slam.

On reflection, that almost mirrors the past ten years in Scottish rugby off the field. If everyone in our game was able to come together, face in the same direction and go forward like one of the driving rucks which became our forte, then we would, I feel, be a force in world rugby once again. There is always room for individuality; but if we want to achieve anything, the desire to show flair must be harnessed to a purpose, an ambitious goal, and in a country as small as Scotland, be part of a united bigger picture.

Becoming a winner is not particularly complicated and, despite the apparent lack of resources, and the doom and gloom we hear about Scottish rugby, consistent success is most certainly attainable in this country; but it requires a change in approach across the Scottish game. We live in hope.

22

Back Down to Earth

The 2001 British and Irish Lions tour was interesting, being the first to come after our 1997 success; I was still involved in the game and fascinated to watch it close at hand. The 2005 tour was the first, however, certainly since my involvement in 1966, that I felt like everyone else, watching and supporting from the outside. And how depressing it was. I can only hope that this is not always what it is like to be a Lions supporter. It is perhaps worse when you have worn the red jersey to watch it being devalued in the way I feel it was by the 2005 tour.

I mean this as no slight to the players, who will all have taken the same immense pleasure as I did from the honour of being handed the British and Irish Lions jersey, but, in truth, there were a lot of people in New Zealand, both on and off the field, who had not earned the right to be a Lion, which was the fault of the management. It is inevitable with a squad of 45 players and 29 officials that many among them will have been handed, without having truly earned, something which hundreds of players over the years have viewed as the achievement of a lifetime, for which they have worked and made great sacrifices.

Calling for replacements is one thing, but going out there with that many and then trying to please them all, to me, makes a mockery of the British and Irish Lions concept. HRH Prince William wandering around with players, having a kicking session and spending time with the head coach; a political spin doctor who clearly had little understanding of Lions rugby making us a laughing stock in New Zealand; a lawyer and referee wandering around in Lions kit. These were all examples of the way in which the honour of reaching the top in British and Irish rugby and becoming a Lion was devalued.

Lions rugby is a serious business. It is not about taking as many players and officials as possible to the other side of the world for an enjoyable holiday. And the Lions paid the price in 2005 for people taking that approach. I fear it has done damage to the Lions reputation that will take some time to repair.

These were all peripheral aspects which might have been eclipsed had the rugby been successful. But we always knew that would be tough to achieve.

Basically, I believe there were three key areas which went wrong in Sir Clive Woodward's tour, the one he frequently told us would feature the 'best-prepared' Lions squad ever. The first was that Woodward and the senior coaches, and perhaps some players, underestimated the standard of rugby in New Zealand – a mistake which is as incredible as it is frequently made on trips to the southern hemisphere. I exclude Ian McGeechan from this because I have spoken with him about the tour and there is little doubt he knew how difficult it would be. I said last year, and would repeat, that perhaps the biggest mistake Clive made was not persuading Ian to be his Test coach, rather than working with the midweek squad. Ian's biggest strength is working with the very best players. Andy Robinson was not as experienced and Eddie O'Sullivan had, to my knowledge, no real experience of Lions rugby and had not really endured very difficult times as Ireland coach, times when you learn a great deal. I understand Ian did not want that role, but they then should have deferred to him at times on the tour and listened to his advice on how to crack the All Blacks. A Lions tour is a hard, uncompromising environment, especially in New Zealand, and you need hard, experienced campaigners in there leading you.

The second issue is that I still feel we had the players to win two Test matches against New Zealand. Yes, the All Blacks were a good side, but they were not a great side. Richie McCaw is by far the most influential forward in world rugby, but with only two specialist jumpers they will struggle in the lineout against some of the top nations. Carl Hayman is world class, but the other front-row players just do the job they are supposed to – win possession and maintain forward momentum. They were not really put under pressure in the backs and so their back line was able to dictate play and had the confidence to try things. Having said that, players like Dan Carter, Sitiveni Sivivato and Tana Umaga were a class apart. More time should have been spent on pulling the Lions combinations together to make the Test team gel as a side before the First Test.

The third reason, I believe, for the whitewash was that we had no clear way of playing the game. We started brilliantly against Bay of Plenty, with the kind of pace, possession and low error-count which would rattle any side. Then we relaxed and found that New Zealand has truckloads of players willing to have a go, players who won't stand for being stuffed and are clever enough not only to come back but also to know how to find weaknesses.

We never really got the momentum or forward domination we needed after that and the First Test was a disgrace. Many of the Lions 'froze'; they seemed to be intimidated. The margin of defeat was not as large as the play warranted because the weather was so poor but we were not close in any of the Test matches.

Of course, Clive had problems, as I had in 1983; every Lions coach has suffered with injured squad members, and losing players like Lawrence Dallaglio, Simon Taylor, Richard Hill and Brian O'Driscoll was very tough. But he made a rod for his own back by ridiculously taking Neil Back, a player serving a month's suspension, and waiting for France-based Gareth Thomas and Stephen Jones to join up after the French club season finally ended in June. I understood Jason Robinson being left at home while his wife was pregnant, but the French lads should have been there from the start or not at all.

The overriding concern I felt at the conclusion, however, was that we had again set too much store by our Six Nations Championship and the English Premiership, believing that we were competing on a level with the Super 12. That idea was shredded by the Lions tour. Hopefully, we will learn this time and realise that the standard of rugby in these competitions has to be improved, which can only happen when all the competing nations develop their rugby. Perhaps even that subject, which I have battered on about for countless years now, moving the game to better-weather months, might finally be addressed and debated seriously. The very idea that our next generation of players might be learning their rugby in a more attractive season when the grounds are firmer, encouraging running rugby, when skills could be honed without the fear of hypothermia taking hold on mud-soaked pitches or the lights going out in midwinter, remains an optimistic dream for me.

But I fear we will once again think mistakenly that the Lions defeat was a one-off, that we were just caught out, that there is little wrong with our approach, that English rugby really is the best there is and the Super 12 can teach us nothing. We wait and watch.

I am not worrying too much about it now. As I said, life has changed for me, and more in these past few months than at any other time, I think. Having enjoyed writing newspaper columns for the *Scotland on Sunday* about the Lions tour – did someone say 'poacher-turned-gamekeeper'? – I was in hospital by the time of the Third Test, a heart operation having been brought forward.

It was something I had tried to keep private, telling only my family, but, to be honest, I was not aware of quite how serious it was until I was admitted to the Royal Infirmary in Edinburgh in early July and it has undoubtedly given me a fresh outlook on life. I have always been a fit and active person, visiting the local gym two or three times a week right up until recent months. But last year, I was finally due to undergo a shoulder operation to sort a rotator-cuff tear which I suffered, I think, playing staff football at Portobello High in the 1970s – probably keeping tacklers away from my wee mate Terry Christie.

I had often had physio on it and, after consulting a physiotherapist I know, Graham Curlewis, I had an operation planned for December 2004 to have it repaired. I had a bit of a cold a week or two beforehand, so I went to see my GP in Selkirk, Dr Jeff Cullen, just to check I was all right for the operation. He detected a heart murmur, however, and the picture changed. He liaised with a consultant at the Royal Infirmary, Richard Nutton, who was to perform the operation, and when a cardiologist at the Borders General Hospital, Dr Neary, discovered my aortic valve wasn't working properly, that was it, the operation was off. I've still not had it, but hopefully the shoulder will be fixed next year.

Instead, I was told to stop the weights, not lift my arms above my head and generally take things easy. Check-ups confirmed it was not improving and I knew by March that an operation was going to happen sooner rather than later. My old friend Dr Donald McLeod, the former SRU doctor, was a great support and, like the other doctors, told me not to worry and that it was a routine operation. It was only after I was in hospital, when Frances told him I felt fine, having seen a poor chap needing a quadruple bypass in the bed beside me, and he said that my operation – which was to remove my aortic valve and replace it with a metal one – was more serious than that, that I realised how 'major' this major surgery was.

In the month or two before going into hospital I had still been coaching the Earlston High School Under-15s, getting organised for taking my Selkirkshire Under-15 squad up to the next level and I had gone on an SRU coaches' course at St Andrews University – that was fun, learning from the development officers I had employed!

The operation, I was warned, would not take place until after the G8 Summit being held at Gleneagles, because they apparently expected the Royal Infirmary's theatres to be busy dealing with people injured in the protests. But a space came up and I was whisked in before the G8, so I watched the demonstrations and the London terrorist bombings from my hospital bed – and kept up to date on the Lions Third Test through phone calls home to Frances. It was a very strange time.

It was tough realising that I faced surgery which, while routine, was not without danger, but I am quite a phlegmatic character and if that was what I needed, fair enough, get on with it. It was harder on my family as they watched somebody who'd been pretty fit all his life weaken and tire and struggle to complete sentences. The operation itself, with an excellent surgeon in Mr Saaid Prasad, was a great success, but I had problems with my blood not thinning quickly enough to pass through the new valve. Despite taking a keen interest in all the problems and the many and various drugs passed my way each day, I will not bore you with the details; suffice to say that what was due to be a ten-day stay became a frustrating five weeks in hospital beds.

The staff at the new Royal Infirmary, Ward 102, namely, and the Borders General Hospital, however, were first class. It struck me that it was not unlike the Scottish Rugby Union operation at Murrayfield. There is an incredible amount of fantastic work done by the people inside those buildings every single day, yet the general public and media hear or report very little of it and focus instead on the small negative aspects which are inevitable in such a massive operation. In both hospitals, I witnessed and benefited from outstanding quality of work and standards of care by wonderful staff dedicated to their professions, and that helped me through what was my longest stay in hospital.

I will need a six-month recovery period and I have been warned by Donald that I will experience a major drop in fitness, which will take some time to reverse, and I may never be as fit again. But that's life, isn't it?

I do not feel old at 65 but life is not something to be taken for granted. I have always tried to value everything that has come my way, whether in rugby or away from the game, but the operation has underlined the fact that having a life as full as mine has been a privilege. I have lost some great friends in recent years and that provides another reminder. I may have to take things a bit slower now but, just like in the game of rugby, even when knocked a bit, there is still plenty of life in the old body. It has been strange but enjoyable looking back on my life, but we are now at the end, and so it is time again to look forward. A pipe and slippers are not yet on my Christmas list.

Appendix 1

My Best Scotland and World XVs

The idea of this is great: simply pick your all-time favourite players and come up with a team which would beat anybody and everybody. No injury worries, no call-offs, no breakdowns in training and . . . no other selectors!

Yet it became apparent pretty quickly that the task of judging those players with whom I played against those whom I coached was tough. I considered listing two sides relevant to the playing and coaching periods in my life, but the challenge of naming an all-encompassing XV ultimately proved too great. Still, I had to pick a second team.

So, purely for some fun at the end of my life story, here are two Scotland teams I would have loved to have seen face each other at Murrayfield, and a World XV which we can dream about seeing in action. I go on to discuss my top four choices for the all-time greatest Scotland players in each position.

SCOTLAND 'BLUES' XV
Andy Irvine; Arthur Smith, Alan Tait, Jim Renwick, Keith Robertson; John Rutherford, Gary Armstrong (captain); Hugh McLeod, Colin Deans, Iain Milne, Gordon Brown, Alastair McHarg, David Leslie, Finlay Calder, Derek White

SCOTLAND 'WHITES' XV
Gavin Hastings (captain); Billy Steele, Scott Hastings, Ian

McGeechan, Roger Baird; Colin Telfer, Roy Laidlaw; Tom Smith, Kenny Milne, Sandy Carmichael, Chris Gray, Alan Tomes, John Jeffrey, Rodger Arneil, Simon Taylor

WORLD XV (NON-SCOTS)

Christian Cullen; Philippe Sella Campese, Jeremy Guscott, Mike Gibson, Jonah Lomu; Mark Ella, Gareth Edwards; Os du Randt, Sean Fitzpatrick (captain), Fran Cotton, Colin Meads, Martin Johnson, Ian Kirkpatrick, Zinzan Brooke, Michael Jones

SCOTLAND'S BEST
Andy Irvine
Gavin Hastings, Ken Scotland, Chris Paterson
Andy was the best attacking player I've ever seen playing for Scotland. A flair player, his pace and power cut defences to pieces and he often won games single-handedly, such was his presence. He was also a very good captain, one who led by example and was popular with his teammates. Gavin was a big, powerful runner, excellent under the high ball and a good counter-attacker – he too was a good Scotland captain. Ken was a very gifted footballer who was the first running full-back I saw, as well as being the first 'round-the-corner' goal-kicker. Chris is an intuitive runner with pace, and excellent sidestep and jink, also a very good goal-kicker.

Arthur Smith
Billy Steele, Sandy Hinshelwood, Tony Stanger
In the right-wing position, Arthur was a beautifully balanced runner with a deceptive change of pace. He was an athlete of note and, while injured, taught himself to kick goals. He was an outstanding captain of Scotland and the Lions. Billy was a slightly built, mesmerising runner who could beat opponents on a sixpence. Sandy was a strong, aggressive player who burst defences but could also outflank them. Tony was a big, deceptively quick winger who also adapted well to playing outside-centre at the highest level.

Alan Tait
Scott Hastings, David Johnston, John Frame
Alan left union after making his Scotland debut in the 1987 World

Cup to follow his father Alan's route to rugby league. Like his father, he was a star there but returned to union and made a huge contribution for Scotland and the Lions. He had a perfect running action for an outside-centre, with long strides and speed on the break, but his angles of running set him apart. Scott was very strong, quick and an excellent tackler. David was quick off the mark, skilful and a good kicker, while John was a big, strong, resolute runner, and a very good sevens player, with an eye for an opening.

Jim Renwick
Ian McGeechan, John Leslie, Jock Turner
The best attacking midfield back I've coached, Jim could cut a defence apart with the move of his head, swerve and injection of pace. He was also a good tactical kicker. Ian was a very neat and tidy footballer, who often acted as a foil for more powerful outside players. He had excellent vision, good hands and was a very good defender. John revolutionised our centre three-quarter play when he arrived from New Zealand in 1998; with quick feet, he got in behind defences and was always looking to offload. Jock, another excellent sevens player, was strong and decisive, with a big boot, not unlike John Rutherford in his style.

Keith Robertson
Roger Baird, Iwan Tukalo, Bruce Hay
Keith was a versatile player who could play wing or centre. He had a good sidestep and break, a willingness to run from anywhere and an engine to support it – an excellent sevens player. Roger was a very fast, silky runner with a deceptive swerve, who started out as a scrum-half and so was a good passer. Iwan was a very elusive, strong runner, with an excellent change of direction. Bruce was a strong player, comfortable at either wing or full-back at the top level, and he possessed a great boot and kicking ability.

John Rutherford
Colin Telfer, Gregor Townsend, Craig Chalmers
A world-class player who started out as a runner and a breaker, John matured into a very good all-round player. With good hands, he developed into a prodigious kicker but retained his ability to

see and go through openings. Hugely underrated, Colin was a little genius of a player and the best reader of a game I've seen in Scotland, with a scything break and very good hands. 'Mercurial' is the word to describe Gregor – quick off the mark, strong in attack and defence, and with an ability to spot opportunities before anyone else. Craig used all his talents to the full. The most dedicated trainer I've come across, he was a fine kicker, read the game well and was an excellent defender.

Gary Armstrong
Roy Laidlaw, Bryan Redpath, Dougie Morgan
Spoilt for choice, I could easily have picked nine great Scotland players at scrum-half – players like Eck Hastie, Dunc Paterson, Andy Nicol, Alan Lawson and Brian Shillinglaw were top quality. Gary was the epitome of what a Scottish rugby player should be. Fearless and very competitive, with a great work rate, he challenged his body to breaking point. An excellent defender and good kicker, Gary had a great break and pass – the ideal scrum-half and a perfect choice for captain. Roy was similar but he was the best breaking scrum-half I've worked with. Bryan developed over the years into an excellent player, with a long service and good kick, an excellent defender. Dougie was a very good all-round scrum-half and also an excellent goal-kicker.

Hugh McLeod
Tom Smith, Ian McLauchlan, David Sole
A non-drinking, dedicated trainer, Hughie dominated Scottish rugby for eight years. He was the consummate professional, he scrummed well on either side and he was very good on a sevens team. Tom, the most skilul prop I have coached, was technically a very good scrummager and though a quiet, thoughtful player, he commanded respect the world over. Ian was the hard man of Scottish rugby throughout the '70s. Not a flamboyant player, he made his presence felt in the scrum and in close-quarter forward exchanges – an excellent captain who led by example. Another good Scotland captain, David was very explosive in the loose and developed into an uncompromising scrummager.

Colin Deans

Kenny Milne, Frank Laidlaw, Gordon Bulloch

The best hooker I have coached in Scotland, Colin was quick off the mark and very effective in attack and defence. An excellent thrower, he captained Scotland 13 times and was unfortunate that his deserved selection as Lions captain in 1986 did not involve a tour. Kenny improved as a Test hooker as he matured; he was a very strong scrummager and very mobile. Frank was a true craftsman, perfectly suited to hooking in his era; very flexible, he could hook the ball at any height, and even used his head on occasions. Gordon worked hard to maintain his position as Scotland's number-one hooker over the last eight years and fended off all challengers before his Test retirement on 75 caps this year. He's a mobile, dynamic hooker who could be used as an extra flanker.

Iain Milne

Sandy Carmichael, David Rollo, Paul Burnell

The rock of the Scottish scrum for ten years, Iain was a huge man, but surprisingly mobile and comfortable with ball in hand. Despite his size and obvious strength, he was a very clean player and actually took pity on some of his opponents in club games. Like Iain, Sandy was a huge prop, a good scrummager, very good around the park and a great tackler. David was similarly strong and mobile, and an able scrummager who could play both sides well. Paul was a great servant to Scottish rugby, very durable and an excellent scrummager.

Gordon Brown

Chris Gray, Bill Cuthbertson, Mike Campbell-Lamerton

A larger-than-life figure, Gordon came into his own among the elite in Lions teams. Hugely competitive, he was very mobile and an excellent lineout player. A good ball player, he scored eight tries on the 1974 Lions tour, which highlighted his rugby skills. Chris was the engine of the Scottish pack in the Grand Slam of 1990. He had a high work rate, was a good front-of-the-lineout jumper and fine tackler, and he scored a lovely try against the All Blacks at Dunedin in 1990. Another vital cog in a Grand Slam triumph, Bill was injured midway through the 1984 campaign but his unselfish play epitomised Scotland's game at that time. Mike was a tireless team player who could play lock or number 8 equally well, a committed leader with good ball skills.

Alastair McHarg
Alan Tomes, Scott Murray, Doddie Weir
Alastair was an outstanding lineout forward who could have graced any era, combining the strengths of tight forward play with an eye for attack in the open. Alan was a very big, strong player, who imposed himself on the opposition, particularly in the lineout and at rucks and mauls. Scott is an excellent jumper, both in attack and defence, and has good ball skills. Doddie was similarly an outstanding lineout player with good skills, who revelled in open play and had an effusive character which was great for squad morale.

David Leslie
John Jeffrey, Jim Calder, Mike Biggar
Technically, David Leslie was the best Scotland forward I have ever coached. Comfortable with the ball in hand, brave to the point of recklessness and a very good leader, he showed his best form in the 1984 Grand Slam success. J.J. was also a brave character who loved the ball in his hands. A good sevens player, the Borders farmer had great energy and was a terrific try-poacher. Jim was an intelligent and combative forward, someone who knew the game and how to play to his strengths very well. Mike was a courageous rugby player, an industrious person who revelled in wet conditions.

Finlay Calder
Rodger Arneil, Budge Pountney, Derrick Grant
Not an orthodox open-side flanker, Finlay was a superb rugby player in the mould of All Blacks flanker Michael Jones. Very adept on the ball, and mentally and physically very hard, Fin was an inspirational captain. Rodger was a very quick player, aggressive and brave; he toured twice with the Lions and emerged as a star of the 1968 tour after being called up as a replacement. Budge was a very committed, intuitive ball-winner; good at close-quarter encounters on the ground, he led by example. Derrick was

a greatly underrated player, a committed flanker who hounded stand-offs relentlessly.

Derek White
Simon Taylor, Iain Paxton, John Beattie
Derek was a quiet, unassuming lad with a huge talent, a very good lineout forward and adept as second row, flanker or number 8. Quick off the back of the scrum, Derek scored some great tries from the number 8 position. Simon is a genuine class player, with good hands, plenty of pace and a very high work rate. Iain was an athletic and very fit forward, a skilful ball player who could play a number of positions. John was a big, explosive number 8 who was good with the ball in his hands and aggressive in attack and defence.

Appendix 2

Playing and Coaching Records

James William Telfer
Born: 17 March 1940
Club: Melrose
Scotland caps: 25
British and Irish Lions Tests: 8

JIM TELFER – THE PLAYER
Melrose RFC

Debut against Heriot's at Goldenacre in October 1957; final competitive appearance against Edinburgh Wanderers in March 1974.

Captained 1st XV in 6 seasons, played in 317 senior club games and scored 144 points, including 42 tries.

Melrose won 3 Border League Championships and 2 unofficial Scottish championships in Telfer's 17 years with them.

He was the fifth Melrose player to pass the 300-appearance mark (Robbie Brown currently holds the club record with 349 appearances).

In sevens rugby, Telfer played in 4 tournament-winning sides and was runner-up on 19 occasions.

South of Scotland/Scottish Border Club

Debut against Scottish Universities at Mansfield Park in March 1959.

Captained South and the Scottish Border Club, making 55 appearances overall.

Barbarians

Toured with the Baa-Baas on numerous occasions, regularly featuring in the traditional Easter matches in Wales, and faced Australia with them in 1968.

Scotland

Made a winning Test debut against France at Murrayfield on 4 January 1964.

Captained Scotland in the last 9 of his 25 Test matches, the last of which was against Ireland at Lansdowne Road on 28 February 1970. He scored 3 Test tries. Jim also played another 9 times for Scotland in non-cap internationals, including twice against Argentina, and scored 2 more tries.

Most memorable match was against England in 1964, when Telfer was involved in all 3 Scottish tries and scored the final one to spark a Murrayfield pitch invasion and seal a 15–6 victory.

Only Scotland internationalist to have played against all the 'big three' southern-hemisphere giants and never lost.

Telfer toured on 20 separate occasions, including to South Africa, New Zealand, Australia, Canada and Argentina.

P	W	D	L	Tries
25	9	2	14	3

British and Irish Lions

Telfer played in two tours: 1966 to Australia and New Zealand; and 1968 to South Africa. The first resulted in a 4–0 series defeat and the second in a 3-0 loss with one drawn Test. His own playing record is noted below:

1966 Lions tour to Australia and New Zealand

P	W	D	L	Tries
22	15	1	6	2

1968 Lions tour to South Africa

P	W	D	L	Tries
11	7	1	3	3

JIM TELFER – THE COACH
Melrose

Telfer started coaching with Melrose as a player and captain around 1966 and went on to coach the South and Scottish Border Club in a similar manner, non-playing coaches having not yet been invented! His first spell in charge after retirement was from 1975 to 1980. The club twice dropped into Division Two and on both occasions won the second division title and returned to the first division.

He took over as a more formally recognised coach in 1988 and steered the club to the top of the domestic game, winning their first official championship in 1989–90 and another three championships before he stepped down. His assistant Rob Moffat took over and duly brought to the Greenyards another two titles in the next three years, as well as the Scottish Cup, the Border League and the Melrose Sevens trophy.

Telfer's coaching record in the period 1988–94 (awarding two points for a win and one for a draw) is detailed below:

1988–94

P	W	D	L	Pts	Success rate (%)
182	150	3	28	293	80

Scotland B

He coached Scotland B from 1975–80, playing France six times and winning twice, and playing Ireland twice and winning once.

Scotland

Telfer enjoyed four periods coaching the national squad, two of which were as head coach and two as forwards coach to Ian McGeechan. In the first three periods, Scotland won two Grand Slams, two Triple Crowns, two Calcutta Cups and the final Five Nations Championship, as well as taking the scalps of Australia home and away, and South Africa at Murrayfield.

1981–84 (Telfer was not involved in 1983 due to Lions commitments)

P	W	D	L	Pts	Success rate (%)
19	11	2	6	24	63

1988–91 (assistant to Ian McGeechan, did not tour)

P	W	D	L	Pts	Success rate (%)
21	14	1	6	29	69

1998–99

P	W	D	L	Pts	Success rate (%)
20	8	0	12	16	40

2002–3 (assistant to Ian McGeechan)

P	W	D	L	Pts	Success rate (%)
15	8	0	7	16	53

British and Irish Lions

Jim Telfer was the sole coach of the Lions on the 1983 tour to New Zealand, when they suffered a 4–0 series whitewash. He returned to the Lions arena in 1997 as assistant to Ian McGeechan, and the Scots duo steered Martin Johnson's men to a 2–1 series victory over South Africa.

1983 to New Zealand

P	W	D	L	Pts	Success rate (%)
18	12	0	6	24	67

1997 to South Africa (assistant to Ian McGeechan)

P	W	D	L	Pts	Success rate (%)
13	11	0	2	22	85

OTHER ACHIEVEMENTS

Member of the British Empire (MBE), 1984
Honorary doctorates in 1998 from Heriot-Watt University and in 2001 from Napier University and Glasgow University
First socialist to get anywhere in the Scottish Rugby Union!